£19.99

Tony Bush is Professor of International and Comparative Education at the University of Reading. He was previously Professor of Educational Management and Director of the Educational Management Development Unit at the University of Leicester and, before that, senior lecturer in educational policy and management at the Open University. He has experience as a teacher and middle manager in secondary schools and colleges and as a professional officer with a local education authority. He has been a visiting professor in China, New Zealand and South Africa and made invited keynote presentations at conferences in Greece, Hong Kong, Portugal and Singapore. He has published extensively on several aspects of educational leadership and management. His main recent books are *Managing People in Education* (with David Middlewood), *Educational Management: Redefining Theory, Policy and Practice* (with Les Bell, Ray Bolam, Ron Glatter and Peter Ribbins) and *The Principles and Practice of Educational Management* (with Les Bell).

Theories of Educational Leadership and Management

Third Edition

Tony Bush

SAGE Publications
London • Thousand Oaks • New Delhi

First published in 1986 by Paul Chapman Publishing
Second Edition published in 1995 by Paul Chapman Publishing
Third Edition published in 2003 by Sage Publications Ltd
Reprinted 2004

SAGE Publications Ltd
6 Bonhill Street
London EC2A 4PU

Sage Publications Inc
2455 Teller Road
Thousand Oaks, California 91320

SAGE Publications India Pvt Ltd
B-42 Panchsheel Enclave
Post Box 4109
New Delhi 110 017

Library of Congress Control Number: 2002109970

A catalogue record for this book is available from the British Library

ISBN 0 7619 4051 0
ISBN 0 7619 4052 9 (pbk)

Typeset by Anneset, Weston-super-Mare, North Somerset
Printed in Great Britain by Cromwell Press, Trowbridge

Contents

v

Contents

Preface

The significance of effective leadership and management for the successful operation of schools and colleges has been increasingly acknowledged during the 1990s and into the twenty-first century. The trend towards self-management in the United Kingdom, and in many other parts of the world, has led to an enhanced appreciation of the importance of managerial competence for educational leaders. More recently, there has been a growing recognition of the differences between leadership and management and an understanding that school principals and senior staff need to be good leaders as well as effective managers. The leadership dimension embraces concepts of vision, values and transformational leadership. Managing capably is an important requirement but leadership is perceived to be even more significant in England, and in some other countries

The first edition of this book was published in 1986, before the seismic changes to the English and Welsh educational system engendered by the Education Reform Act and subsequent legislation. The second edition, published in 1995, referred to the 'tentative steps' being taken to develop the managerial competence of senior staff, particularly headteachers. The School Management Task Force (SMTF, 1990) had set the agenda for management development in its 1990 report but, unlike many other countries, there was no national programme of management training for heads and very little provision of any kind for deputy heads and middle managers. The 'Headlamp' scheme, which provides support for new heads, had just been introduced but this is a funding stream rather than a coherent programme of development.

Only eight years later, the English landscape has been transformed by the opening (in November 2000) and subsequent expansion of the National College for School Leadership (NCSL), based in Nottingham with a second centre in Cranfield, Bedfordshire. The College manages the two national programmes, the National Professional Qualification for Headship, for aspiring heads, and the Leadership Programme for Serving Heads. It is also introducing a raft of provision for new heads, deputy heads (established leaders) and middle level leaders. This ambitious set of programmes is supported by an active research group and by a strong information and communications technology unit known as the 'Virtual College'.

The decision to locate responsibility for leadership development in England in a single national agency contrasts sharply with arrangements in most other developed countries. In the United States and Canada, potential principals and assistant principals must complete a master's degree in educational administration. Similarly, universities are centrally involved in the preparation of school leaders in Australia, Hong Kong, New Zealand and Singapore (Bush and Jackson, 2002). What these countries do have in common with England is an explicit recognition that training and development are essential if school leaders are to carry out their onerous responsibilities successfully. Just as teachers need training to be effective in the classroom, so leaders need preparation for their specialist roles.

There is now a substantial literature on management practice in educational organizations. Most of these books and journals have been written by academics and practitioners in the United States, the United Kingdom and Australia. However, there are still few sources addressing the theoretical foundations of good practice. The aim of this book is to provide conceptual frameworks to guide the practice of educational leaders and managers. The author seeks to present a complex body of theory in clear, straightforward terms and to illustrate the models by reference to examples of leadership and management in educational institutions. In making relevant theory more accessible to practitioners, the intention is to promote both greater understanding of the concepts underpinning effective leadership and management practice and to develop the capability of senior and middle level leaders in schools and colleges.

In preparing this third edition of the book, I have sought to achieve four objectives:

- To integrate leadership theory with the management models featured in the two previous editions.
- To acknowledge the global significance of educational leadership and management by including much more material from a wide range of international settings.
- To update the literature by including many of the major sources published since 1995.
- To scrutinize the material in the previous edition and to remove some of the less significant sources while retaining those texts central to theory development in the 1970s and 1980s.

As a result of this comprehensive review, the content of this third edition is significantly different, although readers of the previous versions will note that the familiar structure is largely unchanged.

Chapter 1 defines educational management and stresses the centrality of aims or goals in guiding managerial practice. It also defines educational leadership and differentiates it from management. The historical development of educational management as a distinct subject is chronicled from its dependence on industrial models in the 1960s to its position in the new millennium as an established discipline with an evolving specialist literature. A new section examines the twin concepts of centralization and decentralization in education and links them to the emergence of self-managing schools in many countries. The debate on whether education should be regarded as simply a different context for the application of general management principles, or a special case justifying a distinct approach, is also reflected in this chapter. Finally, a new section addresses the notion of instructional leadership, a model given additional prominence by its inclusion as one of NCSL's 10 leadership propositions.

Chapter 2 considers the relationship between theory and practice. The prospect of a theory/practice divide can be avoided by an appreciation of the relevance of theory. The nature and characteristics of educational management theory are discussed and the chapter also addresses the relationship between gender and theory. The six management models are introduced and, in a new section, nine leadership models are outlined.

The next six chapters are the heart of the book, each presenting one of the major models of educational management. The six perspectives are analysed in terms of the assumptions made about the goals of educational institutions, the nature of organizational structure, relations with the external environment and the most appropriate modes of leadership. The models are also linked to the nine leadership theories.

Chapter 3 considers 'formal models', including structural, systems, bureaucratic, rational and hierarchical approaches. A new section relates managerial leadership to the formal models.

Chapter 4 outlines the collegial model and applies it to higher education, and to secondary and primary schools. The emphasis on the authority of expertise, the shared values and objectives of professional staff and decision-making based on consensus is noted and subjected to scrutiny. Collegiality is linked to three models of leadership: transformational, participative and inter-personal.

Chapter 5 presents political models with their assumptions of conflict between interest groups and decision-making based on the resources of power deployed by the various factions. It also examines the relationship between micropolitics and transactional leadership.

Chapter 6 examines subjective models with their emphasis on individual interpretation of events and their rejection of the notions of organizational goals and structure. It assesses the relationship between subjectivity and qualitative research. It also introduces postmodern leadership which is remarkably similar to subjective models of management.

Chapter 7 discusses ambiguity models which stress the unpredictability of organizations, the lack of clarity about goals and the fluid nature of participation in decision-making. These are linked to contingent leadership and its focus on adapting leadership styles to the specific context or event.

Chapter 8 considers the significance of culture for educational leadership and management. A new section examines the increasingly important concept of societal culture while the chapter also retains its focus on organizational culture. This model emphasizes the values and beliefs underpinning culture and the symbols and rituals used to reinforce it. A new section links this model to moral leadership.

Chapter 9 compares the six models and considers their validity for particular types of school or college. A new section also provides a comparative analysis of the nine leadership models. The chapter considers several attempts to integrate some of the models and concludes by assessing how to use theory to improve practice.

I am grateful to the many people who have contributed to the development of this volume. Derek Glover carried out a thorough review of the leadership and management literature since 1995 and also provided valuable comments on a draft of the text. Three generations of secretaries, Helen Knowles, Felicity Murray and Margaret King, have provided excellent support for the three volumes and I also received help from Chabala Mwale. Marianne Lagrange has been the commissioning editor for all three editions and has also been centrally involved in the production of many of my other books, including those in the *Educational Management: Research and Practice series*. Latterly, she has also given me support as the new editor of the leading journal, *Educational Management and Administration*. I am grateful for all her help during the past 20 years. Finally, this book has been prepared at a time of great change in my personal life and I am thankful for the support of all those close to me, especially Graham, Orla and Cha.

References

Bush, T. and Jackson, D. (2002) Preparation for school leadership: international perspectives, *Educational Management and Administration*, 30 (4): 417–29.

School Management Task Force (SMTF) (1990) *Developing School Management: The Way Forward*, London: HMSO.

Tony Bush
The University of Reading
February 2003

1

The Importance of Leadership and Management for Education

What is educational management?

Educational management is a field of study and practice concerned with the operation of educational organizations. There is no single generally accepted definition of the subject because its development has drawn heavily on several more firmly established disciplines including sociology, political science, economics and general management. Interpretations drawn from different disciplines necessarily emphasize diverse aspects of educational management and these varying approaches are reflected in subsequent chapters of this book.

Bolam (1999, p. 194) defines educational management as 'an executive function for carrying out agreed policy'. He differentiates management from educational leadership which has 'at its core the responsibility for policy formulation and, where appropriate, organizational transformation' (ibid., p.194). Writing from an Indian perspective, Sapre (2002, p. 102) states that 'management is a set of activities directed towards efficient and effective utilization of organizational resources in order to achieve organizational goals'.

Glatter's (1979, p. 16) definition remains helpful because it serves to identify the scope of the subject. He argues that management studies are concerned with 'the internal operation of educational institutions, and also with their relationships with their environment, that is, the communities in which they are set, and with the governing bodies to which they are formally responsible'. In other words, managers in schools and colleges have to engage with both internal and external audiences in leading their institutions. This statement delineates the boundaries of educational management but leaves open questions about the nature of the subject.

The present author has argued consistently (Bush, 1986; 1995; 1999) that educational management has to be centrally concerned with the purpose or aims of education. These are the subject of continuing debate and disagreement but the principle of linking management activities and tasks to school or college aims and objectives remains vital. These purposes or goals provide the crucial sense of direction which should underpin the management of educational institutions. Management is directed at the achievement of

1

certain educational objectives. Unless this link between purpose and management is clear and close, there is a danger of 'managerialism', 'a stress on procedures at the expense of educational purpose and values' (Bush, 1999, p. 240). The emphasis is on managerial efficiency rather than the aims and purposes of education (Newman and Clarke, 1994; Gunter, 1997). 'Management possesses no super-ordinate goals or values of its own. The pursuit of efficiency may be the mission statement of management – but this is efficiency in the achievement of objectives which others define' (Newman and Clarke, 1994, p. 29).

Placing the emphasis on educational purpose is not to suggest that any particular aims or targets are appropriate, particularly if they are imposed from outside the school by government or other official bodies. Managing towards the achievement of educational aims is vital but these must be purposes agreed by the school and its community. If managers simply focus on implementing external initiatives, they risk becoming 'managerialist'. Successful management requires a clear link between aims, strategy and operational management. As Culbertson (1983) claims, 'defining purpose is a central function of administration'.

The centrality of aims and purposes for the management of schools and colleges is common to most of the different theoretical approaches to the subject. There is disagreement, though, about three aspects of goal-setting in education:

- the value of *formal* statements of purpose;
- whether the objectives are those of the organization or those of particular individuals;
- *how* the institution's goals are determined.

Formal aims

The formal aims of schools and colleges are sometimes set at a high level of generality. They usually command substantial support but, because they are often utopian, such objectives provide an inadequate basis for managerial action. A typical aim in a primary or secondary school might focus on the acquisition by each pupil of physical, social, intellectual and moral qualities and skills. This is worthy but it has considerable limitations as a guide to decision-making. More specific purposes often fail to reach the same level of agreement. A proposal to seek improved performance in one part of the curriculum, say literacy or numeracy, may be challenged by teachers concerned about the implications for other subjects. The introduction of development planning in England and Wales, and elsewhere, provides a vehicle for resolving these dilemmas and determining school and college priorities.

The international trend towards self management has led to a parallel call for managers, staff and other stakeholders to develop a distinctive vision for their schools with clearly articulated and specific aims. Beare, Caldwell and Millikan (1989, p. 99) say that 'outstanding leaders have a vision of their schools – a mental picture of a preferred future – which is shared with all in the school community'. Where educational organizations have such a vision, it is possible for effective managers to link functions with aims and to ensure that all management activity is purposeful. In practice, however, as we shall see later, many 'visions' are simply generalized educational objectives (Bolam et al., 1993).

Organizational or individual aims

Some approaches to educational management are concerned predominantly with organizational objectives while other models strongly emphasize individual aims. There is a range of opinion between these two views. Gray (1979, p. 12), stresses both elements: 'the management process is concerned with helping the members of an organization to attain individual as well as organizational objectives within the changing environment of the organization'. A potential problem is that individual and organizational objectives may be incompatible, or that organizational aims satisfy some, but not all, individual aspirations. It is reasonable to assume that most teachers want their school or college to pursue policies which are in harmony with their own interests and preferences. This issue will be explored later in this book, notably in Chapter 6.

The determination of aims

The process of deciding on the aims of the organization is at the heart of educational management. In some settings, aims are decided by the principal or headteacher, often working in association with senior colleagues and perhaps a small group of lay stakeholders. In many schools and colleges, however, goal-setting is a corporate activity undertaken by formal bodies or informal groups.

School and college aims are inevitably influenced by pressures emanating from the wider educational environment and lead to the questions about the viability of school 'visions', noted above. Many countries, including England and Wales, have a national curriculum and such government prescriptions leave little scope for schools to decide their own educational aims. Institutions may be left with the residual task of interpreting external imperatives rather than determining aims on the basis of their own assessment of student need.

Wright's (2001) discussion of 'bastard leadership' develops this argument, suggesting that visioning is a 'sham' and that school leaders in England and Wales are reduced to implementing the values and policies of the government and its agencies:

> Leadership as the moral and value underpinning for the direction of schools is being removed from those who work there. It is now very substantially located at the political level where it is not available for contestation, modification or adjustment to local variations. (Wright, 2001, p. 280)

The key issue here is the extent to which school leaders are able to modify government policy and develop alternative approaches based on school-level values and vision. Do they have to follow the script, or can they ad lib? Gold et al.'s (2003) research with ten 'outstanding' English principals begins to address this central issue. They 'take for granted that school leaders are essentially "value carriers" ... school improvement is not a technocratic science, but rather a process of seeking ever better ways of embodying particular educational values in the working practices ... of particular schools' (p. 128). These authors assert that their case study principals were developing just such value led approaches to school leadership and management:

> The school leaders in our case study schools were clearly avoiding doing 'bastard leadership' by mediating government policy through their own values systems. We were constantly reminded by those to whom we spoke, of the schools' strong value systems and the extent to which vision and values were shared and articulated by all who were involved in them. (Ibid, p. 131)

Wright's (2003) response to the Gold et al. research questions the extent to which even 'principled' leaders are able to challenge or modify government policies. In his view, these principals are still 'bastard leaders' because their values cannot challenge government imperatives:

> What is not provided [by Gold et al.] is clear evidence of how these values actually impinged at the interface between particular government initiatives and action in these schools ... 'bastard leadership' ... is actually about the lack of scope for school leaders to make decisions that legitimately fly in the face of particular unrealistic and often inadequately researched government initiatives or requirements. (Wright, 2003, p. 140)

This debate is likely to continue but the central issue relates to the relative power of governments and school leaders to determine the aims and purpose of education in particular schools. Governments have the constitutional power to impose their will but successful innovations require the commitment of those who have to implement these changes. If teachers and leaders believe that an initiative is inappropriate for their children or students, they are unlikely to implement it with enthusiasm. Hence, governments would like schools to have visionary leadership as long as the visions do not depart in any significant way from government imperatives.

Furlong (2000) adds that the increased government control of education has significant implications for the status of teachers as professionals. He claims that, in England and Wales, professionalism is allowed to exist only by the grace of central government because of the dominance of a prescriptive national curriculum and the central monitoring of teacher performance.

The nature of the goal-setting process is a major variant in the different models of educational leadership and management to be discussed in subsequent chapters.

What is educational leadership?

There is no agreed definition of the concept of leadership and Yukl (2002, pp. 4–5) argues that 'the definition of leadership is arbitrary and very subjective. Some definitions are more useful than others, but there is no "correct" definition.' Three dimensions of leadership may be identified as a basis for developing a working definition.

Leadership as influence

A central element in many definitions of leadership is that there is a process of influence.

> Most definitions of leadership reflect the assumption that it involves a social influence process whereby intentional influence is exerted by one person [or group] over other people [or groups] to structure the activities and relationships in a group or organisation. (Yukl, 2002, p. 3)

Yukl's use of 'person' or 'group' serves to emphasize that leadership may be exercised by teams as well as individuals.

Cuban's (1988) definition shows that the influence process is purposeful in that it is intended to lead to specific outcomes: 'Leadership, then refers to people who bend the motivations and actions of others to achieving certain goals; it implies taking initiatives and risks' (ibid., 1988, p. 193). Ogawa and Bossert (1995) see this influence as an organizational quality flowing through the differing internal networks of the organization.

Leadership and values

Leadership may be understood as 'influence' but this notion is neutral in that it does not explain or recommend what goals or actions should be sought through this process. However, certain alternative constructs of leadership focus on the need for leadership to be grounded in firm personal and professional values, as we noted earlier. Wasserberg (2000, p. 158) claims that 'the primary role of any leader [is] the unification of people around key values'. Greenfield and Ribbins (1993) add that leadership begins with the 'character' of leaders, expressed in terms of personal values, self-awareness and emotional and moral capability.

Day, Harris and Hadfield's (2001) research in 12 'effective' schools in England and Wales concludes that 'good leaders are informed by and communicate clear sets of personal and educational values which represent their moral purposes for the school' (ibid., p. 53).

Leadership and vision

Vision is increasingly regarded as an essential component of effective leadership. Beare, Caldwell and Millikan (1989) draw on the work of Bennis and Nanus (1985) to articulate ten 'emerging generalizations' about leadership, four of which relate directly to vision:

1 Outstanding leaders have a vision for their organizations.
2 Vision must be communicated in a way which secures commitment among members of the organization.
3 Communication of vision requires communication of meaning.
4 Attention should be given to institutionalizing vision if leadership is to be successful.

These generalizations are essentially normative views about the centrality of vision for effective leadership. However, there is also some empirical support for these prescriptions. Nias, Southworth and Campbell's (1992) study of five primary schools shows that their heads 'provided a vision for the staff and the school' (ibid., p. 46). Southworth (1993, pp. 23–4) suggests that heads are motivated to work hard 'because their leadership is the pursuit of their individual visions' (ibid., p. 47). Dempster and Logan's (1998) study of 12 Australian schools shows that almost all parents (97 per cent) and teachers (99 per cent) expect the principal to express his or her vision clearly while 98 per cent of both groups expect the leader to plan strategically to achieve the vision

These projects show the high level of support for the notion of visionary leadership but Foreman's (1998) review of the concept shows that it remains highly problematic. 'Inspiring a shared vision is the leadership practice with which [heads] felt most uncomfortable' (Kouzes and Posner, 1996, p. 24) while Fullan (1992a, p. 83) adds that 'vision building is a highly sophisticated dynamic process which few organizations can sustain'. Elsewhere, Fullan (1992b) is even more critical, suggesting that visionary leaders may damage rather than improve their schools:

The current emphasis on vision in leadership can be misleading. Vision can blind leaders in a number of ways . . . The high-powered, charismatic principal who 'radically transforms the school' in four or five years can . . . be blinding and misleading as a role model . . . my hypothesis would be that most such schools decline after the leader leaves . . . Principals are blinded by their own vision when they feel they must manipulate the teachers and the school culture to conform to it. (Ibid., p. 19)

The research by Bolam et al. (1993) for the School Management Task Force illustrates a number of problems about the development and articulation of 'vision' in English and Welsh schools. Their study of 12 self-selected 'effective' schools shows that most heads were able to describe 'some sort of vision' but 'they varied in their capacity to articulate the vision and the visions were more or less sophisticated' (ibid., p. 33). Moreover, the visions were rarely specific to the school. They were 'neither surprising nor striking nor controversial. They are closely in line with what one might expect of the British system of education' (ibid., p. 35).

There is contrasting evidence from the research by Greenfield, Licata and Johnson (1992) in the United States. Using a large sample of 1,769 teachers from 62 schools in rural and small communities, they demonstrate strong support for the notion that there was a clear vision for the school and that it was articulated well:

Teachers in this sample seemed to agree that their principals had a vision of what the school ought to be and that it was in the best interest of their students. Moreover, they viewed their principals as relatively effective in advancing this vision. (Ibid., p. 74)

It is evident that the articulation of a clear vision has the potential to develop schools but the empirical evidence of its effectiveness remains mixed. A wider concern relates to whether school leaders are able to develop a specific vision for their schools, given the centrality of government prescriptions of both curriculum aims and content (see page 4).

Distinguishing educational leadership and management

The concept of leadership overlaps with two similar terms, management and administration. 'Management' is widely used in Britain, Europe and Africa, for example, while 'administration' is preferred in the United States, Canada and Australia. Dimmock (1999) differentiates these concepts whilst also acknowledging that there are competing definitions:

School leaders [experience] tensions between competing elements of leadership, management and administration. Irrespective of how these terms are defined, school leaders experience difficulty in deciding the balance between higher order tasks designed to improve staff, student and school performance (leadership), routine maintenance of present operations (management) and lower order duties (administration). (Ibid., p. 442)

Cuban (1988) provides one of the clearest distinctions between leadership and management. He links leadership with change while management is seen as a maintenance activity. He also stresses the importance of both dimensions of organizational activity:

> By leadership, I mean influencing others' actions in achieving desirable ends. Leaders are people who shape the goals, motivations, and actions of others. Frequently they initiate change to reach existing and new goals ... Leadership ... takes ... much ingenuity, energy and skill. (Ibid., p. xx)

> Managing is maintaining efficiently and effectively current organizational arrangements. While managing well often exhibits leadership skills, the overall function is toward maintenance rather than change. I prize both managing and leading and attach no special value to either since different settings and times call for varied responses. (Ibid., p. xx)

Day, Harris and Hadfield's (2001) study of 12 'effective' schools leads to the discussion of several dilemmas in school leadership. One of these relates to management, which is linked to systems and 'paper', and leadership, which is perceived to be about the development of people. 'Development and maintenance' are identified as another tension, linking to the Cuban (1988) distinction identified above.

Bush (1998, p. 328) links leadership to values or purpose while management relates to implementation or technical issues. Fidler (1997, p. 26) argues against a firm distinction between leadership and management, claiming that they have an 'intimate connection' and 'a great deal of overlap, particularly in respect of motivating people and giving a sense of purpose to the organization'.

Leadership and management need to be given equal prominence if schools and colleges are to operate effectively and achieve their objectives. While a clear vision may be essential to establish the nature and direction of change, it is equally important to ensure that innovations are implemented efficiently and that the school's residual functions are carried out effectively while certain elements are undergoing change:

> Methods ... [are] are as important as knowledge, understanding and value orientations ... Erecting this kind of dichotomy between something pure called 'leadership' and something 'dirty' called 'management', or between values and purposes on the one hand and methods and skills on the other, would be disastrous. (Glatter, 1997, p. 189)

8

Leading and managing are distinct, but both are important. Organizations which are over managed but under led eventually lose any sense of spirit or purpose. Poorly managed organizations with strong charismatic leaders may soar temporarily only to crash shortly thereafter. The challenge of modern organizations requires the objective perspective of the manager as well as the flashes of vision and commitment wise leadership provides. (Bolman and Deal, 1997, pp. xiii–xiv)

The dichotomy in Britain and elsewhere is that while leadership is normatively preferred (e.g. Millett, 1996), governments are encouraging a technical–rational approach through their stress on performance and public accountability (Glatter, 1999; Levačić, et al., 1999). In practice, schools and colleges require both visionary leadership, to the extent that this is possible with a centralized curriculum, and effective management.

The chronology of educational leadership and management

The origins and development of educational management as a distinct discipline have been chronicled by Culbertson (1980), Hughes (1985), Hughes and Bush (1991), Bush (1999) and Glatter (1999). It began in the United States in the early part of this century. The work of Taylor (1947) was particularly influential and his 'scientific management movement' is still subject to vigorous debate, particularly by those who oppose a 'managerial' approach to education. Another important contributor to management theory was the French writer Fayol (1916) whose 'general principles of management' are still significant. Weber's (1947) work on 'bureaucracy' remains powerful and this will be given extended treatment in Chapter 3.

All these theories developed outside education and were subsequently applied to schools and colleges, with mixed results. The other models discussed in this book were developed in the educational context or have been applied to schools or colleges in their formative periods.

The development of educational management as a field of study in the United Kingdom came as late as the 1960s but there has been rapid expansion since then. In 1983 the Department of Education and Science (DES) sponsored a programme of management training for heads and established the National Development Centre for School Management Training at Bristol University. University courses on school and college management became increasingly popular (Hughes, Carter and Fidler, 1981; Gunter, 1997).

The British government appointed a School Management Task Force in 1989 and its influential report (SMTF, 1990) set the agenda for school management development for the next few years. Probably its most important legacy was the establishment of mentoring schemes for new headteachers.

The next major development in England and Wales was the establishment of the Teacher Training Agency (TTA) which took an interest in leadership and management development as well as the pre-service training of teachers. The TTA set up the National Professional Qualification for Headship (NPQH), the first national qualification for aspiring heads, in 1997. The Department for Education and Skills is consulting on making NPQH mandatory for new heads from 2004.

The most important stage in this chronology was the setting up of the National College for School Leadership (NCSL) in November 2000. Significantly, the College's title excludes the term 'management', further emphasizing the current normative preference for 'leadership'. The College has taken over responsibility for leadership development programmes, including NPQH, and is introducing new schemes, such as 'New Visions: Induction to Headship' for new heads, and 'Leading from the Middle' for subject leaders and other middle managers.

The College also gives a high priority to information and communications technology, through its 'virtual college', and has an important research role with a Director of Research in its leadership team. Unlike the TTA, it also has a strong international presence as part of its commitment to becoming a 'world class' centre.

The rationale for a specific focus on school leadership and management is articulated in NCSL's prospectus. It reiterates the now firmly established link between effective leadership and high quality:

> The evidence on school effectiveness and improvement during the last 15 years has consistently shown the pivotal role of effective leadership in securing high quality provision and high standards . . . effective leadership is a key to both continuous improvement and major system transformation. (NCSL, 2001a, p. 5)

The English Learning and Skills sector is also giving a high priority to leadership and management and a Leadership Centre for managers in colleges is likely to be established in 2003.

These developments are paralleled in many other countries. The NCSL organized a series of study visits to 'the best leadership centres world wide to inform college strategy' (NCSL, 2001a, p. 9). Each visit involved teams of two or three people, including school principals, NCSL senior staff, and other professionals and academics directly connected with the College. Fifteen centres were visited in seven countries: Australia, Canada, Hong Kong, New Zealand, Singapore, Sweden and the United States.

The report of the visits (Bush and Jackson, 2002) showed that several other countries were well ahead of England and Wales in the development of national or state programmes for prospective principals. In Canada and most of the United States, for example, it is not possible to be appointed as a principal or vice-principal without an approved master's degree in educational administration. Similarly, Singapore has had a national qualification for school principals since 1984.

In summary, the climate for educational leadership and management has never been more buoyant. The recognition that high-quality leadership is central to educational outcomes has led to the view that training is desirable to develop people with the appropriate knowledge, skills and understanding to lead schools and colleges in an increasingly global economy. This require-ment is particularly important for self-managing institutions.

Decentralization and self-management

Educational institutions operate within a legislative framework set down by national, provincial or state parliaments. One of the key aspects of such a framework is the degree of decentralization in the educational system. Highly centralized systems tend to be bureaucratic and to allow little discretion to schools and local communities. Decentralized systems devolve significant powers to subordinate levels. Where such powers are devolved to the insti-tutional level, we may speak of 'self-management'.

Lauglo (1997) links centralization to bureaucracy and defines it as follows:

> Bureaucratic centralism implies concentrating in a central ('top') authority deci-sion-making on a wide range of matters, leaving only tightly programmed routine implementation to lower levels in the organization . . . a ministry could make deci-sions in considerable detail as to aims and objectives, curricula and teaching mate-rials to be used, prescribed methods, appointments of staff and their job descriptions, admission of students, assessment and certification, finance and budg-ets, and inspection/evaluations to monitor performance. (Ibid., pp. 3–4)

Lauglo (1997, p. 5) says that 'bureaucratic centralism is pervasive in many developing countries' and links this to both the former colonial rule and the emphasis on central planning by many post-colonial governments. Tanzania is one example of a former colonial country seeking to reduce the degree of centralism (Babyegeya, 2000).

Centralized systems are not confined to former colonial countries. Derouet (2000, p. 61) claims that France 'was the most centralized system in the world' in the 1960s and 1970s while Fenech (1994, p. 131) states that Malta's edu-cational system is 'highly centralized'. Bottery (1999, p. 119) notes that the United Kingdom education system 'has experienced a continued and intensi-fied centralization for the last 30 years'. In Greece, the public education sys-tem is characterized by centralization and bureaucracy (Bush, 2001).

Decentralization involves a process of reducing the role of central govern-ment in planning and providing education. It can take many different forms:

Decentralization in education means a shift in the authority distribution away from the central 'top' agency in the hierarchy of authority . . . Different forms of decentralization are diverse in their justifications and in what they imply for the distribution of authority. (Lauglo, 1997, p. 3)

The main forms of decentralization are:

- Federalism, for example in Australia, Germany, India and the United States.
- Devolution, for example in the United Kingdom.
- Deregulation, for example in the Czech republic (Karstanje, 1999).
- Deconcentration, for example in Tanzania (Therkildsen, 2000).
- Participative democracy, involving strong participation by stakeholders at the institutional level, for example in Australia, Canada, England and Wales, and South Africa (Sayed, 1999).
- Market mechanism, for example in Britain and the United States.

Two or more of these modes may coexist within the same educational system. For example, the school-based management trend in many countries (England and Wales, Australia, New Zealand, Hong Kong) is underpinned by both participative democracy and the market mechanism. In England and Wales, schools and colleges are at the heart of 'the educational market place' with students and parents as customers, choosing from a range of providers. Caldwell and Spinks's (1992, p. 4) definition provides a clear link between self management and decentralization: 'A self-managing school is a school in a system of education where there has been significant and consistent *decentralization* to the school level of authority to make decisions related to the allocation of resources.'

The research on self-management in England and Wales (Bush, Coleman and Glover, 1993; Levacic, 1995; Thomas and Martin, 1996) largely suggests that the shift towards school autonomy has been beneficial. These UK perspectives are consistent with much of the international evidence on self-management and the Organization for Economic Co-operation and Development (OECD, 1994) concludes that it is likely to be beneficial:

Greater autonomy in schools . . . [leads] to greater effectiveness through greater flexibility in and therefore better use of resources; to professional development selected at school level; to more knowledgeable teachers and parents, so to better financial decisions, to whole school planning and implementation with priorities set on the basis of data about student [outcomes] and needs. (Quoted in Thomas and Martin, 1996, 28)

Autonomous schools and colleges may be regarded as potentially more efficient and effective but much depends on the nature and quality of internal management if these potential benefits are to be realized. Dellar's (1998) research in 30 secondary schools in Australia, for example, shows that 'site-based' management was most successful where there was a positive school climate and the involvement of staff and stakeholders in decision-making.

The significance of the educational context

Educational management as a field of study and practice was derived from management principles first applied to industry and commerce, mainly in the United States (see page 9). Theory development largely involved the application of industrial models to educational settings. As the subject became established as an academic discipline in its own right, its theorists and practitioners began to develop alternative models based on their observation of, and experience in, schools and colleges. By the twenty-first century the main theories, featured in this book, have either been developed in the educational context or have been adapted from industrial models to meet the specific requirements of schools and colleges.

Educational leadership and management has progressed from being a new field dependent upon ideas developed in other settings to become an established discipline with its own theories and significant empirical data testing their validity in education. This transition has been accompanied by lively argument about the extent to which education should be regarded as simply another field for the application of general principles of leadership and management or be seen as a separate discipline with its own body of knowledge.

One strand of opinion asserts that there are general principles of management which can be applied to all organizational settings. 'Schools have much in common with other organizations that bring people together for a purpose – be they hospitals, or businesses or government offices' (Handy, 1984, p. 26). The case for a common approach to the training and development of managers rests largely upon the functions thought to be common to different types of organization. These include financial management, human resource management and relationships with the organization's clients and the wider community.

This long-running debate about the most appropriate relationship between general management and that specific to education was rekindled from 1995 with the TTA's emphasis on the need to take account of 'best practice outside education' in devising professional development programmes. For example, its National Standards document states that 'the standards . . . reflect the work undertaken on management standards by those outside the education profession' (TTA, 1998, p. 1) and 'the knowledge and understanding that headteachers need draw on sources both inside and outside education' (ibid., p. 3).

Taking account of 'best practice outside education' appears uncontentious,

13

but it assumes that definitions of 'best practice' are widely understood and accepted. In practice, there are several problematic issues:

- Who decides what good, let alone 'best', practice is?
- How is such good practice to be adapted for use in training school leaders and managers?
- Is good practice a universal trait or does it depend on the specific school setting?

In addressing this issue, Glatter (1997) concludes with two cautions:

> It is not always clear what constitutes best practice in management outside education. As in education itself, there are different approaches and contending schools of thought . . . My brief overall conclusions are that, first, identifying best practice outside education will require the judgement of a Solomon, and, second, deciding what elements of this would really be of value in education will involve some notions of cultural compatibility. (Glatter, 1997, pp. 187–8)

Glatter and Kydd (2003, p. 240) add that 'we do not suggest that the idea of "best practice" should never be used, simply that it is often employed far too casually with the potential to mislead. It needs to be applied more rigorously and the criteria for assessing what practice is considered "best" should be clearly specified'.

There are several arguments to support the notion that education has specific needs that require a distinctive approach. These include:

- the difficulty of setting and measuring educational objectives;
- the presence of children and young people as the 'outputs' or 'clients' of educational institutions;
- the need for education professionals to have a high degree of autonomy in the classroom;
- the fact that many senior and middle managers, particularly in primary schools, have little time for the managerial aspects of their work.

Even more important than these issues is the requirement for educational leaders and managers to focus on the specifically educational aspects of their work. The overriding purpose of schools and colleges is to promote effective teaching and learning. These core issues are unique to education and 'best practice outside education' is unlikely to be of any help in addressing these central professional issues. The school improvement research (Stoll, 1996) emphasizes the need for leaders to focus on these educational issues rather than the generic tasks of managing staff, finance and marketing (Bush, 1998).

The NCSL has engaged with the business sector, notably in preparing its 'Think Tank' report, but its Leadership Development Framework (NCSL,

2001b) advocates 'instructional leadership' by including it as one of its 10 'leadership propositions'. The business sector has little to offer in this domain, although other ideas have been borrowed for use in education. Such approaches include Total Quality Management (West-Burnham, 2002), human resource management (Bush and Middlewood, 1997) and marketing (Foskett, 2002). However, the special characteristics of schools and colleges imply caution in the application of management models or practices drawn from non-educational settings. As the leading American writer Baldridge suggested more than 20 years ago, careful evaluation and adaptation of such models is required before they can be applied with confidence to educational organizations.

> Traditional management theories cannot be applied to educational institutions without carefully considering whether they will work well in that unique academic setting . . . We therefore must be extremely careful about attempts to manage or improve . . . education with 'modern management' techniques borrowed from business, for example. Such borrowing may make sense, but it must be approached very carefully. (Baldridge, et al., 1978, p. 9)

Instructional leadership

There are several models of educational leadership and these will be introduced in Chapter 2. Most of the models will be discussed in detail in subsequent chapters. However, instructional leadership does not fit the framework for this book, because it focuses on the direction of influence, rather than its nature and source, so it will be addressed here.

The increasing emphasis on managing teaching and learning as the core activities of educational institutions has led to 'instructional leadership' being emphasized and endorsed, notably by the English NCSL, as we noted above. Hallinger (1992) argues that instructional leadership has been supplanted by transformational leadership (see Chapter 4) in the United States but these models are not seen as incompatible by NCSL.

Leithwood, Jantzi and Steinbach (1999) point to the lack of explicit descriptions of instructional leadership in the literature and suggest that there may be different meanings of this concept. Their definition is:

> Instructional leadership . . . typically assumes that the critical focus for attention by leaders is the behaviour of teachers as they engage in activities directly affecting the growth of students. (Ibid., p. 8).

Southworth (2002, p. 79) adds that 'instructional leadership . . . is strongly concerned with teaching and learning, including the professional learning of teachers as well as student growth'. Bush and Glover's (2002) definition stresses the direction of the influence process:

> Instructional leadership focuses on teaching and learning and on the behaviour of teachers in working with students. Leaders' influence is targeted at student learning via teachers. The emphasis is on the direction and impact of influence rather than the influence process itself. (Ibid., 2002, p. 10)

Hallinger and Murphy (1985) state that instructional leadership comprises three broad categories:

- defining the school mission;
- managing the instructional programme;
- promoting school climate.

Blase and Blase's (1998) research with 800 principals in American elementary, middle and high schools suggests that effective instructional leadership behaviour comprises three aspects:

- talking with teachers (conferencing);
- promoting teachers' professional growth;
- fostering teacher reflection.

Southworth's (2002) qualitative research with primary heads of small schools in England and Wales shows that three strategies were particularly effective in improving teaching and learning:

- modelling;
- monitoring;
- professional dialogue and discussion.

Southworth's third category confirms Blase and Blase's (1998) first point but his other strategies introduce new notions of which instructional leadership practices are likely to be successful. He also concurs with Hill (2001, p. 87) that 'school leaders may lack sufficient knowledge of teaching and learning to provide adequate, let alone successful, instructional leadership' and advocates that this dimension should be included in leadership development programmes.

In contrast, Leithwood (1994, p. 499) claims that 'instructional leadership images are no longer adequate' because they are 'heavily classroom focused' and do not address 'second order changes . . . [such as] organization building' (ibid., p. 501). He adds that the instructional leadership image 'is now showing all the signs of a dying paradigm' (ibid., p. 502).

Despite these comments, instructional leadership is a very important dimension because it targets the school's central activities, teaching and learning. It may also be undergoing a renaissance in England, not least because of its specific endorsement by the National College for School Leadership (NCSL, 2001b). However, this paradigm underestimates other aspects of school life, such as socialization, student welfare and self-esteem, as well as the wider school-level issues referred to by Leithwood (1994).

Conclusion

Effective leadership and management are essential if schools and colleges are to achieve the wide-ranging objectives set for them by their many stakeholders, notably the governments which provide most of the funding for public educational institutions. In an increasingly global economy, an educated workforce is vital to maintain and enhance competitiveness. Society expects schools, colleges and universities to prepare people for employment in a rapidly changing environment. Teachers, and their leaders and managers, are the people who are required to deliver higher educational standards.

As these environmental pressures intensify, managers require greater understanding, skill and resilience to sustain their institutions. Heads, principals and senior staff need an appreciation of the theory, as well as the practice, of educational management. Competence comprises an appreciation of concepts as well as a penchant for successful action. The next chapter examines the nature of theory in educational management and its contribution to good practice.

References

Babyegeya, E. (2000) 'Education reforms in Tanzania: from nationalisation to decentralisation of schools', *International Studies in Educational Administration*, 28 (1): 2–10.

Baldridge, J.V., Curtis, D.V., Ecker, G. and Riley, G.L. (1978) *Policy-Making and Effective Leadership*, San Francisco, CA: Jossey-Bass.

Beare, H., Caldwell, B. and Millikan, R. (1989) *Creating an Excellent School*, London: Routledge.

Bennis, W. and Nanus, B. (1985) *Leaders*, New York: Harper and Row.

Blase, J. and Blase, J.R. (1998) *Handbook of Instructional Leadership: How Really Good Principals Promote Teaching and Learning*, London: Sage Publications.

Bolam, R. (1999) Educational administration, leadership and management: towards a research agenda, in T. Bush, L. Bell, R. Bolam, R. Glatter, and P. Ribbins (eds), *Educational Management: Redefining Theory, Policy and Practice*, London: Paul Chapman Publishing.

Bolam, R., McMahon, A., Pocklington, K. and Weindling, D. (1993) *Effective Management in Schools*, London: HMSO.

Bolman, L.G. and Deal, T.E. (1997) *Reframing Organizations: Artistry, Choice and Leadership*, San Francisco, CA: Jossey-Bass.

Bottery, M. (1999) 'Education under the new modernisers: an agenda for centralisation, illiberalism and inequality?', *Cambridge Journal of Education*, 29 (1): 103–20.

Bush, T. (1986) *Theories of Educational Management*, London: Harper and Row.

Bush, T. (1995) *Theories of Educational Management*, 2nd edn, London: Paul Chapman Publishing.

Bush, T. (1998) 'The National Professional Qualification for Headship: the key to effective school leadership?', *School Leadership and Management*, 18 (3): 321–34.

Bush, T. (1999) 'Crisis or crossroads? The discipline of educational management in the late 1990s', *Educational Management and Administration*, 27 (3): 239–52.

Bush, T. (2001) 'School organisation and management: international perspectives', paper presented at the Federation of Private School Teachers of Greece Conference, Athens, May.

Bush, T. and Glover, D. (2002) *School Leadership: Concepts and Evidence*, Nottingham: National College for School Leadership.

Bush, T. and Jackson, D. (2002) 'Preparation for school leadership: international perspectives', *Educational Management and Administration*, 30 (4): 417–29.

Bush, T. and Middlewood, D. (1997) *Managing People in Education*, London: Paul Chapman Publishing.

Bush, T., Coleman, M. and Glover, D. (1993) *Managing Autonomous Schools: The Grant-Maintained Experience*, London: Paul Chapman Publishing.

Caldwell, B and Spinks, J. (1992) *Leading the Self-Managing School*, London: Falmer Press.

Cuban, L. (1988) *The Managerial Imperative and the Practice of Leadership in Schools*, Albany, NY: State University of New York Press.

Culbertson, J. (1980) 'Educational administration: where we are and where we are going', paper presented at fourth International Intervisitation Program in Educational Administration, Vancouver.

Culbertson, J. (1983) 'Theory in educational administration: echoes from critical thinkers', *Educational Researcher*, 12 (10): 15–22.

Day, C., Harris, A. and Hadfield M. (2001) 'Challenging the orthodoxy of effective school leadership', *International Journal of Leadership in Education*, 4 (1): 39–56.

Dellar, G. (1998) 'School climate, school improvement and site-based management', *Learning Environments Research*, 1 (3): 353–67.

Dempster, N. and Logan, L. (1998) 'Expectations of school leaders', in J. MacBeath (ed.), *Effective School Leadership: Responding to Change*, London: Paul Chapman Publishing.

Derouet, J.L. (2000) 'School autonomy in a society with multi-faceted political references: the search for new ways of co-ordinating action', *Journal of Education Policy*, 15 (1): 61–9.

Dimmock, C. (1999) 'Principals and school restructuring: conceptualising challenges as dilemmas', *Journal of Educational Administration*, 37 (5): 441–62.

Fayol, H. (1916) *General and Industrial Management*, London: Pitman.

Fenech, J. (1994) 'Managing schools in a centralised system: headteachers at work', *Educational Management and Administration*, 22 (2): 131–40.

Fidler, B. (1997) 'School leadership: some key ideas', *School Leadership and Management*, 17 (1): 23–37.

Foreman, K. (1998) 'Vision and mission', in D. Middlewood, and J. Lumby (eds), *Strategic Management in Schools and Colleges*, London: Paul Chapman Publishing.

Foskett, N. (2002) 'Marketing', in T. Bush, and L. Bell (eds), *The Principles and Practice of Educational Management*, London: Paul Chapman Publishing.

Fullan, M. (1992a) *Successful School Improvement*, Buckingham: Open University Press.

Fullan, M. (1992b) 'Visions that blind', *Educational Leadership*, 49 (5): 19–20.

Furlong, J. (2000) 'Institutions and the crisis in teacher professionalism in T. Atkinson and G. Claxton, (eds), *The Intuitive Practitioner*, Buckingham: Open University Press.

Glatter, R. (1979) 'Educational policy and management: one field or two?', *Educational Analysis*, 1 (2): 15–24.

Glatter, R. (1997) 'Context and capability in educational management', *Educational Management and Administration*, 25 (2): 181–92.

Glatter, R. (1999) 'From struggling to juggling: towards a redefinition of the field of educational leadership and management', *Educational Management and Administration*, 27 (3): 253–66.

Glatter, R. and Kydd, L. (2003) 'Best practice in educational leadership and management: can we identify it and learn from it?', *Educational Management and Administration*, 31 (3): 231–44.

Gold, A., Evans, J., Earley, P., Halpin, D. and Collarbone, P. (2003) 'Principled principals? Values-driven leadership: evidence from ten case studies of "outstanding" school leaders', *Educational Management and Administration*, 31 (2): 127–38.

Gray, H.L. (1979) *The School as an Organisation*, Nafferton, Yorkshire: Nafferton Books.

Greenfield, T. and Ribbins, P. (eds) (1993) *Greenfield on Educational Administration: Towards a Humane Science*, London: Routledge.

Greenfield, W., Licata, J. and Johnson, B. (1992) 'Towards a measurement of school vision', *Journal of Educational Administration*, 30 (2): 65–76.

Gunter, H. (1997) *Rethinking Education: The Consequences of Jurassic Management*, London: Cassell.

Hallinger, P. (1992) 'The evolving role of American principals: from managerial to instructional to transformational leaders', *Journal of Educational Administration*, 30 (3): 35–48.

Hallinger, P. and Murphy, J. (1985) 'Assessing the instructional management behaviour of principals', *Elementary School Journal*, 86 (2): 217–47.

Handy, C. (1984) *Taken for Granted? Looking at Schools as Organisations*, York: Longman, for the Schools Council.

Hill, P. (2001) 'What principals need to know about teaching and learning', University of Melbourne, paper presented to the National College for School Leadership Think Tank, London.

Hughes, M. (1985) 'Theory and practice in educational management', in M. Hughes, P. Ribbins and H. Thomas (eds), *Managing Education: The System and the Institution*, London: Holt, Rinehart and Winston.

Hughes, M. and Bush, T. (1991) 'Theory and research as catalysts for change', in W. Walker, R. Farquhar and M. Hughes (eds), *Advancing Education: School Leadership in Action*, London: Falmer Press.

Hughes, M., Carter, J. and Fidler, B. (1981) *Professional Development Provision for Senior Staff in Schools and Colleges*, Birmingham: University of Birmingham.

Karstanje, P. (1999) 'Decentralisation and deregulation in Europe: towards a conceptual framework', in T. Bush, L. Bell, R. Bolam, R. Glatter and P. Ribbins (eds),

Educational Management: Redefining Theory, Policy and Practice, London: Paul Chapman Publishing.

Kouzes, J. and Posner, B. (1996) *The Leadership Challenge*, San Francisco, CA: Jossey-Bass.

Lauglo, J. (1997) 'Assessing the present importance of different forms of decentralisation in education', in K. Watson, C. Modgil and S. Modgil (eds), *Power and Responsibility in Education*, London: Cassell.

Leithwood, K. (1994) 'Leadership for school restructuring', *Educational Administration Quarterly*, 30 (4): 498–518.

Leithwood, K., Jantzi, D. and Steinbach, R. (1999) *Changing Leadership for Changing Times*, Buckingham: Open University Press.

Levačić, R. (1995) *Local Management of Schools: Analysis and Practice*, Buckingham: Open University Press.

Levačić, R., Glover, D., Bennett, N. and Crawford, M. (1999) 'Modern headship for the rationally managed school: combining cerebral and insightful approaches', in T. Bush, L. Bell, R. Bolam, R. Glatter and P. Ribbins (eds), *Educational Management: Redefining Theory, Policy and Practice*, London: Paul Chapman Publishing.

Millett, A. (1996) 'A head is more than a manager', *Times Educational Supplement*, 15 July.

National College for School Leadership (NCSL) (2001a) *First Corporate Plan: Launch Year 2001–2004*, Nottingham: (online at www.ncsl.gov.uk).

National College for School Leadership (NCSL) (2001b) *Leadership Development Framework*, Nottingham: NCSL.

Newman, J. and Clarke, J. (1994) 'Going about our business? The managerialism of public services', in J. Clarke, A. Cochrane and E. McLaughlin (eds), *Managing School Policy*, London: Sage Publications.

Nias, J., Southworth, G. and Campbell, P. (1992) *Whole School Curriculum Development in the Primary School*, London: Falmer.

Ogawa, R. and Bossert, S. (1995) 'Leadership as an organizational quality', *Educational Administration Quarterly*, 31 (2): 224–43.

Sapre, P. (2002) 'Realising the potential of educational management in India', *Educational Management and Administration*, 30 (1): 101–8.

Sayed, Y. (1999) 'Discourses of the policy of educational decentralisation in South Africa since 1994: an examination of the South African Schools Act', *Compare*, 29 (2): 141–52.

School Management Task Force (SMTF) (1990) *Developing School Management: The Way Forward*, London: HMSO.

Southworth, G. (1993) 'School leadership and school development: reflections from research', *School Organisation*, 12 (2): 73–87.

Southworth, G. (2002) 'Instructional leadership in schools: reflections and empirical evidence', *School Leadership and Management*, 22: 73–92.

Stoll, L. (1996) 'Linking school effectiveness and school improvement: issues and possibilities', in J. Gray, D. Reynolds, C. Fitz-Gibbon and D. Jesson (eds), *The Future of Research on School Effectiveness and Improvement*, London: Cassell.

Taylor, F.W. (1947) *Principles of Scientific Management*, New York: Harper and Row.

Teacher Training Agency (TTA) (1998) *National Standards for Headteachers;*

National Standards for Subject Leaders: National Standards for Qualified Teacher Status, London: TTA.

Therkildsen, O. (2000) 'Contextual issues in decentralisation of primary education in Tanzania', *International Journal of Educational Development*, 20: 407–21.

Thomas, H. and Martin, J. (1996) *Managing Resources for School Improvement*, London: Routledge.

Wasserberg, M. (2000) 'Creating the vision and making it happen', in H. Tomlinson, H. Gunter and P. Smith (eds), *Living Headship*, London: Paul Chapman Publishing.

Weber, M. (1947) in T. Parsons (ed.), *The Theory Of Social and Economic Organization*, Glencoe, IL: Free Press, and New York: Collier-Macmillan.

West-Burnham, J. (2002) 'Understanding quality', in T. Bush and L. Bell (eds), *The Principles and Practice of Educational Management*, London: Paul Chapman Publishing.

Wright, N. (2001) 'Leadership, "bastard leadership" and managerialism', *Educational Management and Administration*, 29 (3): 275–90.

Wright, N. (2003) 'Principled "bastard leadership"?: A rejoinder to Gold, Evans, Earley, Halpin and Collarbone', *Educational Management and Administration*, 31 (2): 139–44.

Yukl, G.A. (2002) *Leadership in Organizations*, 5th edn, Upper Saddle River, NJ: Prentice-Hall.

2

Models of Educational Leadership and Management

The theory/practice divide

Leadership and management are often regarded as essentially practical activities. The determination of vision, the allocation of resources and the evaluation of effectiveness all involve action. Practitioners tend to be dismissive of theories and concepts for their alleged remoteness from the 'real' school situation. Theory is also unfashionable with policy-makers and government agencies such as the English Office for Standards in Education (OFSTED) and Teacher Training Agency (TTA) (Bush, 1999a, p. 7).

There is some evidence that the explicit and systematic use of theory as a guide to practice is unusual. Some commentators regard management as atheoretical. Willower (1980, p. 2), for example, asserts that 'the application of theories by practising administrators [is] a difficult and problematic undertaking. Indeed, it is clear that theories are simply not used very much in the realm of practice'. Holmes and Wynne (1989, pp. 1–2) are also sceptical about the value of theory in informing practice: 'There can be little genuine theory in educational administration. It is an applied field ultimately dependent on human will acting within a social context . . . So, it is unproductive to look for a set of theories . . . by which educational administrators may guide administrative behaviour'.

The implementation of the Education Reform Act (1988) and subsequent legislation in England and Wales have led to an emphasis on the *practice* of educational leadership and management. Heads and principals have been inundated with advice from politicians, officials, officers of quangos, academics and consultants, about how to lead and manage their schools and colleges. Many of these prescriptions are atheoretical in the sense that they are not underpinned by explicit values or concepts (Bush, 1999b, p. 246).

It is evident from these comments that theory and practice are often regarded as separate aspects of educational leadership and management. Academics develop and refine theory while managers engage in practice. In short, there is a theory/practice divide, or 'gap':

> The theory–practice gap stands as the Gordian Knot of educational administration. Rather than be cut, it has become a permanent fixture of the landscape because it is embedded in the way we construct theories for use . . . The theory–practice gap will be removed when we construct different and better theories that predict the effects of practice. (English, 2002, pp. 1 and 3)

Theory may be perceived as esoteric and remote from practice. Yet in an applied discipline such as educational management the acid test of theory is its relevance to practice. Theory is valuable and significant if it serves to explain practice and provide managers with a guide to action. The emphasis in this book is on the use of theory to inform practice and to guide managers:

> Theories are most useful for influencing practice when they suggest new ways in which events and situations can be perceived. Fresh insight may be provided by focusing attention on possible interrelationships that the practitioner has failed to notice, and which can be further explored and tested through empirical research. If the result is a better understanding of practice, the theory–practice gap is significantly reduced for those concerned. Theory cannot then be dismissed as irrelevant. (Hughes and Bush, 1991, p. 234)

The relevance of theory to good practice

If practitioners shun theory then they must rely on experience as a guide to action. In deciding on their response to a problem they draw on a range of options suggested by previous experience with that type of issue. However, 'it is wishful thinking to assume that experience alone will teach leaders everything they need to know' (Copland et al., 2002, p. 75).

Teachers sometimes explain their decisions as just 'common sense'. However, such apparently pragmatic decisions are often based on implicit theories: 'Common-sense knowledge . . . inevitably carries with it unspoken assumptions and unrecognized limitations. Theorizing is taking place without it being acknowledged as such' (Hughes, 1985, p. 31). When a teacher or a manager takes a decision it reflects in part that person's view of the organization. Such views or preconceptions are coloured by experience and by the attitudes engendered by that experience. These attitudes take on the character of frames of reference or theories which inevitably influence the decision-making process.

The use of the term 'theory' need not imply something remote from the day-to-day experience of the teacher. Rather, theories and concepts can provide a framework for managerial decisions:

> Because organizations are complex, surprising, deceptive, and ambiguous, they are formidably difficult to understand and manage. We have to rely on the tools at

23

hand, including whatever ideas and theories we have about what organizations are and how they work. Our theories, or frames, determine what we see and what we do . . . Managers need better theories, as well as the ability to implement those theories with skill and grace. (Bolman and Deal, 1997, p. 38)

Theory serves to provide a rationale for decision-making. Managerial activity is enhanced by an explicit awareness of the theoretical framework underpinning practice in educational institutions. As a result some academics and practitioners 'vigorously challenge the traditional view that practical on the job experience *on its own* provides adequate management training in education' (Hughes, 1984, p. 5).

There are three main arguments to support the view that managers have much to learn from an appreciation of theory, providing that it is grounded firmly (Glaser and Strauss, 1967) in the realities of practice:

1 Reliance on facts as the sole guide to action is unsatisfactory because all evidence requires *interpretation*. Life in schools and colleges is too complex to enable practitioners to make decisions simply on an event by event basis. Theory provides the framework for interpreting events. It provides 'mental models' (Leithwood, Jantzi and Steinbach, 1999, p. 75) to help in understanding the nature and effects of practice.

2 Dependence on personal *experience* in interpreting facts and making decisions is narrow because it discards the knowledge of others. Familiarity with the arguments and insights of theorists enables the practitioner to deploy a wide range of experience and understanding in resolving the problems of today. Grounded theory emerges by assessing a wide range of practice and developing models which seem to help in explaining events and behaviour. An understanding of theory also helps by reducing the likelihood of mistakes occurring while experience is being acquired.

3 Experience may be particularly unhelpful as the sole guide to action when the practitioner begins to operate in a different *context*. Organizational variables may mean that practice in one school or college has little relevance in the new environment. A broader awareness of theory and practice may be valuable as the manager attempts to interpret behaviour in the fresh situation.

Of course, theory is useful only so long as it has relevance to practice in education. Hoyle (1986) distinguishes between theory-for-understanding and theory-for-practice. While both are potentially valuable, the latter is more significant for practising leaders and managers in education. The relevance of theory should be judged by the extent to which it informs managerial action and contributes to the resolution of practical problems in schools and colleges.

The nature of theory

There is no single all-embracing theory of educational management. In part this reflects the astonishing diversity of educational institutions, ranging from small rural primary schools to very large universities and colleges. It relates also to the varied nature of the problems encountered in schools and colleges, which require different approaches and solutions. Above all, it reflects the multifaceted nature of theory in education and the social sciences: 'Students of educational management who turn to organizational theory for guidance in their attempt to understand and manage educational institutions will not find a single, universally applicable theory but a multiplicity of theoretical approaches each jealously guarded by a particular epistemic community' (Ribbins, 1985, p. 223).

House (1981) argues that theories or 'perspectives' in education are not the same as scientific theories. The latter comprises a set of beliefs, values and techniques that are shared within a particular field of enquiry. The dominant theory eventually comes under challenge by the emergence of new facts which the theory cannot explain. Subsequently a new theory is postulated which does explain these new facts. However, the physical world itself remains constant.

Theories of education and the social sciences are very different from scientific theories. These perspectives relate to a changing situation and comprise different ways of seeing a problem rather than a scientific consensus as to what is true. House (1981, p. 17) suggests that, in this sense, the perspective is a weaker claim to knowledge than a scientific theory. In education several perspectives may be valid simultaneously:

> Our understanding of knowledge utilization processes is conceived not so much as a set of facts, findings, or generalizations but rather as distinct perspectives which combine facts, values and presuppositions into a complex screen through which knowledge utilization is seen . . . Through a particular screen one sees certain events, but one may see different scenes through a different screen. (Ibid.)

The models discussed in this book should be regarded as alternative ways of portraying events, as House suggests. The existence of several different perspectives creates what Bolman and Deal (1997, p. 11) describe as 'conceptual pluralism: a jangling discord of multiple voices'. Each theory has something to offer in explaining behaviour and events in educational institutions. The perspectives favoured by managers, explicitly or implicitly, inevitably influence or determine decision-making.

Griffiths (1997) provides strong arguments to underpin his advocacy of 'theoretical pluralism'.

> The basic idea is that all problems cannot be studied fruitfully using a single theory. Some problems are large and complex and no single theory is capable of encompassing them, while others, although seemingly simple and straightforward, can be better understood through the use of multiple theories . . . particular theories are appropriate to certain problems, but not others. (Griffiths, 1997, p. 372)

Morgan (1997) discusses the concept of organizational culture and emphasizes the diversity of theories of management and organization. He uses 'metaphors' to explain the complex and paradoxical character of organizational life and describes theory in similar terms to House (1981):

> All theories of organization and management are based on implicit images or metaphors that lead us to see, understand and manage organizations in distinctive yet partial ways . . . the use of metaphor implies *a way of thinking* and *a way of seeing* that pervades how we understand our world . . . We have to accept that any theory or perspective that we bring to the study of organization and management, while capable of creating valuable insights, is also incomplete, biased and potentially misleading. (Morgan, 1997, pp. 4–5)

One of the confusing aspects of educational management theory is the use of different terms to explain similar phenomena. While House (1981) prefers 'perspective', Bolman and Deal (1997) choose 'frame' and Morgan (1986) opts for 'metaphor'. Boyd (1992, p. 506) adds to the confusion by referring to 'paradigms', a term he admits to using 'loosely': 'By paradigm is meant a model or theory; with models or theories often guiding, consciously or subconsciously, our thinking about such things as organizations, leadership and policy.' These terms are broadly similar and reflect the preferences of the authors rather than any significant differences in meaning. They will be used interchangeably in this book.

The various theories of educational leadership and management reflect very different ways of understanding and interpreting events and behaviour in schools and colleges. They also represent what are often ideologically based, and certainly divergent, views about how educational institutions ought to be managed. Waite (2002, p. 66) refers to 'paradigm wars' in describing disagreements between academics holding different positions on theory and research in educational administration.

Theories of educational leadership and management are endowed with different terminology but they all emanate from organization theory or management theory. The former tends to be theory for understanding while management theory has more direct relevance for practice. Hoyle (1986, pp. 1 and 20) distinguishes between these two broad approaches:

> Organization theory is theory-for-understanding. We can thus make a broad distinction between organization theory and management theory, which is practical

theory and hence has a narrower focus. However, the distinction cannot be pressed too hard since management theory is grounded in, and the research which it generates contributes to, organization theory . . . the case for organization theory is that it enhances our understanding of the management component and . . . that it provides a loose organizing framework for a variety of studies of schools.

Holmes and Wynne (1989, p. 29) take a much more critical view of the value of organization theory for educational management: 'Unfortunately, there is no empirically proven theory of school organization so such texts [of school administration] are reduced to describing scattered pieces of research held together with inconclusive argument.' This assessment is dated and much too pessimistic, greatly undervaluing the theory development and related empirical research on aspects of schools and colleges as organizations.

The models discussed in this book are broad compilations of the main theories of educational leadership and management and are largely based on organization theory. However, by applying theory to practice throughout the text, management theories are developed and tested for their applicability to schools and colleges, and to their leaders.

The characteristics of theory

Most theories of educational leadership and management possess three major characteristics:

1 Theories tend to be *normative* in that they reflect beliefs about the nature of educational institutions and the behaviour of individuals within them. Theorists tend to express views about how schools and colleges should be managed as well as, or instead of, simply describing aspects of management or explaining the organizational structure of the school or college. When, for example, practitioners or academics claim that decisions in schools are reached following a participative process they may be expressing normative judgements rather than analysing actual practice.

  Simkins (1999) stresses the importance of distinguishing between descriptive and normative uses of theory:

> This is a distinction which is often not clearly made. The former are those which attempt to describe the nature of organizations and how they work and, sometimes, to explain why they are as they are. The latter, in contrast, attempt to prescribe how organizations should or might be managed to achieve particular outcomes more effectively. (Ibid., p. 270)

  The remaining chapters of this book will distinguish between the normative and descriptive aspects of theory.

2 Theories tend to be *selective* or partial in that they emphasize certain aspects of the institution at the expense of other elements. The espousal

27

of one theoretical model leads to the neglect of other approaches. Schools and colleges are arguably too complex to be capable of analysis through a single dimension. An explanation of educational institutions using a political perspective, for example, may focus on the formation of interest groups and on the bargaining between groups and individuals. This approach offers valuable insights, as we shall see in Chapter 5, but this emphasis necessarily means that other valid theories of school and college management may be underestimated. In the 1980s, a few writers (Enderud, 1980; Davies and Morgan, 1983; Ellstrom, 1983;) attempted syntheses of different approaches but with only limited success.

3 Theories of educational management are often based on, or supported by, *observation* of practice in educational institutions. English (2002, p. 1) says that observation may be used in two ways. First, observation may be followed by the development of concepts which then become theoretical frames. Such perspectives based on data from systematic observation are sometimes called 'grounded theory'. Because such approaches are derived from empirical inquiry in schools and colleges, they are more likely to be perceived as relevant by practitioners. As Glaser and Strauss (1967, p. 3) aptly claim, 'generating grounded theory is a way of arriving at theory suited to its supposed uses'.

Secondly, researchers may use a specific theoretical frame to select concepts to be tested through observation. The research is then used to 'prove' or 'verify' the efficacy of the theory (English, 2002, p. 1).

While many theories of educational management are based on observation, advocates of the subjective model are sceptical of this stance. As we shall see in Chapter 6, subjective theorists prefer to emphasize the perceptions and interpretations of individuals within organizations. In this view observation is suspect because it does not reveal the meanings placed on events by participants.

Theory in educational management thus tends to be normative, selective and often based on observation in educational settings. These qualities overlap and interpenetrate, as Theodossin (1983, p. 89) demonstrates: 'Inevitably . . . research involves selection; selection is determined by, and determines, perspective; perspective limits vision; vision generates questions; and questions in turn, help to shape and influence the answers.'

Gender and educational leadership and management

Women are greatly underrepresented in senior posts in education as in many other occupations. 'It has become part of our taken-for-granted understanding that men dominate numerically in senior positions in all phases of education with the exception of nursery and infant schools. Analysts of education management acknowledge the disparity between women's numbers in the teaching profession and their representation at senior levels' (Hall, 1999, p. 159).

In English and Welsh secondary schools in 1993, 49.6 per cent of all teachers, but only 21.9 per cent of the headteachers, were women. In nursery and primary schools, 81.5 per cent of teachers were women but only 50.3 per cent of the headteachers were women (Coleman, 1997). By 1999, the position in secondary schools had improved with 27.9 per cent of headships held by women but this still compares unfavourably with classroom teachers where 54.7 per cent are women (Coleman, 2002, p. 3).

The position may be worse in many other countries. Davies (1990, p. 62) notes that 'formal decision-making is in the hands of men . . . Educational administration is still seen as a masculine occupation in many countries'. Research by Coleman, Qiang and Li (1998) shows that there were no women principals in any of the 89 secondary schools in three counties of the Shaanxi province of China.

Among the reasons advanced for the low proportion of women in senior posts is the alleged 'male' image of management which may be unappealing to women. This model includes 'aggressive competitive behaviours, an emphasis on control rather than negotiation and collaboration, and the pursuit of competition rather than shared problem-solving' (Al-Khalifa 1992, p. 100). The male domination, or 'androcentricity', of educational management is evident in the United States where school administration evolved into a largely male profession disconnected from the mainly female occupation of teaching. Boyd (1992, p. 509) implies that this led to discrimination in the allocation of administrative posts: 'The abilities and values of women were passed over, as careers in school administration were more driven by male sponsorship than by merit and open competition . . . school administration became far more concerned with hierarchy, control and efficiency than with issues of curriculum, pedagogy, and educational values.'

The androcentricity of educational management has led certain writers (Shakeshaft, 1987; Ozga, 1993) to claim that theory has failed to acknowledge the different values of women and remains largely rooted in a male perspective. The difficulty is that there is little clarity about what constitutes a distinctive female theory of educational management. Hall (1993, p. 43) concludes that:

> There is relatively little to date in research about women managers that can be used to challenge theories of educational management or lead to their reconceptualization to include both women and men . . . Research is needed that challenges

traditional stereotypes of what constitutes appropriate management behaviour and process. The association of management and masculinity has not been established as a fact yet it is treated as such, with negative consequences for women in education . . . theory and prescriptions for action [would be] transformed by the inclusion of gender as a relevant concept for understanding educational management.

Wallace and Hall's (1994, p. 39) research on senior management teams in secondary schools suggests that it is possible for management to incorporate both female and male styles: 'The decision to adopt a team approach seems to signify a shift in leadership style towards an "androgynous" model which posits the possibility for leaders to exhibit the wide range of qualities which are present in both men and women.' Gray (1989) adopts a similar approach in distinguishing between 'feminine' and 'masculine' paradigms in school management. Feminine characteristics include 'caring', 'creative' and 'intuitive' dimensions, while the masculine paradigm features 'competitive', 'highly regulated' and 'disciplined' elements. Individual managers may possess qualities from both paradigms, regardless of their gender. This view is supported by the large-scale research on male and female secondary heads carried out by Coleman (2002). She shows that there is little difference in the ways that male and female heads respond to the Gray descriptors and concludes that 'the paradigms are not perceived as relevant in distinguishing women from men' (ibid., p. 103).

A number of the six models presented in this book have been aligned with 'male' or 'female' qualities. The gender implications of the theories will be discussed at appropriate points in the text.

Models of educational management: an introduction

Many different theories of educational management have been presented by various writers. These perspectives overlap in several respects. A further complication is that similar models are given different names or, in certain cases, the same term is used to denote different approaches. A degree of integration of these theories is required so that they can be presented in a clear and discrete manner. Cuthbert (1984, p. 39) explains why there is a lack of clarity:

The study of management in education is an eclectic pursuit. Models have been borrowed from a wide range of disciplines, and in a few cases developed specifically to explain unique features of educational institutions. To comprehend the variety of models available we need some labels and categories that allow us to consider different ideas in a sensible order.

The approach to theory adopted in this book has certain similarities with Cuthbert's (1984) presentation of models in five distinct groups. Cuthbert's categories are analytic-rational, pragmatic-rational, political, models that stress ambiguity, and phenomenological and interactionist models. The latter three groups are the same as three of the models discussed in this text although I prefer the term subjective rather than phenomenological or interactionist. Cuthbert compares his models in the following terms:

- the level of agreement among people in the organization about the objectives of their joint efforts;
- different ideas about the way in which performance can and should be evaluated;
- different ideas about the concept and the meaning of organization structure.

Two of the criteria used by Cuthbert are similar to two of the four main elements used in this text to distinguish between the models.

Several writers have chosen to present theories in distinct groups or bundles but they differ in the models chosen, the emphasis given to particular approaches and the terminology used to describe them. Two of the best known are those by Bolman and Deal (1997) and Morgan (1997).

- Bolman and Deal (1997); four 'perspectives or frames' – structural, human resource, political, symbolic.
- Morgan (1997); eight images or metaphors of organizations – as machines, organisms, brains, cultures, political systems, psychic prisons, flux and transformation, instruments of domination.

In this book the main theories are classified into six major models of educational management. While this division differs somewhat from the categorization of other writers, these models are given significant attention in the literature of educational management and have been subject to a degree of empirical verification in British education. The six theories are illustrated extensively by examples of practice drawn from primary schools, secondary schools and colleges in England and Wales, and in many other countries.

The six models are:

- formal;
- collegial;
- political;
- subjective;
- ambiguity;
- cultural.

In the first edition of this book only five models were identified. A chapter on the cultural model was added to the second edition because of the increasing significance of this approach in the literature and because some empirical work had been undertaken in British schools and elsewhere in the English speaking world.

Analysing the models

The analysis of these six models includes consideration of four main elements which are valuable in distinguishing the theories. These criteria are as follows:

1 The level of agreement about the *goals* or objectives of the institution. There is increasing emphasis on goals in the literature on school improvement (Blum and Butler, 1989, p. 19). Cheng (2002, p. 51) also shows that goal orientation is one of only two common factors within the numerous definitions of leadership.

   The theories differ in that some emphasize organizational aims, while others focus on individual purposes. Certain models feature agreement about objectives but others stress conflict over aims or point to difficulties in defining purpose within educational organizations.

2 The meaning and validity of organizational *structures* within educational institutions. Hoyle (1986) refers to the twin dimensions of people and structure. An emphasis on structure leads to the notion of individuals being defined by their roles, while a focus on people leads to the predominance of personality in determining behaviour.

   According to some theorists, structure is an objective fact while others believe that it is the subjective creation of individuals within the institution. Another group argues that structure is a matter for negotiation or dispute while others claim that the structure is one of the many ambiguous features of schools and colleges.

3 The relationship between the institution and its external *environment*. The shift to self-managing schools and colleges, discussed in Chapter 1, increases the significance of the relationships that staff and governors must have with a wide range of external groups and individuals. The nature of these external relationships is a key element in the differences between models. Some writers regard the head or principal as the sole or major contact with the outside world, while others suggest a wider range of contacts. Links may be regarded as essentially co-operative in nature or they may be thought of as political, with conflict between the institution and external agencies. Other approaches emphasize the ambiguity of such relationships.

4 The most appropriate *leadership* strategies for educational institutions. Analysts have different views about the nature of educational leadership

according to the theories they espouse. Some assume that heads take the lead in establishing objectives and in decision-making while others regard the head as one figure within a participative system. Certain approaches stress conflict inside institutions and emphasize the head's role as negotiator while others point to the limitations of an active leadership role within essentially ambiguous institutions.

Given the heightened interest in the concept of educational leadership since the second edition of this volume, this subject will be given extended treatment in this edition. The main theories of leadership are introduced below and will also be addressed alongside the six management models, to demonstrate the links between these twin concepts.

These four criteria serve to emphasize the great differences in approach between the various models and reinforce the view that theories are normative and selective. In subsequent chapters of this book we examine these different interpretations of the nature of leadership and management in schools and colleges.

Models of educational leadership: an introduction

As with educational management, the vast literature on leadership has generated a number of alternative, and competing, models. Some writers have sought to cluster these various conceptions into a number of broad themes or 'types'. The best known of these typologies is that by Leithwood, Jantzi and Steinbach (1999), who identified six 'models' from their scrutiny of 121 articles in four international journals. Bush and Glover (2002) extended this typology to eight models. These are among the nine leadership models shown in Table 2.1, alongside the management models introduced earlier in this chapter.

Table 2.1   Typology of management and leadership models

Management model	Leadership model
Formal	Managerial
Collegial	Participative
	Transformational
	Interpersonal
Political	Transactional
Subjective	Post-modern
Ambiguity	Contingency
Cultural	Moral
	Instructional

Source: adapted from Bush and Glover, 2002

Instructional leadership does not link to any of the management models because it focuses on the direction of influence, learning and teaching, rather than the nature of the influence process. This model was discussed in Chapter 1 while the other eight leadership models will be addressed alongside the appropriate management model in subsequent chapters of this book.

References

Al-Khalifa, E. (1992) 'Management by halves: women teachers and school management', in N. Bennett, M. Crawford and C. Riches (eds), *Managing Change in Education: Individual and Organizational Perspectives*, London: Paul Chapman Publishing.

Blum, R.E. and Butler, J.A. (1989) 'The role of school leaders in school improvement', in R.E. Blum and J.A. Butler (eds), *School Leader Development for School Improvement*, Leuven: Acco.

Bolman, L.G. and Deal, T.E. (1997) *Reframing Organisations: Artistry, Choice and Leadership*, San Francisco, CA: Jossey-Bass.

Boyd, W. (1992) 'The power of paradigms: reconceptualizing educational policy and management', *Educational Administration Quarterly*, 28 (4): 504–28.

Bush, T. (1999a) 'Introduction: setting the scene, in T. Bush, L. Bell, R. Bolam, R. Glatter and P. Ribbins (eds), *Educational Management: Redefining Theory, Policy and Practice*, London: Paul Chapman Publishing.

Bush, T. (1999b) 'Crisis or crossroads? The discipline of educational management in the late 1990s', *Educational Management and Administration*, 27 (3): 239–52.

Bush, T. and Glover, D. (2002) *School Leadership: Concepts and Evidence*, Nottingham: NCSL.

Cheng, Y.C. (2002) 'Leadership and strategy', in T. Bush and L. Bell (eds), *The Principles and Practice of Educational Management*, London: Paul Chapman Publishing.

Coleman, M. (1997) 'Managing for equal opportunities: the gender issue', in T. Bush and D. Middlewood (eds), *Managing People in Education*, London: Paul Chapman Publishing.

Coleman, M. (2002) *Women as Headteachers: Striking the Balance*, Stoke-on-Trent: Trentham Books.

Coleman, M., Qiang, H. and Li, Y. (1998) 'Women in educational management in China: experience in Shaanxi province, *Compare*, 28 (2): 141–54.

Copland, M., Darling-Hammond, L., Knapp, M., McLaugghlin, M. and Talbert, J. (2002) *Leadership for Teaching and Learning: A Framework for Research and Action*, April, New Orleans: American Educational Research Association.

Cuthbert, R. (1984) *The Management Process, E324 Management in Post Compulsory Education, Block 3, Part 2*, Buckingham: Open University Press.

Davies, J.L. and Morgan, A.W. (1983) 'Management of higher education in a period of contraction and uncertainty', in O. Boyd-Barrett, T. Bush, J. Goodey, I. McNay and M. Preedy (eds), *Approaches to Post School Management*, London: Paul Chapman Publishing.

Davies, L. (1990) *Equity and Efficiency? School Management in an International Context*, London: Falmer Press.

Ellstrom, P.E. (1983) 'Four faces of educational organisations', *Higher Education*, 12: 231–41.

Enderud, H. (1980) 'Administrative leadership in organised anarchies', *International Journal of Institutional Management in Higher Education*, 4 (3): 235–53.

English, F. (2002) 'Cutting the Gordian Knot of educational administration: the theory–practice gap, *The Review*, 44 (1): 1–3.

Glaser, B.G. and Strauss, A.L. (1967) *The Discovery of Grounded Theory*, London: Weidenfeld and Nicolson.

Gray, H. (1989) 'Gender considerations in school management: masculine and feminine leadership styles', in C. Riches and C. Morgan (eds), *Human Resource Management in Education*, Buckingham: Open University Press.

Griffiths, D. (1997) 'The case for theoretical pluralism', *Educational Management and Administration*, 25 (4): 371–80.

Hall, V. (1993) 'Women in educational management: a review of research in Britain', in J. Ouston (ed.), *Women in Educational Management*, Harlow: Longman.

Hall, V. (1999) 'Gender and education management: duel or dialogue?', in T. Bush, L. Bell, R. Bolam, R. Glatter and P. Ribbins (eds), *Educational Management: Redefining Theory, Policy and Practice*, London: Paul Chapman Publishing.

Holmes, M. and Wynne, E. (1989) *Making the School an Effective Community: Belief Practice and Theory in School Administration*, Lewes: Falmer Press.

House, E.R. (1981) 'Three perspectives on innovation', in R. Lehming and M. Kane (eds), *Improving Schools: Using What We Know*, Beverly Hills, CA: Sage Publications.

Hoyle, E. (1986) *The Politics of School Management*, Sevenoaks: Hodder and Stoughton.

Hughes, M. (1984) 'Educational administration; pure or applied', *Studies in Educational Administration*, 35: 1–10.

Hughes, M. (1985) 'Theory and practice in educational management', in M. Hughes, P. Ribbins and H. Thomas (eds), *Managing Education: The System and the Institution*, London: Holt, Rinehart and Winston.

Hughes, M. and Bush, T. (1991) 'Theory and research as catalysts for change', in W. Walker, R. Farquhar and M. Hughes (eds), *Advancing Education: School Leadership in Action*, London: Falmer Press.

Leithwood, K., Jantzi, D. and Steinbach, R. (1999) *Changing Leadership for Changing Times*, Buckingham: Open University Press.

Morgan, G. (1997) *Images of Organization*, Newbury Park, CA: Sage Publications.

Ozga, J. (1993) *Women in Educational Management*, Buckingham: Open University Press.

Ribbins, P. (1985) 'Organisation theory and the study of educational institutions', in M. Hughes, P. Ribbins and H. Thomas (eds), *Managing Education: The System and the Institution*, London: Holt, Rinehart and Winston.

Shakeshaft, C. (1987) *Women in Educational Administration*, Newbury Park, CA: Sage Publications.

Simkins, T. (1999) 'Values, power and instrumentality: theory and research in education management', *Educational Management and Administration*, 27 (3):

267–81.

Theodossin, E. (1983) 'Theoretical perspectives on the management of planned educational change', *British Education Research Journal*, 9 (1): 81–90.

Waite, D. (2002) 'The "paradigm wars" in educational administration: an attempt at transcendence', *International Studies in Educational Administration*, 30 (1): 66–81.

Wallace, M. and Hall, V. (1994) *Inside the SMT: Teamwork in Secondary School Management*, London: Paul Chapman Publishing.

Willower, D.J. (1980) 'Contemporary issues in theory in educational administration', *Educational Administration Quarterly*, 16 (3): 1–25. Copyright © 1980 D. J. Willower. Reprinted by permission of Sage Publications, Inc.

3
Formal Models

Central features of formal models

Formal model is an umbrella term used to embrace a number of similar but not identical approaches. The title 'formal' is used because these theories emphasize the official and structural elements of organizations. There is a focus on pursuing institutional objectives through rational approaches. The definition suggested below incorporates the main features of these perspectives:

> Formal models assume that organizations are hierarchical systems in which managers use rational means to pursue agree goals. Heads possess authority legitimized by their formal positions within the organization and are accountable to sponsoring bodies for the activities of their institutions.

The various formal models have several common features:

1 They tend to treat organizations as *systems*. A system comprises elements that have clear organizational links with each other. Within schools and colleges, for example, departments and other sub-units are systemically related to each other and to the institution itself.
2 Formal models give prominence to the *official structure* of the organization. Formal structures are often represented by organization charts which show the authorized pattern of relationships between members of the institution. Structural models do not adequately reflect the many informal contacts within schools and colleges but they do help to represent the more stable and official aspects of organizations.
3 In formal models the official structures of the organization tend to be *hierarchical*. Organization charts emphasize vertical relationships between staff. In secondary schools and colleges staff are responsible to heads of department who, in turn, are answerable to heads and principals for the activities of their departments. The hierarchy thus represents a means of control for leaders over their staff.
4 All formal approaches typify schools and colleges as *goal-seeking* organizations. The institution is thought to have official purposes which

are accepted and pursued by members of the organization. Cheng (2002, p. 52) claims that goal development and achievement is one of two main general elements in leadership: 'How to set goals, create meanings, direct actions, eliminate uncertainty or ambiguity and achieve goals is also a core part of leadership activities in education.' Increasingly, goals are set within a broader vision of a preferred future for the school (Beare, Caldwell and Millikan, 1989).

5 Formal models assume that managerial decisions are made through a *rational* process. Typically, all the options are considered and evaluated in terms of the goals of the organization. The most suitable alternative is then selected to enable those objectives to be pursued. The essence of this approach is that decision-making is thought to be an objective, detached and intellectual process.

6 Formal approaches present the *authority* of leaders as essentially a product of their official positions within the organization. Heads and principals possess authority over other staff because of their formal roles within schools and colleges. Their power is regarded as positional and is held only while they hold these senior posts.

7 In formal models there is an emphasis on the *accountability* of the organization to its sponsoring body. Most schools remain responsible to the local education authority (LEA). Colleges in England are accountable to the Learning and Skills Council. In many centralized systems, school principals are accountable to national or provincial ministries of education. In decentralized systems, heads and principals are increasingly answerable to their governing bodies which have enhanced responsibility for finance and staff management.

These seven basic features are present to a greater or lesser degree in each of the individual theories which together comprise the formal models. These are:

- structural models;
- systems models;
- bureaucratic models;
- rational models;
- hierarchical models.

These different theories overlap significantly and the main elements are often very similar despite their different titles. There are variations in emphasis but the central components appear in most of the individual theories.

Structural models

> Structure refers to the formal pattern of relationships between people in organizations. It expresses the ways in which individuals relate to each other in order to achieve organizational objectives. (Bush, 1997, p. 45)

Structural models stress the primacy of organizational structure but the key elements are compatible with the central features of any formal model. Bolman and Deal (1991, p. 48) argue that the structural perspective is based on six core assumptions:

1 Organizations exist primarily to accomplish established goals.
2 For any organization, a structural form can be designed and implemented to fit its particular set of circumstances.
3 Organizations work most effectively when environmental turbulence and the personal preferences are constrained by norms of rationality.
4 Specialization permits higher levels of individual expertise and performance.
5 Co-ordination and control are essential to effectiveness.
6 Organizational problems typically originate from inappropriate structures or inadequate systems and can be resolved through restructuring or developing new systems.

The structural assumptions identified by Bolman and Deal, including the goal orientation, the rationality, the exercise of authority and the reference to systems, are consistent with the central features of formal models discussed earlier.

Becher and Kogan (1992) propose a structural model which has four levels. These are as follows:

1 The *Central Level*, including the various national and local authorities who are between them charged with overall planning, resource allocation and the monitoring of standards.
2 The *Institution* as defined in law and convention. This includes all schools and colleges.
3 The *Basic Unit* which corresponds with departments or faculties in colleges and with departments and pastoral units in schools.
4 The *Individual Level* comprises teachers, students or pupils and support staff, but Becher and Kogan focus mainly on teachers because 'it is they who normally play the main role in shaping academic and curricular policy' (Becher and Kogan, 1992, p. 9).

This structural model features normative and operational modes. The normative mode relates to the monitoring and maintenance of values within the system as a whole. The operational mode refers to the business of carrying out practical tasks at different levels within the system.

Relationships between levels can be categorized as either normative or operational. Normative relationships involve appraisal or judgement while operational relationships relate to the allocation of resources, responsibilities and tasks.

Becher and Kogan leave open the nature of the relationships between their four levels. Their structural model does not assume hierarchical relationships. However, school and college structures are usually portrayed as vertical and hierarchical. Evetts (1992, p. 84), for example, stresses the hierarchical nature of school structures and reinforces the authority of the head: 'A high degree of authority is vested in the headteacher and transmitted through heads of departments/years . . . [it implies] agreement about the headteacher's ability to direct the management of the school without disagreement or opposition.'

The structures of English further education colleges have traditionally been hierarchical and Hall (1994) notes that the departmental, pyramid structure has dominated in colleges for 30 years. Lumby's (2001) research with post-incorporation colleges shows that many are adopting different metaphors for structure including the 'Christmas tree', 'a less stark image than a pyramid' (ibid., pp. 91–2), and a series of concentric circles. However, she concludes that 'some degree of bureaucratic hierarchy will always assert itself' (ibid., p. 92).

Structures are not inevitably hierarchical. Those which are apparently hierarchical may be used to facilitate delegation and participation in decision-making. This may occur, for example, where budgets are delegated to departments.

The resilience of structure

It is easy to dismiss organizational structures as a rigid, over-formal presentation of relationships in educational institutions. All schools and colleges benefit from informal contacts not represented on organization charts. In addition, formal structures conceal a range of different styles of management. Yet structures remain powerful influences on the nature and direction of development within institutions, as Clark (1983, p. 114) makes clear:

> Academic structures do not simply move aside or let go: what is in place heavily conditions what will be. The heavy hand of history is felt in the structures and beliefs that development has set in place. As systems grow larger and more complex, their internal structures acquire greater momentum, thrusting themselves powerfully into the future and snapping back with considerable resilience after

imposed changes seemingly altered their ways . . . We do not begin to know the score in the study of academic change until we understand how current structures stack the deck.

Systems models

Systems theories emphasize the unity and integrity of the organization and focus on the interaction between its component parts, and with the external environment. These models stress the unity and *coherence* of the organization. Schools and colleges are thought to have integrity as prime institutions. Members of the organization, and those external to it, recognize the school or college as a meaningful entity. Staff and students may feel that they 'belong' to the place where they teach or learn. However, there are dangers in too great an emphasis on the organization rather than the people within it because of the risk of attributing human characteristics to schools and colleges. Greenfield (1973; 1975) has been the most persistent critic of this tendency to reify organizations as we shall see in Chapter 6.

Systems approaches share with other formal models the emphasis on agreed organizational *objectives*. It is assumed that the total system has objectives which have the support of its members. The institution is thought to develop policies in pursuit of these objectives and to assess the effectiveness of such policies. Systems theories play down or ignore the possibility that goals may be contested or that individuals may have purposes independent of the formal aims of the organization.

Systems models emphasize the concept of a system *boundary*. The boundary is an essential element in the definition of the system, distinguishing the organization and its members from the external environment:

> Environment is typically seen as everything outside the boundaries of an organisation, even though the boundaries are often nebulous and poorly drawn. It is the environment that provides raw materials to an organisation and receives the organisation's outputs . . . Schools receive students from the community and later return graduates to the community. (Bolman and Deal, 1989, p. 24)

Closed or open systems

Systems theories are usually categorized as either *closed* or *open* in terms of the organization's relationships with its environment. Closed systems tend to minimize transactions with the environment and to take little account of external opinion in determining the purposes and activities of the organization. Bolman and Deal's (1991) structural assumptions, noted earlier, imply a 'closed systems' approach:

> These assumptions depict organizations as relatively closed systems pursuing fairly explicit goals. Such conditions make it possible for organizations to operate rationally, with high degrees of certainty, predictability and efficiency. Organizations highly dependent on the environment are continually vulnerable to external influence or interference. To reduce this vulnerability, a variety of structural mechanisms are created to protect central activities from fluctuation and uncertainty. (Bolman and Deal, 1991, pp. 48–9)

The shift to self-management in many countries, and the associated requirement to interact closely with many groups and individuals, has made it more difficult to sustain a closed systems approach, as Boyd (1999) stresses in respect of the United States:

> The increasing environmental turbulence and external challenges to educational organisations . . . showed that the closed systems . . . approach was inadequate for understanding or dealing with the most pressing problems of school administrators . . . Failing the test of practical relevance, the closed systems model was abandoned and the search was on for more useful models. (Boyd, 1999, p. 286)

The alternative theory, identified by Boyd and others, is that of 'open systems' which assumes permeable boundaries and an interactive two-way relationship between schools and colleges, and their environments:

> As a result of the search for more practically relevant models, organisations such as school systems are now viewed as open systems, which must adapt to changing external conditions to be effective and, in the long term, survive. The open-system concept highlights the vulnerability and interdependence of organisations and their environments. (Hoy and Miskel, 1987, p. 29)

As this extract implies, open systems encourage interchanges with the environment, both responding to external influences and, in turn, seeking support for the objectives of the organization. In education, open systems theory shows the relationship between the institution and external groups such as parents, employers and the local education authority. In this model, schools and colleges have wide-ranging links across an increasingly permeable boundary but organizations are able to influence their environment and are not simply responding to external demands.

Educational institutions vary considerably in the extent to which they may be regarded as closed or open systems. English further education colleges have extensive and vital links with employers, who sponsor students on many part-time and some full-time courses, and with the Learning and Skills Councils which largely determine their levels of funding. Most schools may also be regarded as open systems because of the constant interaction with various groups and individuals in the neighbourhood. Selective schools and certain universities, which enjoy high reputations and which do not have to compete vigorously for students, may be sufficiently impervious to external influences to be categorized as closed systems.

The distinction between open and closed systems is more blurred in practice than it is in theory. It may be more useful to think of a continuum rather than a sharp distinction between polar opposites. All schools and colleges have a measure of interaction with their environments but the greater the dependence of the institution on external groups the more 'open' it is likely to be.

The educational reforms of the 1980s and 1990s, in Britain and elsewhere, have increased the salience of the open systems model. Schools have to compete for pupils and their income is tied closely to their levels of recruitment. To be attractive to potential parents, it is important to be responsive to their requirements. This can lead to permeable boundaries with parents and others influencing school policies and priorities.

Systems theorists believe that organizations can be categorized as systems with their parts interacting to achieve systemic objectives. However, caution should be exercised in attributing these qualities to educational institutions. Schools and colleges are complex human organizations and systems models may be inadequate, as Hoyle (1981, p. 12) emphasizes: 'Schools are certainly not organizations consisting of carefully articulated parts functioning harmoniously in the pursuit of agreed objectives. They are characterized by conflict, malintegration and the pursuit of individual and group interests. Nevertheless a certain degree of systematic integration is necessary for their effective function.'

Bureaucratic models

The bureaucratic model is probably the most important of the formal models. There is a substantial literature about its applicability to schools and colleges. It is often used broadly to refer to characteristics which are generic to formal organizations. Some writers suggest that bureaucracy is an almost inevitable consequence of increasing size and complexity (Packwood, 1989). The 'pure' version of the bureaucratic model is associated strongly with the work of Weber who argued that, in formal organizations, bureaucracy is the most efficient form of management:

> The purely bureaucratic type of administrative organization . . . is, from a technical point of view, capable of attaining the highest degree of efficiency and is in this sense formally the most rational means of carrying out imperative control over human beings. It is superior to any other form in precision, in stability, in the stringency of its discipline, and in its reliability. (Weber, 1989, p. 16)

Bureaucracy, then, describes a formal organization which seeks maximum efficiency through rational approaches to management. Its main features are as follows:

1 It stresses the importance of the *hierarchical authority structure* with formal chains of command between the different positions in the hierarchy. This pyramidal structure is based on the legal authority vested in the officers who hold places in the chain of command. Office holders are responsible to superordinates for the satisfactory conduct of their duties. In educational institutions teachers are accountable to the head or principal.

2 In common with other formal models, the bureaucratic approach emphasizes the *goal orientation* of the organization. Institutions are dedicated to goals which are clearly delineated by the officers at the apex of the pyramid. In colleges or schools goals are determined largely by the principal or head and endorsed without question by other staff.

3 The bureaucratic model suggests a *division of labour* with staff specializing in particular tasks on the basis of expertise. The departmental structure in secondary schools and colleges is an obvious manifestation of division of labour with subject specialists teaching a defined area of the curriculum. In this respect, English primary schools do not resemble bureaucracies because staff are typically class teachers who work with one group of children for much of their time.

4 In bureaucracies decisions and behaviour are governed by *rules and regulations* rather than personal initiative. Schools typically have rules to regulate the behaviour of pupils and often guide the behaviour of teachers through bureaucratic devices such as the staff handbook. These rules may extend to the core issues of teaching and learning. In South Africa, 'the teachers . . . were subjected to tight bureaucratic regulation, especially in the matter of the curriculum' (Sebakwane, 1997, p. 397). In Greece, bureaucratic control extends to prescribing school textbooks (Bush, 2001).

5 Bureaucratic models emphasize *impersonal* relationships between staff, and with clients. This neutrality is designed to minimize the impact of individuality on decision-making. Good schools depend in part on the quality of personal relationships between teachers and pupils, and this aspect of bureaucracy has little influence in many schools. Yet where staff are required to make an appointment to see the head, this may be regarded as an example of bureaucracy in action.

6 In bureaucracies the recruitment and career progress of staff are determined on *merit*. Appointments are made on the basis of qualifications and experience, and promotion depends on expertise demonstrated in present and previous positions. Schools and colleges fulfil this criterion in that formal competitive procedures are laid down for the appointment of new staff and for some promoted posts. Internal promotions, however, depend on the recommendation of the head or principal and there may be no formal process.

Applying the bureaucratic model to education

All large organizations contain some bureaucratic elements and this is true of educational institutions:

> Schools and colleges have many bureaucratic features, including a hierarchical structure with the headteacher or principal at the apex. Teachers specialise on the basis of expertise in secondary schools and colleges and, increasingly, in primary schools also. There are many rules for pupils and staff, whose working lives are largely dictated by 'the tyranny of the timetable'. Heads and senior staff are accountable to the governing body and external stakeholders for the activities of the school or college. Partly for these reasons, bureaucratic theories pervade much of the literature on educational management. (Bush, 1994, p. 36)

Hughes (1985, p. 8) concludes that the bureaucratic model applies to education: 'Schools and colleges, particularly if they are large, conform to a considerable degree to Weber's specification of bureaucracy, as judged by their division of work, their hierarchical structures, their rules and regulations, their impersonal procedures and their employment practices based on technical criteria.' The recognition that bureaucracy applies to many aspects of education is tempered by concern about its procedures becoming too dominant an influence on the operation of schools and colleges. There is a fear that the bureaucracy itself may become the *raison d'être* of the organization rather than being firmly subordinated to educational aims:

> All schools are bureaucracies. There are rules governing the behaviour of the members. There is a hierarchy and there are formal and informal norms of behaviour associated with the various roles . . . One difficulty with a bureaucratic school system is that the bureaucracy and its survival become ends in themselves, and the goals of schooling become subsidiary. (Holmes and Wynne, 1989, pp. 63–4)

> While not applicable in a pure form, the notion of bureaucracy provides powerful insights into the managerial processes and ideology of large parts of the education service. The management of our schools has been conditioned by both the ideology and practice of hierarchy and control to a point at which, in some cases, it must attract the pejorative term of *managerialism*, (original emphasis) a condition under which the artificial needs of managers, organisations, systems, bureaucracies or routines assume dominance over the real needs of children. (Osborne, 1990, pp. 9–10)

Bureaucracy is the preferred model for many education systems, including the Czech Republic (Svecova, 2000), China (Bush, Coleman and Si, 1998), Greece (Kavouri and Ellis, 1998), Israel (Gaziel, 1998), Poland (Klus-Stanska and Olek, 1998), South Africa (Sebakwane, 1997), Slovenia (Becaj, 1994) and much of South America (Newland, 1995). Two of these authors point to some of the weaknesses of bureaucracy in education:

> The excessive centralization and bureaucratization, which continue to exist [in South America] in spite of the reforms undertaken, affect the efficiency of the system. (Newland, 1995, p. 113)

> The Greek state should start moving towards restructuring the organization of schools. Less complexity, formalization and centralization of the system, and more extended professionalism and autonomy of teachers and headteachers would be beneficial. (Kavouri and Ellis, 1998, p. 106)

Lungu (1985, p. 173) acknowledges several of these sceptical views but concludes that the bureaucratic model remains valid and appropriate for education: 'There is . . . a formidable tradition that views bureaucracy in pejorative terms . . . bureaucracy as described by Weber is still the most appropriate form of organization to facilitate the attainment of educational goals.'

The bureaucratic model has certain advantages for education but there are difficulties in applying it too enthusiastically to schools and colleges because of the professional role of teachers. If teachers do not 'own' innovations but are simply required to implement externally imposed changes, they are likely to do so without enthusiasm, leading to possible failure.

Rational models

Rational approaches differ from other formal models in that they emphasize managerial *processes* rather than organizational structure or goals. The focus is on the process of decision-making instead of the structural framework which constrains but does not determine managerial decisions. Although the distinctive quality of rational models is their emphasis on process, they share several characteristics with the other formal theories. These include agreed organizational objectives and a bureaucratic organizational structure. The decision-making process thus takes place within a recognized structure and in pursuit of accepted goals.

The process of rational decision-making is thought to have the following sequence:

1 Perception of a problem or a choice opportunity.
2 Analysis of the problem, including data collection.
3 Formulation of alternative solutions or choices.
4 Choice of the most appropriate solution to the problem to meet the objectives of the organization.
5 Implementation of the chosen alternative.
6 Monitoring and evaluation of the effectiveness of the chosen strategy.

The process is essentially iterative in that the evaluation may lead to a redefinition of the problem or a search for an alternative solution (see Figure 3.1).

In Chapter 2 we noted that theories tend to be *normative* in that they reflect views about how organizations and individuals ought to behave. The rational model is certainly normative in that it presents an idealized view of the decision-making process. It has serious limitations as a portrayal of the decision-making process in education:

- There may be dispute over objectives and the definition of the 'problem' is likely to be dependent on the particular standpoint of the individuals involved.
- Some of the data needed to make a decision may not be available.
- Most problematic of all is the assumption that the choice of solution can be detached and impartial. In practice, individuals and groups are likely to promote their own favoured solutions which in turn may reflect individual rather than organizational objectives.
- The perceived effectiveness of the chosen solution may also vary according to the preferences of the people concerned.

Despite these practical limitations, Levačić (1995) shows that the rational model provides the basis for the management of schools in England and

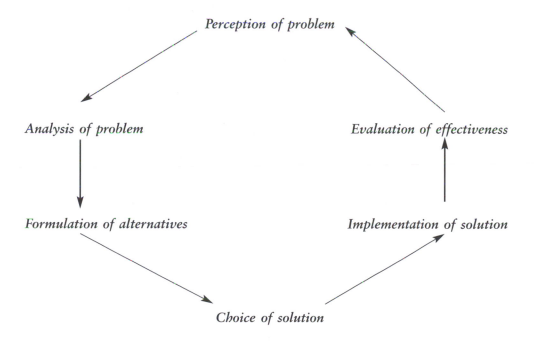

Figure 3.1   The rational process

Wales. She refers to the management consultancy report by Coopers and Lybrand (1988) which was influential in the introduction of local management in the early 1990s:

> The model of good management practice contained in the Coopers and Lybrand report is essentially a rational one. It advocates a system for allocating resources which is directed at the explicit achievement of institutional objectives. This requires clarity in the specification of objectives, gathering and analysing information on alternative ways of attaining the objectives, evaluating the alternatives and selecting those actions judged most likely to maximize achievement of the objectives. (Levačić, 1995, p. 62)

Watson and Crossley (2001, p. 114) show that similar principles underpin the management of further education in England and Wales: 'Many of the basic assumptions underpinning the [former] Further Education Funding Council's directives on strategy are rooted in a rational–scientific model that proposes the creation of a [strategic management process] that is sequential, linear and controllable.'

The application of rational principles to education can be illustrated through examining internal resource allocation in schools. There are five core principles (Bush, 2000, pp. 105–6):

1) *Aims and priorities*. Resource allocation should be informed by clearly articulated aims and by determining priorities among these aims.
2) *Long-term planning*. Budgetary decisions should reflect an awareness of their long-term implications. This means going beyond the typical annual budget cycle to a consideration of the longer-term aims of the organisation.
3) *Evaluating alternatives*. There should be a thorough consideration of alternative patterns of expenditure based on evaluation of past actions and assessment of the opportunity costs of different spending options.
4) *Zero-based budgeting*. This involves taking a fresh look at all areas of expenditure rather than simply making incremental changes to previous spending patterns.
5) *Selecting the most appropriate options*. Once the possible alternative spending patterns have been scrutinized, with an element of zero-basing, rational models require a choice of the most appropriate option linked to organisational objectives.

Levačić et al. (1999) conducted a large-scale review of inspection reports prepared by the Office for Standards in Education (OFSTED) in England and then carried out detailed case studies of 13 schools deemed by OFSTED to be offering good value for money. These authors cautiously conclude that applying the rational model is beneficial:

> Both OFSTED inspection report and case-study evidence showed that teachers are

increasingly following the rational model in establishing aims for their schools and then endeavouring through planning processes to involve all staff ... we have found a tendency for schools which have sound planning approaches and developed monitoring and evaluation procedures to be more successful in relation to the quality of teaching and learning, student behaviour and attendance. (Levačić et al., 1999, pp. 25–6)

Hierarchical models

Hierarchical approaches stress vertical relationships within organizations and the accountability of leaders to external sponsors. The organizational structure is emphasized with particular reference to the authority and responsibility of the managers at the apex of the structure. Packwood (1989, pp. 9–10) provides a precise definition of the hierarchical model and locates it firmly within the bureaucratic framework:

> One of the basic properties of bureaucratic organisation is the way in which occupational roles are graded in a vertical hierarchy. Authority to prescribe work passes from senior to junior roles, while accountability for the performance of work passes in the reverse direction from junior to senior. Authority and accountability are impersonal in that they are attached to roles, not to the personalities of the individuals who occupy the roles. The headteacher has authority to define the work of the deputy headteacher in a school because he or she occupies the role of headteacher not because of who he or she is as an individual.

This view subordinates individuals to the organizational hierarchy. Subjective theorists are very critical of this stance, as we shall see in Chapter 6.

Hierarchical models emphasize *vertical communication* patterns. Information is passed down the hierarchy to all appropriate levels and subordinates are expected to implement the decisions made by the senior managers. Difficult issues may be referred upwards until they reach a level where they can be resolved. In schools and colleges the head or principal is thought to inform heads of department or other staff about policies and is the final arbiter of problems incapable of resolution at lower levels in the hierarchy.

Horizontal communication also plays a part in the hierarchy but Packwood (1989) argues that such contacts are for co-ordination rather than management. The subject leader role in English primary schools is an example of a lateral relationship. These staff communicate with class teachers about aspects of their subject but they do not have managerial authority over them.

Central to hierarchical models is the concept of *accountability*. Leaders are responsible to external agencies for the performance of subordinates and the activities of the organization. In schools, the accountability of heads to the governing body, and to the local education authority, serves to underpin their internal authority.

Mortimore and Mortimore's (1991, p. 168) research on English secondary heads shows the extent to which they have used the hierarchy to delegate tasks and the substantial degree of discretion they have in determining the management structure of the school:

> We have been struck by the amount of thought and effort the headteachers put into the organization and management of schools. The size and complexity of the schools and the wide-ranging responsibilities carried out by today's headteachers necessitates a considerable degree of delegation. Different management structures have been devised, according to the priorities and preferred management styles of the heads.

Hierarchical models have certain limitations when applied to educational institutions. Teachers as professionals claim discretion in their classroom work and there is increasing participation in decision-making on wider school issues. As a result, the significance of the hierarchy may be modified by notions of collegiality (see Chapter 4) and teacher autonomy. However, because of the clear legal authority of heads and principals, hierarchical models remain significant for schools and colleges.

In certain societies, the significance of the hierarchy is further reinforced by the tendency to accept unequal concentrations of power (Walker and Dimmock, 2002). Bush and Qiang (2000; 2002), for example, show that China is the archetypal high power-distance society and that teachers have considerable respect for the positional authority of principals.

Formal models: goals, structure, environment and leadership

Goals

Formal models characterize schools and colleges as *goal oriented*. There is an assumption that institutions pursue specific objectives. These goals are invariably determined by heads and senior staff and formal theories do not regard the support of other teachers as problematic. All members of the organization are thought to be working towards the achievement of these official aims. Everard and Morris (1990, pp. 149 and 151) stress the significance of goals:

> We believe that all organizations, including educational ones, should be actively managed against goals; in other words, not only should there be a clear sense of direction in which the organization is being steered, but also markers whereby we can assess progress . . . Organizational aims . . . nurture and steer creative tension and release and harness human energy; they keep the organization on the move, heading in a certain direction.

The activities and procedures of institutions are evaluated in terms of their relevance to the approved objectives, as Harling (1984, p. 7) suggests: 'The distinctive characteristic of an organisation is . . . that it has been formally established for the explicit purpose of achieving certain goals. Every organisation has a formally instituted pattern of authority and an official body of rules and procedures which are intended to aid the achievement of those goals.'

Cheng (2002, p. 61) stresses the role of leaders in goal development and achievement. He argues that leaders should be 'goal developer' and 'goal leader' and should have two main strategies to promote quality:

- Develop appropriate institutional mission and goals.
- Lead members to achieve goals, implement plans and programmes, and meet standards.

The portrayal of schools and colleges as organizations actively pursuing official goals set out in formal statements is modified by certain writers who acknowledge the existence of multiple objectives in institutions: 'Organizations usually have more than one objective . . . schools that make their aims explicit usually find that they are having to harmonize different though compatible aims' (Everard and Morris, 1990, p. 152). The diverse goals of schools and colleges often emanate from different parts of the organization. For example, one can distinguish between individual, departmental and school goals. In a secondary school an official goal may refer to the fulfilment of the potential of all pupils. A departmental goal might relate to the attainment of particular standards of competence in certain subjects. Individual goals may well reflect personal career ambitions. These goals are not necessarily compatible.

Despite the recognition that goals may exist at different levels, there remains the clear implication that personal and sub-unit goals should be subordinated to the official aims. Everard and Morris (1990, p. 152), for example, argue that the aims of constituent parts of the school – departments, teams and committees – 'should be kept aligned with those of the school'. This assumption underpins the notion of development planning in schools and colleges where sub-unit plans are expected to be consistent with those of the institutional level.

Fishman (1999) makes a further distinction between external and internal goals in commenting on the differences between Russian and Western education. In centralized educational systems, there may be limited scope for institutional leaders to determine school aims because these are set by national or local government. However, even in highly directive systems, there has to be some scope for local interpretation, as Fishman (1999, p. 73) demonstrates:

51

> Goal formulation cannot set one and the same result for all (that would be nothing but totalitarianism in education). Such goal setting should take into account the interests of the children, their abilities, the peculiarities of the social environment and the capabilities of the school itself . . . the goal-setting process inside an educational system is not merely a banal transmission of the external goals

The organization's official goals may be a product of both external imperatives and internal requirements, but the assumption that they necessarily guide the behaviour and decisions of staff may be unrealistic or naive. As we shall see in subsequent chapters, formal goals may be contested or may provide only a limited guide to action.

Organizational structure

Formal models present organizational *structure* as an objective fact. Schools and colleges are 'real' institutions which imbue teachers and pupils with a sense of belonging. Staff are thought to define their professional lives in terms of their position within the school or college. Structures may be typified in physical terms that imply permanence. Individuals are accorded a place in the structure such as teacher of class 2 or head of the science department. The work of teachers and other staff is defined in terms of their roles within the formal structure. The structure is assumed to influence the behaviour of the individuals holding particular roles in the organization. Structure dominates and individuality is de-emphasized: 'The role structure remains relatively stable whilst different incumbents of the roles come and go' (Hoyle, 1986, p. 5).

As noted earlier, the organizational structure tends to be hierarchical and vertical, with staff being accountable to their superordinate in the hierarchy. In schools, teachers are accountable to the principal, often through a middle manager such as a head of department. The 'ethos of top-down management' (Johnson, 1995, p. 224) is evident in South African schools: 'It [is] important to bear in mind the nature of power relations within schools. In most cases power resides with the principal who has legal authority and is legally accountable' (Johnson, 1995, p. 225).

The external environment

Formal approaches differ in the way they typify relationships between the organization and its environment. The more rigid models, such as 'closed systems' or structural theories, tend to limit environmental links to the minimum required to sustain accountability. These perspectives characterize relationships in terms of the official links between the head or principal and such formal groups as national and local governments and the governing body.

Interaction with other groups, such as parents, employers and other educational institutions, is de-emphasized. 'Closed systems' models assume that schools and colleges are impervious to such influences.

A significant aspect of bureaucracy, and particularly of closed systems, is that accountability to officials is regarded as more important than responsibility to clients such as students or parents. This is well illustrated by Becaj's discussion of schools in Slovenia:

> Heads know that parents and children are important but in fact they have been used to accepting the superior institutions and authorities as the real and powerful 'customers' on which they are really dependent. At the same time, parents and children have been used to seeing the school and its teachers as authorities who should be obeyed ... This kind of relationship between heads and parents also suits and supports bureaucratic organisation and head centred leadership very well. (Becaj, 1994, p. 11)

Other formal models, such as 'open systems', postulate wide-ranging links with the environment. Educational institutions are portrayed as interactive organizations, responding to a changing environment and displaying their achievements to the local community. Everard and Morris (1990, pp. 155–6) stress the need for schools and colleges to be responsive to the wider system:

> Those who manage organizations should remember that they are part of a bigger system; they are interdependent with the rest of society, which they serve as society serves them ... Many long-serving heads ... have remarked how much ... the nature of their jobs has changed to one of boundary management: that is they spend much more of their time managing transactions between the school and its environment.

Schools and colleges in self-managing systems are increasingly adopting a more 'open' stance, conscious of the need for a good reputation with present and prospective parents, employers and the local community. Few educational institutions justify the label 'closed' in the twenty-first century.

Leadership

Within formal models leadership is ascribed to the person at the apex of the hierarchy. It is assumed that this individual sets the tone of the organization and establishes the major official objectives. Baldridge et al. (1978, p. 44) discuss the nature of formal leadership:

> Under the bureaucratic model the leader is seen as the hero who stands at the top of a complex pyramid of power. The hero's job is to assess the problems, consider alternatives, and make rational choices. Much of the organisation's power is held by the hero, and great expectations are raised because people trust him [sic] to solve problems and fend off threats from the environment.

The leader is expected to play a key part in policy-making, and adoption of innovations is assumed to follow. The possibility of opposition, or indifference, to change is not acknowledged. It is believed that implementation is unproblematic.

In education there are several features that support this characteristic of unidimensional leadership. Official bodies and individuals behave as if the head or principal is the fount of all knowledge and authority. The head is the focal point for most external communications, and parents and community leaders generally expect to contact the school via the head. Many other groups tend to regard the principal as the public face of the institution and behave accordingly. In primary schools, in particular, there is a perceived identity between the head and the school which reinforces the 'top down' perspective on leadership. 'Because of his [*sic*] formal authority the head represents and symbolizes the school both to people inside it and to members of the community' (Coulson, 1985, p. 9).

The assumption of an all-powerful leader at the apex of schools and colleges has several limitations. While formal authority resides with heads, they require the consent of colleagues if policy initiatives are to be carried through into departmental and classroom practice. It is now a truism that staff must 'own' decisions if they are to be implemented successfully.

Heads of self-managing schools and colleges have to share power with other staff in order to cope with the sheer volume of work arising from their enhanced responsibility for managing finance, staff and external relations. This pragmatic response to change serves to modify the notion of all-powerful heads but in many cases the effect has been to increase the role of the senior management team and not to empower more junior staff. The hierarchy remains intact but the apex comprises a team rather than a single individual (Wallace and Hall, 1994).

Managerial leadership

Various types of leadership have been identified in the literature, as we noted in Chapter 2. The type of leadership most closely associated with formal models is 'managerial'. Leithwood, Jantzi and Steinbach (1999, p. 14) define it as follows:

> Managerial leadership assumes that the focus of leaders ought to be on functions, tasks and behaviours and that if these functions are carried out competently the work of others in the organisation will be facilitated. Most approaches to managerial leadership also assume that the behaviour of organizational members is largely rational. Authority and influence are allocated to formal positions in proportion to the status of those positions in the organizational hierarchy.

This definition is remarkably close to that given for 'formal models' in this volume (see page 37) and in earlier editions of the book.

Dressler's (2001, p. 175) review of leadership in Charter schools in the United States shows the significance of managerial leadership: 'Traditionally, the principal's role has been clearly focused on management responsibilities.'

Myers and Murphy (1995) identify six specifically managerial functions for school principals. Four of these are described as 'hierarchical':

* supervision;
* input controls (e.g. teacher transfers);
* behaviour controls (e.g. job descriptions);
* output controls (e.g. student testing).

The remaining two are non-hierarchical:

* selection/socialization;
* environmental controls (e.g.community responsiveness).
  (Myers and Murphy, 1995, p. 14)

Caldwell (1992, pp. 16–17) argues that managers and leaders of self managing schools must be able to develop and implement a cyclical process involving seven managerial functions:

* goal-setting;
* needs identification;
* priority-setting;
* planning;
* budgeting;
* implementing;
* evaluating.

It is significant to note that this type of leadership does not include the concept of vision which is central to most leadership models. Managerial leadership is focused on managing existing activities successfully rather than visioning a better future for the school.

The limitations of formal models

The various formal models pervade much of the literature on educational management. They are normative approaches in that they present ideas about how people in organizations ought to behave. So schools and colleges are typified as goal-seeking organizations employing rational means to achieve the objectives established by official leaders. Packwood (1989, p. 9) argues that the dramatic changes in England and Wales in the 1980s served to increase the significance of formal models:

> The last decade has also seen fundamental changes in the way in which education is provided . . . many of these changes can only be understood and accommodated in the context of a bureaucratic theory of educational organisation . . . If schools are to make the best of the new demands that have, to a great extent, been imposed upon them, they have no choice but to make the best of bureaucracy.

Packwood seems to be arguing that, because a top-down model is operating in imposing change on schools and colleges, their leaders should respond by managing their establishments in the same way. This is also the assumption underpinning the educational reforms of the 1990s and the twenty-first century, as Levačić et al. demonstrate:

> A major development in educational management in the last decade has been much greater emphasis on defining effective leadership by individuals in management posts in terms of the effectiveness of their organisation, which is increasingly judged in relation to measurable outcomes for students. In the UK both major political parties have pursued educational policies which seek to diminish the traditional ambiguity and lack of coupling between inputs, process and outcomes in educational organisations. This is argued to require a rational–technicist approach to the structuring of decision-making. (Levačić et al., 1999, p. 15)

The 'measurable outcomes' include, in England and Wales, league tables, target setting and benchmarking, leaving schools vulnerable to a range of bureaucratic pressures. MacBeath (1999) points to the resultant tension between meeting the requirements of a centrally determined agenda and the specific needs of the school as an educational community.

Formal models are selective as well as normative. In focusing on the bureaucratic and structural aspects of organizations they necessarily ignore or underestimate other salient features:

> Rationalistic-bureaucratic notions . . . have largely proven to be sterile and to have little application to administrative practice in the 'real world'. (Owens and Shakeshaft, 1992, p. 4)

> A classical, rationalist model . . . fails to take into account the wider dimensions of organisational history, culture and context. There has been a failure of management . . . to understand that an apparently rational [process] may be a chimera in practice. (Watson and Crossley, 2001, p. 123).

There are five specific weaknesses associated with formal models:

1 It may be unrealistic to characterize schools and colleges as *goal-oriented* organizations. It is often difficult to ascertain the goals of educational institutions. Formal objectives may have little operational relevance because they are often vague and general, because there may be many different goals competing for resources, and because goals may emanate

56

from individuals and groups as well as from the leaders of the organization.

Even where the purposes of schools and colleges have been clarified, there are further problems in judging whether objectives have been achieved. Many of the goals associated with education are very difficult to measure. Policy-makers, practitioners and researchers often rely on examination performance to assess schools, but this is only one dimension of the educational process.

2 The portrayal of decision-making as a *rational* process is fraught with difficulties. The belief that managerial action is preceded by a process of evaluation of alternatives and a considered choice of the most appropriate option is rarely substantiated. Decisions in schools and colleges are made by teachers, who draw on a whole range of experience as they respond to events. Much human behaviour is irrational and this inevitably influences the nature of decision-making in education. Weick (1976, p. 1) asserts that rational practice is the exception rather than the norm:

> People in organisations, including educational organisations, find themselves hard pressed either to find actual instances of those rational practices or to find rationalized practices whose outcomes have been as beneficent as predicted, or to feel that those rational occasions explain much of what goes on within the organisation. Parts of some organisations are heavily rationalized but many parts also prove intractable to analysis through rational assumptions.

Educational institutions, in common with other organizations staffed by professionals, depend on decisions made by individuals and subunits. Professional judgement is based as much on the expertise of the individual as on rational processes conditioned by the rule book.

3 Formal models focus on the organization as an entity and ignore or underestimate the contribution of *individuals*. They assume that people occupy preordained positions in the structure and that their behaviour reflects their organizational positions rather than their individual qualities and experience. Critics argue that formal perspectives treat organizations as if they are independent of the people within them. Greenfield (1973, p. 571) has been particularly critical of this view:

> Most theories of organisation grossly simplify the nature of the reality with which they deal. The drive to see the organisation as a single kind of entity with a life of its own apart from the perceptions and beliefs of those involved in it blinds us to its complexity and the variety of organisations people create around themselves.

Greenfield's alternative approach to organizations is discussed in Chapter 6 but the essence of his argument is that organizations are the creation of the people within them. He claims that formal models greatly underestimate individual variables and thus produce an inaccurate portrayal of schools and colleges. Samier (2002, p. 40) takes a similar view, expressing concern 'about the role technical rationality plays in crippling the personality of the bureaucrat, reducing him [sic] to a cog in a machine'.

4 A central assumption of formal models is that power resides at the apex of the pyramid. Heads and principals possess authority by virtue of their positions as the appointed leaders of their institutions. This focus on official authority leads to a view of institutional management which is essentially *top down*. Policy is laid down by senior managers and implemented by staff lower down the hierarchy. Their acceptance of managerial decisions is regarded as unproblematic.

The hierarchical aspect of the formal model is most relevant to organizations which depend on tight discipline for their effectiveness. The armed forces, for example, are expected to carry out their orders without any questioning or elaboration. The situation is assumed to require compliance with instructions from superordinates.

Organizations with large numbers of professional staff tend to exhibit signs of tension between the conflicting demands of professionalism and the hierarchy. Formal models assume that leaders, because they are appointed on merit, have the competence to issue appropriate instructions to subordinates. This is supported by the authority vested in them by virtue of their official position. Professional organizations have a rather different ethos with expertise distributed widely within the institution. Osborne (1990, p. 10) refers to the conflict between professionalism and bureaucracy: 'The great weight of evidence is that the employment of large numbers of professionals in an organisation poses "problems" for the application of the bureaucratic or hierarchical model.'

Where professionals specialize, as in secondary schools and colleges, the ability of leaders to direct the actions of subordinates may be questionable. A head who is a humanities graduate lacks the specific competence to supervise teaching in the faculty of technology. In professional organizations there is an authority of expertise which may come into conflict with positional authority.

Heads are responsible for the quality of teaching and learning in their schools, but their authority over teachers may be ambiguous. Professional staff claim zones of autonomy based on their specialist expertise. The classroom is still largely the domain of the teacher and pedagogic matters are primarily the responsibility of the practitioner as a qualified professional. These areas of discretion may lead to conflict between heads and other staff. Such difficulties can be avoided only if there is at least tacit acceptance of the head's overall responsibility for the activities of the school. This involves recognition by teachers of the head's right to take the initiative in many areas of school policy.

5 Formal approaches are based on the implicit assumption that organizations are relatively *stable*. Individuals may come and go but they slot into pre-determined positions in a static structure. Bureaucratic and structural theories are most appropriate in stable conditions as Bolman and Deal (1991, p. 77) suggest: 'Organisations operating in simpler and more stable environments are likely to employ less complex and more centralized structures, with authority, rules and policies as the primary vehicles for co-ordinating the work.'

It can be argued that assumptions of stability are unrealistic in many organizations and invalid in most schools and colleges. March and Olsen (1976, p. 21) are right to claim that 'Individuals find themselves in a more complex, less stable and less understood world than that described by standard theories of organisational choice'. Rational perspectives require a measure of predictability to be useful as portrayals of organizational behaviour. The validity of formal models may be limited during phases of rapid and multiple change, such as that affecting most educational systems in the twenty-first century. The notion of a thorough analysis of a problem followed by identification of alternatives, choice of the preferred option and a process of implementation and evaluation may be unrealistic during periods of turbulence.

Conclusion: are formal models still valid?

These criticisms of formal models suggest that they have serious limitations in respect of schools and colleges. The dominance of the hierarchy is compromised by the expertise possessed by professional staff. The supposed rationality of the decision-making process requires modification to allow for the pace and complexity of change. The concept of organizational goals is challenged by those who point to the existence of multiple objectives in education and the possible conflict between goals held at individual, departmental and institutional levels.

Despite these limitations, it would be inappropriate to dismiss formal approaches as irrelevant to schools and colleges. The other models discussed in this book were all developed as a reaction to the perceived weaknesses of formal theories. However, these alternative perspectives have not succeeded in dislodging the formal models which remain valid as *partial* descriptions of organization and management in education. Formal models are inadequate but still have much to contribute to our understanding of schools and colleges as organizations. Owens and Shakeshaft (1992) refer to a reduction of

confidence in bureaucratic models and a 'paradigm shift' to a more sophisticated analysis. In subsequent chapters we examine several alternative
perspectives and assess the extent to which they have supplanted forma
models as the principal means of understanding and managing schools and
colleges.

References

Baldridge, J.V., Curtis, D.V., Ecker, G. and Riley, G.L. (1978) *Policy-Making and Effective Leadership*, San Francisco, CA: Jossey-Bass.

Beare, H., Caldwell, B. and Millikan, R. (1989) *Creating an Excellent School*, London: Routledge.

Becaj, J. (1994) 'Changing bureaucracy to democracy', *Educational Change and Development*, 15 (1): 7–14.

Becher, T. and Kogan, M. (1992) *Process and Structure in Higher Education*, London: Routledge.

Bolman, L. and Deal, T. (1989) 'Organisations, technology and environment', in R. Glatter, *Educational Institutions and their Environments: Managing the Boundaries*, Buckingham: Open University Press.

Bolman, L. and Deal, T. (1991) *Reframing Organisations: Artistry, Choice and Leadership*, San Francisco, CA: Jossey-Bass.

Boyd, W. (1999) 'Environmental pressures, management imperatives and competing paradigms in educational administration', *Educational Management and Administration*, 27 (3): 283–97.

Bush, T. (1994) 'Theory and practice in educational management', in T. Bush and J. West-Burnham (eds), *The Principles of Educational Management*, Harlow: Longman.

Bush, T. (1997) 'Management structures', in T. Bush and D. Middlewood (eds), *Managing People in Education*, London: Paul Chapman Publishing.

Bush, T. (2000) 'Management styles: impact on finance and resources', in M. Coleman and L. Anderson (eds), *Managing Finance and Resources in Education*, London: Paul Chapman Publishing.

Bush, T. (2001) 'School organisation and management: international perspectives', paper presented at the Federation of Private School Teachers' Annual Conference, Athens, May.

Bush, T. and Qiang, H. (2000) 'Leadership and culture in Chinese education', *Asia Pacific Journal of Education*, 20 (2): 58–67.

Bush, T. and Qiang, H. (2002) 'Leadership and culture in Chinese education', in A. Walker and C. Dimmock (eds), *School Leadership and Administration: Adopting a Cultural Perspective*, London: RoutledgeFalmer.

Bush, T., Coleman, M. and Si, X. (1998) 'Managing secondary schools in China', *Compare*, 28 (2): 183–96.

Caldwell, B. (1992) 'The principal as leader of the self-managing school in Australia', *Journal of Educational Administration*, 30 (3): 6–19.

Cheng, Y.C. (2002) 'Leadership and strategy', in T. Bush and L. Bell (eds), *The*

Principles and Practice of Educational Management, London: Paul Chapman Publishing.

Clark, B.R. (1983) 'The contradictions of change in academic systems', *Higher Education*, 12, 101–16.

Coopers and Lybrand (1988) *Local Management of Schools: A Report to the DES*, London: HMSO.

Coulson, A. (1985) *The Managerial Behaviour of Primary School Heads*, Collected Original Resources in Education, Abingdon: Carfax.

Dressler, B. (2001) 'Charter school leadership', *Education and Urban Society*, 33 (2): 170–85.

Everard, B. and Morris, G. (1990) *Effective School Management*, London: Paul Chapman Publishing.

Evetts, J. (1992) 'The organisation of staff in secondary schools: headteachers' management structures', *School Organisation*, 12 (1): 83–98.

Fishman, L. (1999) 'The cultural imperative and how we consider educational leadership', *International Journal of Leadership in Education*, 2 (2): 69–79.

Gaziel, H. (1998) 'School-based management as a factor in school effectiveness', *International Review of Education*, 44 (4): 319–33.

Greenfield, T.B. (1973) 'Organisations as social inventions: rethinking assumptions about change', *Journal of Applied Behavioural Science*, 9 (5): 551–74.

Greenfield T.B. (1975) 'Theory about organisation: a new perspective and its implications for schools', in M. Hughes (ed.), *Administering Education: International Challenge*, London: Athlone Press.

Hall, V. (1994) *Further Education in the United Kingdom*, London: Collins Educational.

Harling, P. (1984) 'The organisational framework for educational leadership', in P. Harling (ed.), *New Directions in Educational Leadership*, Lewes: Falmer Press.

Holmes, M. and Wynne, E. (1989) *Making the School an Effective Community: Belief Practice and Theory in School Administration*, Lewes: Falmer Press.

Hoy, W. and Miskel, C. (1987) *Educational Administration: Theory, Research and Practice*, New York: McGraw-Hill.

Hoyle, E. (1981) *The Process of Management, E323 Management and the School, Block 3, Part 1*, Buckingham: Open University Press.

Hoyle, E. (1986) *The Politics of School Management*, Sevenoaks: Hodder and Stoughton.

Hughes, M. (1985) 'Theory and practice in educational management', in M. Hughes, P. Ribbins and H. Thomas (eds), *Managing Education: The System and the Institution*, London: Holt, Rinehart and Winston.

Johnson, D. (1995) 'Developing an approach to educational management development in South Africa', *Comparative Education*, 31 (2): 223–41.

Kavouri, P. and Ellis, D. (1998) 'Factors affecting school climate in Greek primary schools', *Welsh Journal of Education*, 7 (1): 95–109.

Klus-Stanska, D. and Olek, H. (1998) 'Private education in Poland: breaking the mould', *International Review of Education*, 44 (2–3): 235–49.

Leithwood, K., Jantzi, D. and Steinbach, R. (1999) *Changing Leadership for Changing*

Times, Buckingham: Open University Press.

Levačić, R. (1995) *Local Management of Schools: Analysis and Practice*, Buckingham: Open University Press.

Levačić, R., Glover, D., Bennett, N. and Crawford, M. (1999) 'Modern headship for the rationally managed school: combining cerebral and insightful approaches', in T. Bush and L. Bell (eds), *The Principles and Practice of Educational Manage-ment*, London: Paul Chapman Publishing.

Lumby, J. (2001) *Managing Further Education: Learning Enterprise*, London: Paul Chapman Publishing.

Lungu, G. (1985) 'In defence of bureaucratic organisation in education', *Educational Management and Administration*, 13: 172–8.

MacBeath, J. (1999) *Schools Must Speak for Themselves: The Case for School Self-Evaluation*, London: Routledge.

March, J.G. and Olsen, J.P. (1976) 'Organisational choice under ambiguity', in J.G. March and J.P. Olsen, *Ambiguity and Choice in Organisations*, Bergen: Universitetsforlaget.

Mortimore, P. and Mortimore, J. (1991) *The Secondary Head: Roles, Responsibilities and Reflections*, London: Paul Chapman Publishing.

Myers, E. and Murphy, J. (1995) 'Suburban secondary school principals' perceptions of administrative control in schools', *Journal of Educational Administration*, 33 (3): 14–37.

Newland, C. (1995) 'Spanish American elementary education 1950–1992: bureaucracy, growth and decentralisation', *International Journal of Educational Development*, 15 (2): 103–14.

Osborne, A. (1990) 'The nature of educational management', in B. Davies, L. Ellison, A. Osborne and J. West-Burnham (eds), *Education Management for the 1990s*, Harlow: Longman.

Owens, R. and Shakeshaft, C. (1992) 'The new "revolution" in administrative theory', *Journal of Educational Management*, 30 (9): 4–17.

Packwood, T. (1989) 'Return to the hierarchy', *Educational Management and Administration*, 17 (1): 9–15.

Samier, E. (2002) 'Weber on education and its administration: prospects for leadership in a rationalised world', *Educational Management and Administration*, 30 (1): 27–45.

Sebakwane, S. (1997) 'The contradictions of scientific management as a mode of controlling teachers' work in black secondary schools: South Africa', *International Journal of Educational Development*, 17 (4): 391–404.

Svecova, J. (2000) 'Privatisation of education in the Czech Republic', *International Journal of Educational Development*, 20: 127–33.

Walker, A. and Dimmock, C. (2002) 'Cross-cultural and comparative insights into educational administration and leadership', in A. Walker and C. Dimmock (eds), *School Leadership and Administration: Adopting a Cultural Perspective*, London: RoutledgeFalmer.

Wallace, M. and Hall, V. (1994) *Inside the SMT: Teamwork in Secondary School Management*, London: Paul Chapman Publishing.

Watson, G. and Crossley, M. (2001) 'Beyond the rational: the strategic management process, cultural change and post-incorporation further education', *Educational Management and Administration*, 29 (1): 113–25.

Weber, M. (1989) 'Legal authority in a bureaucracy', in T. Bush (ed.), *Managing Education: Theory and Practice*, Buckingham: Open University Press.

Weick, K. E. (1976) 'Educational organisations as loosely coupled systems', *Administrative Science Quarterly*, 21 (1): 1–19.

4
Collegial Models

Central features of collegial models

Collegial models include all those theories which emphasize that power and decision-making should be shared among some or all members of the organization. These approaches range from a 'restricted' collegiality where the leader shares power with a limited number of senior colleagues to a 'pure' collegiality where all members have an equal voice in determining policy. The definition suggested below captures the main features of these perspectives:

> Collegial models assume that organizations determine policy and make decisions through a process of discussion leading to consensus. Power is shared among some or all members of the organization who are thought to have a shared understanding about the aims of the institution.

The notion of collegiality became enshrined in the folklore of management as the most appropriate way to run schools and colleges in the 1980s and 1990s. It was closely associated with school effectiveness and school improvement (Campbell and Southworth, 1993) and was then regarded as 'the official model of good practice' (Wallace, 1989, p. 182). Subsequently, in England and Wales, there has been a re-emphasis on the power of the leader, who is expected to 'deliver' by meeting government targets as part of a centralized agenda. Latterly, however, there has been renewed interest in 'distributed leadership' (Harris, 2003; Lumby, 2003), which shares many features with collegiality.

Brundrett (1998, p. 305) says that 'collegiality can broadly be defined as teachers conferring and collaborating with other teachers'. Little (1990, p. 166) discusses the benefits of this approach:

> The reason to pursue the study and practice of collegiality is that, presumably, something is gained when teachers work together and something is lost when they do not; in effect, the perceived benefits must be great enough that the time teachers spend together can compete with time spent in other ways, on other priorities

that are equally compelling or more immediate.

The time required to implement collegial approaches is a significant constraint as we shall see later in this chapter (pp. 81–82).

Collegial models have the following major features:

1 They are strongly *normative* in orientation. We noted in Chapter 2 that all theories tend to be normative but collegial approaches in particular reflect the prescriptive view that management ought to be based on agreement. Their advocates believe that decision-making should be based on democratic principles but do not necessarily claim that these principles actually determine the nature of management in action. It is an idealistic model rather than one that is founded firmly in practice:

> Those who advocate collegiality do so on the basis of prescription rather than description [but] ... it may not be simply an act of faith. (Campbell and Southworth, 1993, p. 62)

> The advocacy of collegiality is made more on the basis of prescription than on research-based studies of school practice. (Webb and Vulliamy, 1996, p. 443)

> Credible evidence regarding the nature of participatory structures and processes in schools ... is thinner than one might expect. (Brown, Boyle and Boyle, 1999, p. 320)

The normative dimension of collegiality is particularly evident in post-Apartheid South Africa. There is a powerful commitment to democratic institutions fuelled by an understandable reaction to the injustices and inequities of the past. This is particularly evident in the decision to establish governing bodies in all schools, and in the representation of both teachers and, in secondary schools, students, on these bodies. The South African government links governance to wider democratic objectives in its advice to school governors:

> Just like the country has a government, the school that your child and other children in the community attend needs a 'government' to serve the school and the school community. (Department of Education, 1997, p. 2)

The empowerment of school level governing bodies is largely a matter of faith (Bush and Heystek, 2003) and there is only limited evidence that this change is being matched by professional collegiality in schools.

2 Collegial models seem to be particularly appropriate for organizations such as schools and colleges that have significant numbers of professional staff. Teachers possess authority arising directly from their knowledge and skill. They have an *authority of expertise* that contrasts with the positional

authority associated with formal models. Professional authority occurs where decisions are made on an individual basis rather than being standardized. Education necessarily demands a professional approach because pupils and students need personal attention. Teachers require a measure of autonomy in the classroom but also need to collaborate to ensure a coherent approach to teaching and learning. 'Professionalism has the effect of allowing teachers to come together with respect for one another's professional ability' (Brundrett, 1998, p. 307).

Collegial models assume that professionals also have a right to share in the wider decision-making process. Shared decisions are likely to be better informed and are also much more likely to be implemented effectively. Collegiality is also 'acclaimed as a way for teachers to benefit from the support and expertise of their colleagues' (Brown, Boyle and Boyle, 1999, p. 320).

3 Collegial models assume a *common set of values* held by members of the organization. These may arise from the socialization which occurs during training and the early years of professional practice. These common values guide the managerial activities of the organization and, in particular, are thought to lead to shared educational objectives. Campbell and Southworth (1993, p. 66) refer to 'jointly held beliefs and values' in reporting their study of staff relationships in primary schools.

The common values of professionals form part of the justification for the optimistic assumption that it is always possible to reach agreement about goals and policies. Brundrett (1998, p. 308) goes further in referring to the importance of 'shared vision' as a basis for collegial decision-making.

4 The *size* of decision-making groups is an important element in collegial management. They have to be sufficiently small to enable everyone to be heard. This may mean that collegiality works better in primary schools, or in sub-units, than at the institutional level in secondary schools and colleges. Meetings of the whole staff may operate collegially in small schools but may be suitable only for information exchange in larger institutions.

The collegial model deals with this problem of scale by building-in the assumption that staff have *formal representation* within the various decision-making bodies. Significant areas of policy are determined within the official committee system rather than being a prerogative of individual leaders. The democratic element of formal representation rests on the allegiance owed by participants to their constituencies. A teacher representing the English department on a committee is accountable to colleagues who may have the right to nominate or elect another person if they are not happy about the way they are being represented.

Informal consultations with staff do not constitute collegiality. Where heads seek the advice of colleagues before making a decision the process is one of consultation, whereas the essence of collegiality is participation in decision-making. Power is shared with staff in a democracy rather than remaining the preserve of the leader. Formal representation confers the right to participate in defined areas of policy while informal consultation is at the sole discretion of the leader who is under no obligation to act on the advice received.

5 Collegial models assume that decisions are reached by *consensus* rather than division or conflict. The belief that there are common values and shared objectives leads to the view that it is both desirable and possible to resolve problems by agreement. There may be differences of opinion but they can be overcome by the force of argument. The decision-making process may be elongated by the search for compromise but this is regarded as an acceptable price to pay to maintain the aura of shared values and beliefs.

The case for consensual decision-making rests in part on the ethical dimension of collegiality. It is regarded as wholly appropriate to involve people in the decisions which affect their professional lives. Imposing decisions on staff is considered morally repugnant, and inconsistent with the notion of consent. Williams (1989, p. 80) outlines this moral argument:

> The moral character of an exercise of authority is based on the presence of consent on the part of those subject to its jurisdiction . . . the consent of the obligated is necessary for authority to assume moral status . . . Where consent is not made a condition of authority, then we are not speaking of moral authority, but of the exercise of power, or of purely formal or legal authority.

These considerations also provide the rationale for the concept of 'moral leadership' which will be examined in Chapter 8.

These five central features of collegiality appear to a greater or lesser extent in each of the main sectors of education. We turn now to consider its application in higher education.

Collegial models in higher education

Collegial approaches in British education originated within the colleges of Oxford and Cambridge universities (Becher and Kogan, 1992, p. 72): 'Collegium designates a structure or structures in which members have equal authority to participate in decisions which are binding on each of them. It usually implies that individuals have discretion to perform their main operations in their own way, subject only to minimal collegial controls.'

The collegial model has been adopted by most universities. Authority of expertise is widespread within these institutions of scholarship and research. Glatter (1984, p. 23) describes universities as 'bottom-heavy institutions' and the nature of management should reflect this wide distribution of knowledge and competence. 'Any organisation which depends on high-level professional skills operates most efficiently if there is a substantial measure of collegiality in its management procedures' (Williams and Blackstone, 1983, p. 94).

The collegial model is most evident within the extensive committee system. Decisions on a whole range of academic and resource allocation issues take place within a labyrinth of committees rather than being the prerogative of the vice-chancellor. Issues are generally resolved by agreement or compromise rather than by voting or dissent: 'The members of a college take their own collective decisions, which have an authority legitimized by consensus, or at least compromise, amongst those to whom they apply' (Williams and Blackstone, 1983, p. 94).

Collegial approaches may have originated within higher education but in many universities democracy is compromised by a limited franchise. Certain institutions give full voting rights to all academic staff and some representation to students and, perhaps, also non-academic staff. Elsewhere membership of senate and the key committees is the preserve of senior staff. This restricted franchise serves to limit the extent to which universities can be regarded as collegial and many might be regarded as elitist rather than democratic.

There is a dichotomy in universities and colleges between academic policy, which is generally the responsibility of the collegial senate or academic board, and resource management which is usually the preserve of the vice-chancellor and heads of faculty. The committee system fits the collegial model while the powers accorded directly to senior managers suggest one of the formal models.

The rapid growth of higher education in the 1990s may have made it more difficult for the collegial aspects of universities to maintain their previous significance in the decision-making process. Middlehurst and Elton (1992, p. 261) argue that collegiality is threatened by the increased emphasis on competition:

> [Universities] have not only survived the 1980s, but in certain ways have prospered . . . by becoming more managerial . . . There is no doubt that in the short run this has worked, but we have quite serious doubts concerning the long term, particularly as one of the effects . . . has been a considerable loss in collegiality across the higher education system, with the resulting loss of a sense of ownership and shared professional responsibility for the operation of the institution.

The threat to collegiality noted by Middlehurst and Elton (1992) has intensified during the 1990s and the early part of the twenty-first century. Warren (1994, p. 52) notes that 'in the new universities [collegiality] is being challenged by the rise of the academic manager and the movement towards top-down hierarchical control'. Similarly, Deem's (2000, p. 48) large-scale research with academic managers suggest that 'the UK higher education system was now highly managerial and bureaucratic'.

The desire to maintain staff participation in decision-making is increasingly in conflict with external demands for accountability, notably in respect of funding, quality control and research assessment. This tension between participation and accountability is also evident in schools.

Collegial models in secondary schools

The introduction of collegial approaches in secondary schools has been slower, less complete and more piecemeal than in higher education. The tradition of all powerful heads, with authority over staff and accountability to external bodies, has stifled several attempts to develop participative modes of management. The formal position is that principals alone are responsible for the organization and management of schools. This consideration has acted as a brake on some heads who wish to share their power and as a convenient justification for those reluctant to do so.

An early example of a collegial model in operation was seen at Countesthorpe College in Leicestershire (England) in the 1970s. The main policy-making body was the 'moot' which was open to all staff and students. It met every six weeks and all other decision-making bodies were responsible to it. The main standing committee held office for one quarter of the year and comprised one-quarter of the staff with student representation. All meetings were advertised and open. Proposals could emanate from any group or individual. The former principal, John Watts, outlines the main collegial features at Countesthorpe:

> The major policy decisions that have shaped the curriculum and discipline of the school have been made by the consensus of the staff. Increasingly, students have contributed to this consensus, and in some cases parents and governors have participated. I accepted the headship in 1972 because I found the policies and the means of determining them attractive. (Watts, 1976, pp. 130–1)

The Countesthorpe approach incorporated all the central elements of collegial models, including acknowledgement of teachers' authority of expertise and the emphasis on consensual decision-making by all the staff with student input. This example also illustrates the normative nature of collegiality because Watts regarded the approach as 'attractive'.

Brown, Boyle and Boyle (1999) carried out research on collegial models of management in 21 secondary schools in the north-west of England. The first phase involved interviews with middle managers in each school. Subsequently, the researchers interviewed the headteachers in 12 of these schools. Their analysis is thus based on paired responses from heads and middle managers in these schools.

The research was undertaken in the context of conflicting pressures on schools to be both collegial and managerial. The authors note that 'collegiality, or at least collaborative management, has become one of the biggest international trends in education' (ibid., p. 320) but also point out that such developments may not be genuine:

> Headteachers may construct decision-making processes that seem on the surface to be participatory in order to gain greater acceptance of decisions and greater teacher satisfaction. However, they may be reluctant to extend genuine influence to teachers, assuming that they do not have the expertise to make valuable contributions, or because they do not trust them to make decisions which are in the best interest of the school. (Ibid., p. 319)

Brown, Boyle and Boyle (1999) found that only four of the 12 case-study schools could be categorized as 'operating fully' in a collegial way. These 'type A' schools had the following features:

- a commitment to regular formal opportunities for collaboration with other heads of department and colleagues from different subject areas;
- departmental priorities correlated closely with the School Development Plan, with themes and issues identified and agreed collectively;
- heads of department were actively involved and consulted in whole-school policy and decision-making;
- the headteacher saw the heads of department as having a wider whole-school management role.

The participants explained why shared decision-making is desirable:

> You need the collective support of your staff to implement any worthwhile change, so involvement in the decision-making process is vital. (Headteacher) (Ibid., p. 322)

> Team work is the crucial ingredient for this school to be effective. There is no mystique and feeling of intimidation. It is almost a collaboration of equals. (Middle manager) (Ibid., p. 323)

Type A schools overcame the problem of size by adopting flexible structures. One school changed its senior management team into a school management team and included representation from all areas of the teaching staff. Working parties or curriculum groups with cross-department and voluntary representation were also favoured ways of widening involvement.

Despite these strategies, the authors conclude that it is difficult to achieve collegiality in practice:

> Collegial models of education management are becoming the dominant paradigm in the literature ... There are, however, pragmatic and ideological factors which raise the question of the attainability of collegiality. Collegiality offers many persuasive benefits but is, in reality, difficult to attain. (Ibid., p. 329)

The concept of collegiality is similar to that of the 'jiaoyanzu' in Chinese schools. Paine and Ma (1993) refer to an 'assumption that teachers would work together in virtually every aspect of their work' and explain how the jiaoyanzu works:

> Many decisions about curriculum and instruction are made jointly through the jiaoyanzu ... teachers have a structured time to work together ... Teachers ... work together ... in an office that belongs to their jiaoyanzu. (Ibid., p. 679)

Unlike their English equivalents, teachers have substantial non-contact time to facilitate collaborative working. Research in secondary schools in the Shaanxi province of China (Bush, Coleman and Si, 1998) shows that departmental jiaoyanzu work collegially to discuss teaching materials, provide demonstration lessons, and observe and comment on each other's lessons. However, these discussions occur under the supervision of the teaching dean who, in turn, is appointed by the principal. This suggests a hierarchical dimension to the operation of jiaoyanzu.

Collegial models in primary schools

Collegiality became established during the 1980s and 1990s as the most appropriate way to manage primary schools. It remains the normative model of good practice in this phase of education in England and Wales, despite the contrary pressures arising from government imperatives. Little (1990, pp. 177–80) describes how collegiality operates in practice:

- Teachers talk about teaching.
- There is shared planning and preparation.
- The presence of observers in classrooms is common.
- There is mutual training and development.

The model outlined by Little (1990) appears to depend on shared professional values leading to the development of trust and a willingness to give and receive criticism in order to enhance practice. It is a demanding approach which requires commitment from staff if it is to become an effective vehicle for beneficial change. It is also an elusive model to operate even where staff are committed to the concept.

Webb and Vulliamy (1996) examined the tension between collegiality and managerialism in their study of a national sample of 50 primary schools in England and Wales. They note the 'ideal type' of collegiality emerging in numerous reports in the 1980s and 1990s and state that 'aspirations for collaborative approaches to whole-school change still pervade much current advice to primary schools' (ibid., pp. 441–2). However, the pressures for external accountability means that many schools are 'resorting to managerialism' (ibid., p. 442). They express concern that 'tension between collegiality and managerialism is resulting in concepts like "whole school" being hijacked by a managerialist ethic'.

These authors report that all 50 heads in their sample 'spoke of the growth in openness, discussion and sharing among teachers since the introduction of the National Curriculum' (ibid., p. 444). Subject leaders were viewed as playing a vital role in curriculum planning despite the lack of non-contact time for them to visit or work in colleagues' classrooms. Other difficulties reported by participants include:

- the time-consuming nature of meetings where 'the discussion phase seemed to go on and on' and 'I felt we weren't getting anywhere';
- lack of agreement led to non-action;
- the pace at which the external changes were introduced meant that teachers had insufficient time for critical reflection on existing practice (Webb and Vulliamy, 1996, p. 446).

They add that the policy climate 'encourages headteachers to be powerful and, if necessary, manipulative leaders' (ibid., p. 448) and conclude that collegiality is being damaged by external demands and the pressures on headteachers to ensure compliance with national directives:

> We have documented a growing tension between collegial and top-down approaches to whole-school change . . . strong . . . forces appear to be combining to promote what we have termed managerialism and the directive management styles of headteachers associated with it, which undermine the feasibility and credibility of teachers working together collegially to formulate policies and promote continuity of practice . . . The tensions generated by trying to create conditions for co-operative working in the context of increased managerialism were present to some extent in all schools. (Webb and Vulliamy, 1996, pp. 455–6)

We shall return to these issues in examining the limitations of collegial models.

Collegial models: goals, structure, environment and leadership

Goals

Collegial models assume that members of an organization agree on its *goals*.

There is a belief that staff have a shared view of the purposes of the institution. Agreement on aims is perhaps the central element in all participative approaches to school and college management. Goals have three main functions:

- They provide a general guide to activity, enabling teachers to link their work to school objectives.
- Goals serve as a source of legitimacy, enabling activities to be justified if they contribute to achievement of the goals.
- They are a means of measuring success; a school is effective if it achieves its objectives.

Campbell and Southworth (1993, p. 72) emphasize the need for staff to 'purpose the same' and quote from their research in primary schools: 'Teachers felt that it was important that they should have compatible ideals, agree the same aims and share the same purpose . . . "If you are aiming for a whole-school . . . then everybody has got to agree about aims and purposes".' However, agreement on goals is likely to be achieved only under certain conditions. One such circumstance is where staff have been chosen by the head and possess a common educational philosophy.

In universities and colleges, and perhaps also in secondary schools, the various academic disciplines often have rather different ideas about the central purpose of their institutions. In these circumstances, as Baldridge et al. (1978, pp. 20–1) demonstrate, agreement on aims may be achieved only by obfuscation: 'Most organisations know what they are doing . . . By contrast, colleges and universities have vague, ambiguous goals . . . As long as goals are left ambiguous and abstract, people agree; as soon as they are concretely specified and put into operation, disagreement arises.'

The acknowledgement of possible conflict over the goals of educational institutions threatens one of the central planks of collegial theory. The belief that staff can always reach agreement over institutional purposes and policies lies at the heart of all participative approaches. Recognition of goal conflict serves to limit the validity of collegial models.

Organizational structure

Collegial models share with formal approaches the view that organizational *structure* is an objective fact which has a clear meaning for all members of the institution. The major difference concerns the relationships between different elements of the structure. Formal models present structures as vertical or hierarchical with decisions being made by leaders and then passed down the structure. Subordinates are accountable to superiors for the satisfactory performance of their duties. In contrast, collegial models assume structures to be lateral or horizontal with participants having an equal right to determine policy and influence decisions.

In education, collegial approaches are often manifested through systems of committees, which may be elaborate in the larger and more complex institutions. The decision-making process inside committees is thought to be egalitarian with influence dependent more on specific expertise than an official position. The assumption is that decisions are reached by consensus or compromise rather than acquiescence to the views of the head or principal.

In schools, ad hoc working parties may be more effective than standing committees. Brown, Boyle and Boyle (1999) report on the usefulness of such groups in their case study secondary schools, as one of their respondents illustrates:

> We have working parties who report back to faculties after consultation with the senior management team and collaborative policies are produced and implemented. (Ibid., p. 323)

The external environment

There are several difficulties in assessing the nature of relationships between the organization and its *external environment*. Collegial models characterize decision-making as a participative process with all members of the institution having an equal opportunity to influence policy and action. However, where decisions emerge from an often complex committee system, it is no easy task to establish who is responsible for organizational policy.

The ambiguity of the decision-making process within collegial organizations creates a particular problem in terms of accountability to external bodies. The head or principal is invariably held responsible for the policies of the school or college. The assumptions of the formal models are in line with these expectations. Leaders are thought to determine or strongly influence decisions and are accountable to external bodies for these policies.

Collegial models do not fit comfortably with these formal accountability assumptions. Are principals expected to justify school policies determined within a participatory framework even where they do not enjoy their personal support? Or is the reality that collegial policy-making is limited by the head's responsibility to external agencies? Heads must agree with, or at minimum acquiesce in, decisions made in committee if they are not to be placed in a very difficult position.

Collegial models tend to overlook the possibility of conflict between internal participative processes and external accountability. The often bland assumption that issues can be resolved by consensus leads to the comfortable conclusion that heads are always in agreement with decisions and experience no difficulty in explaining them to external bodies. In practice, it may be that the head's accountability leads to a substantially modified version of collegiality in most schools and colleges. There is also the risk of tension for the principal who is caught between the conflicting demands of participation and accountability.

These pressures have intensified in England and Wales following the implementation of the National Curriculum, its associated assessment requirements, and a national inspection regime headed by the Office for Standards in Education (OFSTED). As we noted earlier, these external demands have made it more difficult for schools to operate collegially. This is equally true for primary (Webb and Vulliamy, 1996) and secondary (Brown, Boyle and Boyle, 1999) schools.

Leadership

In collegial models the style of *leadership* both influences, and is influenced by, the nature of the decision-making process. Because policy is determined within a participative framework, the head or principal is expected to adopt strategies which acknowledge that issues may emerge from different parts of the organization and be resolved in a complex interactive process. Heroic models of leadership are inappropriate when influence and power are widely distributed within the institution:

> The collegial leader is at most a 'first among equals' in an academic organization supposedly run by professional experts . . . The basic idea of the collegial leader is less to command than to listen, less to lead than to gather expert judgements, less to manage than to facilitate, less to order than to persuade and negotiate . . . the collegial leader is not so much a star standing alone as the developer of consensus among the professionals who must share the burden of the decision. (Baldridge et al., 1978, p. 45)

Collegial theorists ascribe the following qualities to leaders in schools and colleges:

1 They are responsive to the needs and wishes of their professional colleagues. Heads and principals acknowledge the expertise and skill of the teachers and seek to harness these assets for the benefit of the pupils and students. Invariably, they have been appointed to leadership posts after a long period as successful practitioners. Their experience makes them 'sensitive to the informal codes of professional practice which govern expectations for relations among teachers and between teachers and head' (Coulson, 1985, p. 86).

2 Collegial heads seek to create formal and informal opportunities for the

testing and elaboration of policy initiatives. This is done to encourage innovation and to maximize the acceptability of school decisions. The headteacher of 'Uplands' school, for example, promotes and nurtures a culture of shared values and a modified form of collegiality:

> She believes in the importance of high quality human relationships and is very accessible. She teaches regularly, does bus duty every afternoon when she is in school, continually walks round the school talking to staff and pupils and partakes in social activities . . . She consults and wants to involve staff in decision-making, although the ultimate decisions clearly rest with the senior management team. (Glover, 1996, p. 146)

3 Collegial models emphasize the authority of expertise rather than official authority. It follows that authority in professional organizations such as schools or colleges resides as much with the staff as with the head. Instead of exerting authority over subordinates, the leader seeks to influence the decisions and actions of professional colleagues. The head also allows and encourages heads of department and subject leaders to become co-leaders. The following passage develops this point in relation to primary schools: '[Collegial] leadership draws much of its justification from the authority of expertise of professional staff. The process of subject coordination reinforces this authority and establishes a cadre of specialists who are able to influence decisions by virtue of their accumulated knowledge of their subjects' (Bush, 1988, p. 42).

In collegial models, then, the head or principal is typified as the facilitator of an essentially participative process. Their credibility with their colleagues depends on providing leadership to staff and external stakeholders while valuing the contributions of specialist teachers:

> The picture of a 'good' headteacher which emerged from the teachers' comments on a 'whole school' was of a person to whom they could talk and with whom they could discuss, who did not dictate, who was effectively a part of the staff group and whose philosophy was clear and shared by colleagues. (Campbell and Southworth, 1993, p. 75)

Transformational leadership

As we noted in Chapter 2, the six management models are compared with leadership models throughout this book. Three of these leadership models appear particularly relevant for collegiality. The first of these is 'transformational leadership'.

> This form of leadership assumes that the central focus of leadership ought to be the commitments and capacities of organisational members. Higher levels of personal commitment to organisational goals and greater capacities for accomplishing

those goals are assumed to result in extra effort and greater productivity. (Leithwood, Jantzi and Steinbach, 1999, p. 9)

Leithwood (1994) conceptualizes transformational leadership along eight dimensions:

- building school vision;
- establishing school goals;
- providing intellectual stimulation;
- offering individualized support;
- modelling best practices and important organizational values;
- demonstrating high performance expectations;
- creating a productive school culture;
- developing structures to foster participation in school decisions.

Caldwell and Spinks (1992, pp. 49–50) argue that transformational leadership is essential for autonomous schools: 'Transformational leaders succeed in gaining the commitment of followers to such a degree that . . . higher levels of accomplishment become virtually a moral imperative. In our view a powerful capacity for transformational leadership is required for the successful transition to a system of self-managing schools.'

Leithwood's (1994) research suggests that there is some empirical support for the essentially normative transformational leadership model. He reports on seven quantitative studies and concludes that:

> Transformational leadership practices, considered as a composite construct, had significant direct and indirect effects on progress with school-restructuring initiatives and teacher-perceived student outcomes. (Ibid., p. 506)

The transformational model is comprehensive in that it provides a normative approach to school leadership which focuses primarily on the process by which leaders seek to influence school outcomes rather than on the nature or direction of those outcomes. However, it may also be criticized as being a vehicle for control over teachers and more likely to be accepted by the leader than the led (Chirichello, 1999).

Allix (2000) goes further and alleges that transformational leadership has the potential to become 'despotic' because of its strong, heroic and charismatic features. He believes that the leader's power ought to raise 'moral qualms' and serious doubts about its appropriateness for democratic organizations. His conception suggests a political (see Chapter 5) rather than a collegial stance:

> Leadership [is] a special form of power embodied in a structure of action, in which the acceptance of 'superior' values by followers is forged through social conflict

in a context charged by emotional elevation, rather than reason . . . there lurk(s) implicitly . . . the necessary – though not sufficient – conditions for the development of despotic forms of social organisation and control . . . this conceptualisation of education carries with it the seeds of psychological manipulation, in which the indoctrination of falsehoods, and the cultivation of ignorance, is all too possible. (Allix, 2000, pp. 17–18)

The contemporary policy climate within which schools have to operate also raises questions about the validity of the transformational model, despite its popularity in the literature. The English system increasingly requires school leaders to adhere to government prescriptions which affect aims, curriculum content and pedagogy as well as values. There is 'a more centralized, more directed, and more controlled educational system [that] has dramatically reduced the possibility of realising a genuinely transformational education and leadership' (Bottery, 2001, p. 215).

Transformational leadership is consistent with the collegial model in that it assumes that leaders and staff have shared values and common interests. When it works well, it has the potential to engage all stakeholders in the achievement of educational objectives. The aims of leaders and followers coalesce to such an extent that it may be realistic to assume a harmonious relationship and a genuine convergence leading to agreed decisions. When 'transformation' is a cloak for imposing the leader's values, then the process is political rather than collegial, as we shall see in Chapter 5.

Participative leadership

The second leadership model relevant to collegiality is 'participative leadership'.

Participative leadership . . . assumes that the decision-making processes of the group ought to be the central focus of the group. (Leithwood, Jantzi and Steinbach, 1999, p. 12)

As with collegiality itself, this is a normative model which is based on three criteria:

- Participation will increase school effectiveness.
- Participation is justified by democratic principles.
- In the context of site-based management, leadership is potentially available to any legitimate stakeholder (ibid., p. 12).

Sergiovanni (1984, p. 13) points to the importance of a participative approach. This will succeed in 'bonding' staff together and in easing the pressures on school principals: 'The burdens of leadership will be less if leadership functions and roles are shared and if the concept of *leadership density* were to emerge as a viable replacement for principal leadership' (ibid.).

Copland (2001) makes a similar point in claiming that participative leadership has the potential to ease the burden on principals and avoid the expectation that the formal leader will be a 'superhead':

> Leadership is embedded in various organisational contexts within school communities, not centrally vested in a person or an office . . . exciting work is under way that explores specific ways in which schools might distribute leadership more broadly . . . [There is] a need to identify and support aspects of leadership beyond the role of the principal. (Ibid., p. 6)

Savery, Soutar and Dyson (1992) demonstrate that deputy principals in Western Australia wish to participate in school decision-making but their desire to do so varied across different types of decision. A majority of their 105 respondents wanted joint decision-making in school policy, student discipline, teaching load, general policy and time allocation but fewer were interested in participating in what were described as 'economic variables', including budgets and staff selection, and in responding to parental complaints. The authors conclude that 'people are more likely to accept and implement decisions in which they have participated, particularly where these decisions relate directly to the individual's own job' (ibid., p. 24).

Interpersonal leadership

The third leadership model relevant to collegiality is the relatively new concept of interpersonal leadership. West-Burnham (2001, p. 1) argues that 'interpersonal intelligence is the vital medium. It is impossible to conceptualize any model of leadership that does not have interpersonal intelligence as a key component'. His definition is:

> Interpersonal intelligence is the authentic range of intuitive behaviours derived from sophisticated self-awareness, which facilitates effective engagement with others. (p. 2)

Interpersonal leadership links to collegiality in that it stresses the importance of collaboration and interpersonal relationships, a theme taken up by Tuohy and Coghlan (1997, p. 67):

> Much of the teachers' day is taken up in an intensity of relationships. Understanding the changing nature of relationships with young students, the changing context of their lives, and developing appropriate and effective responses to both their personal and academic needs requires constant reflection and adjustment.

These pressures are even more evident in the work of school leaders and suggests a requirement for high level personal and interpersonal skills

(Johnston and Pickersgill, 1992) and a need for a collaborative approach to relationships with staff, students and other stakeholders.

Bennett et al.'s (2000) research with nine English primary schools provides evidence about the significance of interpersonal leadership and its contribution to a collegial approach to school management:

> In four of the sample schools the headteacher was seen as leading from within the staff with strong interpersonal relationships. Here, staff interviewees referred to 'teams', 'friends working together' and 'certainty of consultation and support'. In this situation . . . collegiality may be more readily achieved. (Ibid., p. 347)

Collegiality and gender

The trend towards collegial management has been particularly noticeable in primary schools and most of the relevant literature refers to this sector. There may be several reasons for this disparity, including the fact that primary schools are generally small enough for 'whole-school' collegiality and have simple, unstratified structures. It may also be influenced by gender. Women invariably form the majority in primary schools and some have an all-female staff. There is also a much higher proportion of women leaders in primary schools than in secondary schools or colleges.

Al-Khalifa (1989, p. 89) claims that women adopt different management styles from men with a much greater emphasis on collaboration, co-operation and other 'feminine' behaviours. These styles, which are compatible with collegiality, are contrasted with 'masculine' aspects of management: 'Women managers pinpoint aspects of management practice which they find dysfunctional – namely aggressive competitive behaviours, an emphasis on control rather than negotiation and collaboration, and the pursuit of competition rather than shared problem-solving' (ibid.).

Nias, Southworth and Yeomans (1989, pp. 70–1) discuss the applicability of a gender perspective to the collegial culture prevalent in many primary schools but conclude on the basis of their research that this view is 'simplistic':

> It could be argued that the 'culture of collaboration', with its emphasis on concern for the individual and on cohesion, its legitimation of emotionality, its validation of control both by peers and by the head, its denial of competition, is a 'woman's culture' . . . [but] to argue that a collaborative culture is gender-specific is simplistic. (Ibid.)

Nias, Southworth and Yeomans (1989) refer to examples of successful collaborative behaviour involving both women and men. However, Coleman (1994) presents evidence that women managers in education tend to be more democratic than men, demonstrating qualities of warmth, empathy and co-operation. Subsequently, her large scale research with male and female secondary school heads suggests, on the basis of self-reporting data, that there is 'very little difference in the qualities . . . identified by women and men in terms of how they perceive their management style' (Coleman, 2002, p. 106). Further qualitative research with male and female leaders is required before firm conclusions can be drawn with confidence.

Limitations of collegial models

Collegial models have been popular in the literature on educational leadership and management, and in official pronouncements about school development, since the 1980s. Brundrett (1998, p. 307) argues that it has become 'one of the ubiquitous megatrends in education'. Advocates of collegiality believe that participative approaches represent the most appropriate means of conducting affairs in educational institutions. However, critics of collegial models point to a number of flaws which serve to limit their validity in schools and colleges. There are seven significant weaknesses of collegial perspectives.

1 Collegial models are so strongly *normative* that they tend to obscure rather than portray reality. Precepts about the most appropriate ways of managing educational institutions mingle with descriptions of behaviour. While collegiality is increasingly advocated, the evidence of its presence in schools and colleges tends to be sketchy and incomplete, leading Webb and Vulliamy (1996, p. 443) to state that 'the advocacy of collegiality is made more on the basis of prescription than on research-based studies of school practice'. Baldridge et al. (1978, p. 33) present a powerful critique of collegial models in higher education which may also apply to schools:

> The collegial literature often confuses *descriptive* and *normative* enterprises. Are the writers saying that the university *is* a collegium or that it *ought* to be a collegium? Frequently, the discussions of collegium are more a lament for paradise lost than a description of present reality. Indeed, the collegial idea of round table decision making does not accurately reflect the actual processes in most institutions. (original emphases)

2 Collegial approaches to decision-making tend to be *slow and cumbersome*. When policy proposals require the approval of a series of committees, the process is often tortuous and time-consuming. The participative ethic requires that a decision should be made by agreement where possible rather than by resorting to a voting process. The attempts to achieve consensus may lead to procedural delays such as a reference back to the sponsoring committee, or to consultation with other committees, individuals or external agencies. Participants may have to endure many lengthy meet-

ings before issues are resolved. This requires patience and a considerable investment of time. Several primary school heads interviewed by Webb and Vulliamy (1996, pp. 445–6) refer to 'the time-consuming nature of meetings where 'the discussion phase seemed to go on and on' and 'I felt we weren't getting anywhere'.

Hellawell (1991, p. 335) concludes that lack of time could be a serious constraint in primary schools: 'My own experience of collegial structures in higher education is that they are extremely time-consuming and they certainly demand a level of meetings that primary school personnel could only fulfil by using considerable time outside the school teaching hours.' The sheer length of the process may be a major factor in the relatively limited adoption of collegial approaches in schools. Most staff are engaged in classroom activities for much or all of the day. Meetings tend to be held after school when staff are tired and unprepared for a protracted attempt to achieve consensus on aspects of school policy.

3 A fundamental assumption of democratic models is that decisions are reached by *consensus*. It is believed that the outcome of debate should be agreement based on the shared values of participants. In practice, though, committee members have their own views and there is no guarantee of unanimity on outcomes. In addition, participants often represent constituencies within the school or college. Individuals may be members of committees as representatives of the English department or the science faculty. Inevitably these sectional interests have a significant influence on committees' processes. The participatory framework may become the focal point for disagreement between factions. Baldridge et al. (1978, pp. 33-4) argue that democratic models greatly underestimate the significance of conflict within education:

> The collegial model ... fails to deal adequately with the problem of *conflict* ... [it] neglects the prolonged battles that precede consensus and the fact that the consensus actually represents the prevalence of one group over another. Collegial proponents are correct in declaring that simple bureaucratic rule making is not the essence of decision making, but in making this point they take the equally indefensible position that major decisions are reached primarily by consensus (original emphasis).

4 Collegial models have to be evaluated in relation to the special features of educational institutions. The participative aspects of decision-making exist alongside the structural and bureaucratic components of schools and colleges. Often there is tension between these rather different modes of management. The participative element rests on the authority of expertise possessed by professional staff but this rarely trumps the positional authority of official leaders. Brundrett (1998) points to the inevitable con-

tradiction between collegiality and bureaucracy in the English educational system:

> In an era of a national curriculum, centralised testing and increased bureaucratisation of education, it is interesting to note that collegiality is the preferred style of school-based management . . . collegiality is inevitably the handmaiden of an ever increasingly centralised bureaucracy. (Ibid., pp. 312–13).

5 Collegial approaches to school and college decision-making may be difficult to sustain in view of the requirement that heads and principals remain accountable to the governing body and to various external groups. Participation represents the internal dimension of democracy. *Accountability* may be thought of as the external aspect of democracy. Governors and external groups seek explanations of policy and invariably turn to the head or principal for answers to their questions. Heads may experience considerable difficulty in defending policies which have emerged from a collegial process but do not enjoy their personal support. Brundrett (1998, p. 310) is right to argue that 'heads need to be genuinely brave to lend power to a democratic forum which may make decisions with which the headteacher may not themselves agree'.

6 The effectiveness of a collegial system depends in part on the attitudes of staff. If they actively support participation then it may succeed. If they display apathy or hostility, it seems certain to fail. Hellawell (1991, p. 334) refers to the experience of one primary head who sought to introduce collegial approaches:

> I have worked very hard over the last few years, as the number of staff has grown, to build up a really collegial style of management with a lot of staff input into decisions that affect the school and they are saying that they don't like this. They would like an autocracy. They would like to be told what to do.

Wallace (1989) argues that teachers may not welcome collegiality because they are disinclined to accept any authority intermediate between themselves and the head. This has serious implications for the role of the curriculum co-ordinator: 'Potential tension is . . . embedded in the relationship between the roles of curriculum consultant and class-teacher. Many teachers expect a high degree of autonomy over the delivery of the curriculum in their classrooms, yet their professional judgement may conflict with that of the consultant' (Wallace, 1989, p. 187).

A related consideration is the limited time available to work collegially. Secondary teachers have only limited 'free' time while, as Webb and Vulliamy (1996, p. 445) note, 'there is little or no contact time for [primary teachers] to visit or work in colleagues' classrooms'.

7 Collegial processes in schools depend even more on the attitudes of heads

than on the support of teachers. In colleges, the academic board provides a legitimate forum for the involvement of staff in decision-making and principals have to recognize and work with this alternative power source. In schools, participative machinery can be established only with the support of the head, who has the legal authority to manage the school. Wise heads take account of the views of their staff but this is a consultative process and not collegiality. Hoyle (1986, p. 91) concludes that its dependence on the head's support limits the validity of the collegiality model: 'Collegiality is not inherent in the system but is a function of leadership style whereby teachers are given the opportunity to participate in the decision-making process by benevolent heads rather than as of right.'

Contrived collegiality

Hargreaves (1994) makes a more fundamental criticism of collegiality, arguing that it is being espoused or 'contrived' by official groups in order to secure the implementation of national policy in England and Wales, and elsewhere. He claims that genuine collegiality is spontaneous, voluntary, unpredictable, informal and geared to development. Contrived collegiality, in contrast, has the following contradictory features:

- administratively regulated rather than spontaneous;
- compulsory rather than discretionary;
- geared to the implementation of the mandates of government or the headteacher;
- fixed in time and place;
- designed to have predictable outcomes (Hargreaves, 1994, pp. 195–6).

Within the post-Education Reform Act context in England and Wales, this analysis is persuasive. Brundrett (1998) and Webb and Vulliamy (1996) both argue that collegial frameworks may be used for essentially political activity, the focus of the next chapter:

> What is actually happening in many institutions where collaboration is espoused, is not a genuine collegial environment but rather an adept use of micro-political manipulation . . . In effect individuals and groups seek to realise their values and goals at the expense of others but seek to legitimate their power through assuming the cloak of the moral legitimacy lent to them by the apparent use of democratic procedures. (Brundrett, 1998, p. 311)

> The current climate . . . encourages headteachers to be powerful and, if necessary, manipulative leaders in order to ensure that policies and practices agreed upon are ones that they can wholeheartedly support and defend. (Webb and Vulliamy, 1996, p. 448)

These views are also consistent with the comments made by Allix (2000), noted earlier, about the potentially manipulative aspects of transformational leadership.

Conclusion: is collegiality an unattainable ideal?

Collegial models are highly normative and idealistic. Their advocates believe that participative approaches represent the most appropriate means of managing educational institutions. Teachers exhibit that authority of expertise which justifies their involvement in the decision-making process. In addition, they are able to exercise sufficient discretion in the classroom to ensure that innovation depends on their co-operation. Collegial theorists argue that active support for change is more likely to be forthcoming where teachers have been able to contribute to the process of policy formulation.

Collegial models contribute several important concepts to the theory of educational management. Participative approaches are a necessary antidote to the rigid hierarchical assumptions of the formal models. However, collegial perspectives provide an incomplete portrayal of management in education. They underestimate the official authority of the head and present bland assumptions of consensus which often cannot be substantiated. Hoyle (1986, p. 100) argues that bureaucratic and political realities mean that collegiality does not exist in schools: 'In the absence of a true collegium, a situation which the existing law and external expectations preclude, the head either carries a fully-participating staff or fails to do so thus creating a situation of direct conflict.' This view may be too pessimistic but it remains true that those who aspire to collegiality often find that it cannot be implemented effectively. Little (1990, p. 187), following substantial research in the United States, concludes that collegiality 'turns out to be rare'.

A generation ago almost all schools and colleges could have been categorized as formal. Since the 1990s, many have developed collegial frameworks. There is a discernible trend towards collegiality and participative leadership despite the bureaucratic pressures imposed by central government. It may also exist in pockets, for example in subject teams, within bureaucratic organizations. Despite Hargreaves's (1994) justifiable criticisms of 'contrived collegiality', the advantages of participation in professional organizations remain persuasive. Collegiality is an elusive ideal but a measure of participation is essential if schools are to be harmonious and creative organizations.

References

Al-Khalifa, E. (1989) 'Management by halves: women teachers and school management', in H. De Lyon and F. Migniuolo (eds), *Women Teachers: Issues and Experiences*, Buckingham: Open University Press.

Allix, N.M. (2000) 'Transformational leadership: democratic or despotic?', *Educational Management and Administration*, 28 (1): 7–20.

Baldridge, J.V., Curtis, D.V., Ecker, G. and Riley, G.L. (1978) *Policy Making and Effective Leadership*, San Francisco, CA: Jossey-Bass.

Becher, T. and Kogan, M. (1992) *Process and Structure in Higher Education*, 2nd edn, London: Routledge.

Bennett, N., Crawford, M., Levačić, R., Glover, D. and Earley, P. (2000) 'The reality of school development planning in the effective primary school: technicist or guiding plan?', *School Leadership and Management*, 20 (3): 333–51.

Bottery, M. (2001) 'Globalisation and the UK competition state: no room for transformational leadership in education?', *School Leadership and Management*, 21 (2): 199–218.

Brown, M., Boyle, B. and Boyle, T. (1999) 'Commonalities between perception and practice in models of school decision-making in secondary schools', *School Leadership and Management*, 19 (3): 319–30.

Brundrett, M. (1998) 'What lies behind collegiality, legitimation or control?', *Educational Management and Administration*, 26 (3): 305–16.

Bush, T. (1988) *Action and Theory in School Management, E325 Managing Schools*, Buckingham: Open University Press.

Bush, T. and Heystek, J. (2003) 'School governance in the new South Africa', *Compare*, 33 (2): 127–38.

Bush, T., Coleman, M. and Si, X. (1998) 'Managing secondary schools in China', *Compare*, 28 (2): 183–96.

Caldwell, B. and Spinks, J. (1992) *Leading the Self-Managing School*, London: Falmer Press.

Campbell, P. and Southworth, P. (1993) 'Rethinking collegiality: teachers' views', in N. Bennett, M. Crawford and C. Riches (eds), *Managing Change in Education: Individual and Organizational Perspectives*, London: Paul Chapman Publishing.

Chirichello, M. (1999) 'Building capacity for change: transformational leadership for school principals', paper presented at ICSEI Conference, 3–6 January, San Antonio.

Coleman, M. (1994) 'Women in educational management', in T. Bush and J. West-Burnham (eds), *The Principles of Educational Management*, Harlow: Longman.

Coleman, M. (2002) *Women as Headteachers: Striking the Balance*, Stoke-on-Trent: Trentham Books.

Copland, M. (2001) 'The myth of the superprincipal', *Phi Delta Kappan*, 82, 528–32.

Coulson, A. (1985) *The Managerial Behaviour of Primary School Heads*, Collected Original Resources in Education, Abingdon: Carfax Publishing Company.

Deem, R. (2000) ' "New Managerialism" and the management of UK universities', end of award report of the findings of an Economic and Social Research Council funded project, Lancaster University.

Department of Education (1997) *Understanding the SA Schools Act*, Pretoria: Department of Education.

Glatter, R. (1984) *Managing for Change, E324 Management in Post Compulsory Education, Block 6*, Buckingham: Open University Press.

Glover, D. (1996) 'Leadership, planning and resource management in four very effective schools. Part one: setting the scene', *School Organisation*, 16 (2): 135–48.

Hargreaves, A. (1994) *Changing Teachers, Changing Times: Teachers' Work and Culture in the Postmodern Age*, London: Cassell.

Harris, A. (2002) *Distributed leadership in schools: leading or misleading?*, paper presented at the British Educational Leadership, Management and Administration Society, Birmingham, September.

Hellawell. D. (1991) 'The changing role of the head in the primary school in England', *School Organisation*, 11, (3): 321–37.

Hoyle, E. (1986) *The Politics of School Management*, Sevenoaks: Hodder and Stoughton.

Johnston, J. and Pickersgill, S. (1992) 'Personal and interpersonal aspects of effective team oriented headship in the primary school', *Educational Management and Administration*, 20 (4): 239–48.

Leithwood, K. (1994) 'Leadership for school restructuring', *Educational Administration Quarterly*, 30 (4): 498–518.

Leithwood, K., Jantzi, D. and Steinbach, R. (1999) *Changing Leadership for Changing Times*, Buckingham: Open University Press.

Little, J. (1990) 'Teachers as colleagues', in A. Lieberman (ed.), *Schools as Collaborative Cultures: Creating the Future Now*, Basingstoke: Falmer Press.

Lumby, J. (2003) *Distributed leadership in colleges: leading or misleading?*, Educational Management and Administration, 31 (3): 283–93.

Middlehurst, R. and Elton, L. (1992) 'Leadership and management in higher education', *Studies in Higher Education*, 17, (3): 251–64.

Nias, J., Southworth, G. and Yeomans, R. (1989) *Staff Relationships in the Primary School*, London: Cassell.

Paine, L. and Ma, L. (1993) 'Teachers working together: a dialogue on organisational and cultural perspectives of Chinese teachers', *International Journal of Educational Research*, 19, 675–97.

Savery, L., Soutar, G. and Dyson, J. (1992) 'Ideal decision-making styles indicated by deputy principals', *Journal of Educational Administration*, 30 (2): 18–25.

Sergiovanni, T. (1984) 'Leadership and excellence in schooling', *Educational Leadership*, 41 (5): 4–13.

Tuohy, D. and Coghlan, D. (1997) 'Development in schools: a systems approach based on organisational levels', *Educational Management and Administration*, 25 (1): 65–77.

Wallace, M. (1989) 'Towards a collegiate approach to curriculum management in primary and middle schools', in M. Preedy (ed.), *Approaches to Curriculum Management*, Buckingham: Open University Press.

Warren, R. (1994) 'The collegiate ideal and the organisation of the new universities', *Reflections*, 6, 39–55.

Watts, J. (1976) 'Sharing it out: the role of the head in participatory government', in R.S. Peters (ed.), *The Role of the Head*, London: Routledge and Kegan Paul.

Webb, R. and Vulliamy, G. (1996) 'A deluge of directives: conflict between collegiality and managerialism in the post-ERA primary school', *British Educational*

Research Journal, 22 (4): 441–58.

West-Burnham, J. (2001) 'Interpersonal leadership', *NCSL Leading Edge Seminar*, Nottingham: National College for School Leadership.

Williams, K. (1989) 'The case for democratic management in schools', *Irish Educational Studies*, 8, (2): 73–86.

Williams, G. and Blackstone, T. (1983) *Response to Adversity*, Guildford: Society for Research into Higher Education.

5
Political Models

Central features of political models

Political models embrace those theories which characterize decision-making as a bargaining process. They assume that organizations are political arenas whose members engage in political activity in pursuit of their interests. Analysis focuses on the distribution of power and influence in organizations and on the bargaining and negotiation between interest groups. Conflict is regarded as endemic within organizations and management is directed towards the regulation of political behaviour. The definition suggested below incorporates the main elements of these approaches:

> Political models assume that in organizations policy and decisions emerge through a process of negotiation and bargaining. Interest groups develop and form alliances in pursuit of particular policy objectives. Conflict is viewed as a natural phenomenon and power accrues to dominant coalitions rather than being the preserve of formal leaders.

Political models in schools and other educational institutions are often described as 'micropolitics' (Ball, 1987; Hoyle, 1999). Mawhinney (1999, p. 161) defines micropolitics as 'the interaction and political ideologies of social systems of teachers, administrators, teachers and pupils within school buildings. These may be viewed as internal organizational subsystems. Micropolitical analysis is also concerned with external system issues such as those arising in the interaction between professional and lay subsystems'. Micropolitics are important examples of political models but there are other political approaches that are not described as 'micropolitical'. Hence the wider concept of 'political models' is used in this volume.

Politics tend to be regarded as the concern of central and local government and to be associated strongly with the political parties who compete for our votes at national, provincial and local elections. It is useful to loosen this close identity between government and politics before seeking to apply political metaphors to educational institutions.

National and local politics strongly influence the context within which schools and colleges operate. In most societies, central government determines the broad character of the educational system and this is inevitably under-pinned by the political views of the majority party. In England and Wales, for example, the 1988 Education Reform Act and subsequent legislation, set the framework within which schools and colleges must operate.

Local politics have become less influential in England and Wales since the 1988 Act which allocated many former local education authority (LEA) responsibilities to central government or to the educational institutions. However, LEAs retain the power to determine the financial position of most schools through their control over the funding formula. The elements of the formula, and their weighting, are the product of the political judgements of the majority party, within the limitations laid down in the legislation.

While national and local government determine the broad framework for education, political models apply to schools, colleges and other organizations just as much as they relate to political parties:

> I take schools, in common with virtually all other social organizations, to be riven with actual or potential conflict between members; to be poorly coordinated; to be ideologically diverse. I take it to be essential that if we are to understand the nature of schools as organizations, we must achieve some understanding of these conflicts. (Ball, 1987, p. 19)

West (1999) points out that the international trend towards self-management in education expands the scope for political activity. As schools have greater responsibility for their own affairs, so the potential for conflict inevitably increases:

> The majority of decisions that concern teachers, and the responsibility for plan-ning the individual school's future, now reside within the school . . . schools in England and Wales have never offered more scope for micropolitical influence than they do now – within the self-managing school. We can speculate, therefore, that there has never been a time when an awareness of micropolitical processes and interactions was more useful to headteachers. (West, 1999, p. 190)

Hoyle (1999) makes a useful distinction between policy and management micropolitics:

> The concerns of policy micropolitics are essentially transboundary; how microp-olitics constitute the means by which school staff respond to external pressures, e.g. resistance, retreatism, ritualism. Management micropolitics faces in the direc-tion of the strategies whereby school leaders and teachers pursue their interests in the context of the management of the school . . . although micropolitics is con-cerned with strategies deployed in the conflict of interests between teachers, per-haps the main focus is the conflict of interests between school leaders and teachers. (Hoyle, 1999, p. 214)

Baldridge (1971, pp. 19–20) conducted research in universities in the United

States and concluded that the political model, rather than the formal or collegial perspectives, best captured the realities of life in higher education:

> When we look at the complex and dynamic processes that explode on the modern campus today, we see neither the rigid, formal aspects of bureaucracy nor the calm concensus-directed elements of an academic collegium. On the contrary . . . [interest groups] emerge . . . These groups articulate their interests in many different ways, bringing pressure on the decision-making process from any number of angles . . . Power and influence, once articulated, go through a complex process until policies are shaped, reshaped and forged out of the competing claims of multiple groups.

Political models may be just as valid for schools and further education as they are for universities.

Political models have the following major features:

1 They tend to focus on *group activity* rather than the institution as a whole. The emphasis is on the basic unit (Becher and Kogan, 1992) not the school or college level. Interaction between groups is at the heart of political approaches whereas formal and collegial models stress the institutional level: 'The basic unit of traditional political analysis is the sub group . . . the basic unit of an apolitical perspective is the total system' (Bacharach and Lawler, 1980).

Most schools and colleges are complex organizations and there are several different types of group. West (1999) distinguishes between formal and informal groups. The former 'are created in order to fulfil specific goals and carry on specific tasks which are clearly linked to the school's overall mission' (ibid., p. 190). Formal groups may be either permanent (the senior management, subject departments, etc.) or temporary (working parties or task forces). Informal groups exist to meet teachers' need for affiliation and can take many forms. Typically, they have their own leader and certain norms or rituals that underpin group behaviour (West, 1999).

Ball (1987, p. 221) refers to 'baronial politics' and discusses the nature of conflict between the leaders of subgroups: 'In the middle ages the conflicts between English barons were essentially concerned with two matters: wealth and power. In the school the concerns and interests of academic and pastoral barons are fundamentally the same: allocations from the budget . . . and influence over school policies.'

Lindle (1999) also stresses the significance of the competition for resources in fuelling political activity. 'The perennially scarce resources of schools . . . provide the nutrients for school-based political activity' (ibid., p. 171). Wallace and Hall's (1994) research on school management teams

(SMTs) in England and Wales shows how issues of power and resources were strongly evident in the work of SMTs and in their relationships with other staff in the school.

2 Political models are concerned with *interests* and *interest groups*. Individuals are thought to have a variety of interests which they pursue within the organization. Morgan (1997) explains their significance within the political model:

> In talking about 'interests', we are talking about pre-dispositions embracing goals, values, desires, expectations, and other orientations and inclinations that lead a person to act in one way rather than another. In everyday life, we tend to think of interests in a spatial way: as areas of concern that we wish to preserve or enlarge or as positions that we wish to protect or achieve ... the flow of politics is intimately connected with this way of positioning ourselves. (Morgan, 1997, p. 161)

Hoyle (1986, p. 128) distinguishes between personal and professional interests: 'Professional interests ... centre on commitments to a particular curriculum, syllabus, mode of pupil grouping, teaching method, etc ... professional interests become part of the micropolitical process according to the strategies used to further them. Personal interests focus on such issues as status, promotion and working conditions.' Hoyle (1982, p. 89) points to the development of interest groups as a principal means of seeking and achieving individual aims:

> Interests are pursued by individuals but frequently they are most effectively pursued in collaboration with others who share a common concern. Some of these may have the qualities of a group in that they are relatively enduring and have a degree of cohesion, but others ... will be looser associations of individuals who collaborate only infrequently when a common interest comes to the fore.

The more permanent formal groups, such as departments, tend to be cohesive because of shared values and beliefs. The individuals within such groups often have common attitudes towards many of the central issues in schools and colleges, although this was not the case with the departments in Brown, Boyle and Boyle's (2000) 'Type C' secondary schools where there was only limited co-operative working between and among staff colleagues. However, there are usually greater differences in goals and values *between* interest groups, leading to fragmentation rather than organizational unity. On particular issues, groups may form alliances to press for policies which reflect their joint interests. These coalitions may well be temporary, disbanding when certain objectives have been achieved, while the interest groups themselves often have enduring significance.

3 Political models stress the prevalence of *conflict* in organizations. Interest groups pursue their independent objectives which may contrast sharply with the aims of other subunits within the institution and lead to conflict between them: 'Micropolitics is about conflict, and how people compete to get what they want in the face of scarce resources' (Mawhinney, 1999, pp. 167–8).

An important feature of political perspectives is the view that conflict is a normal feature of organizations. Collegial models have a strong harmony bias and the possibility of disagreement is ignored or assumed away. In contrast, Morgan argues that conflict is the inevitable outcome of a clash of interests and interest groups:

> Conflict arises whenever interests collide. The natural reaction to conflict in organisational contexts is usually to view it a as a dysfunctional force that can be attributed to some regrettable set of circumstances or causes. 'It's a personality problem' ... Conflict is regarded as an unfortunate state that in more favourable circumstances would disappear ... [In practice] conflict will always be present in organisations ... its source rests in some perceived or real divergence of interests. (Morgan, 1997, p. 167)

Milliken's (2001) study of a business school within a United Kingdom university illustrates the prevalence of conflict. The school is divided into four specific divisions, each with its own goals. The interaction between these groups often generates conflict:

> The interest groups cluster around the divergent values and this clustering is socially evident even to the organisation of their coffee breaks when members within a division often have their breaks together in the staff common room – a form of micropolitical apartheid. (Ibid., p. 78)

4 Political models assume that the *goals* of organizations are unstable, ambiguous and contested. Individuals, interest groups and coalitions have their own purposes and act towards their achievement. Goals may be disputed and then become a significant element in the conflict between groups. Certain subunits succeed in establishing their goals as the objectives of the institution while other interests seek to supplant the official purposes with their own objectives. Bolman and Deal (1991) explain the fluid nature of goals in political settings:

> Traditional views of organisations ... assume that organisations have, or ought to have, clear and consistent goals. Generally, the goals are presumed to be established by those in authority ... The political frame, however, insists that organisational goals are set through negotiations among the members of coalitions. Different individuals and groups have different objectives and resources, and each attempts to bargain with other members or coalitions to influence goals and decision-making process. (Bolman and Deal, 1991, p. 190)

Interest groups are likely to promote their objectives in a variety of ways until they are supported by the policy-makers. This does not necessarily end the conflict because the endorsement of one set of purposes tends to be at the expense of other goals, whose proponents may continue to lobby for their own ideas. Disagreement over goals is a continuing feature of the policy process in organizations.

5 As noted above, decisions within political arenas emerge after a complex process of *bargaining and negotiation*. Formal models assume that decisions follow a rational process. Options are evaluated in terms of the objectives of the organization and the most appropriate alternative is selected.

Policy-making in political settings is a more uncertain business. Interests are promoted in committees and at numerous unofficial encounters between participants. Policies cannot easily be judged in terms of the goals of the institution because these are subject to the same process of internal debate and subsequent change. The objectives are a moving target, as Bolman and Deal (1991, p. 186) suggest:

> Organisational goals and decisions emerge from ongoing processes of bargaining, negotiation, and jockeying for position among members of different coalitions

The emphasis on the several stages of decision-making is significant because it multiplies the opportunities available to interest groups to exert influence on the policy process. Decisions on a subject at one forum do not necessarily resolve the issue because the unsuccessful groups are likely to pursue the matter whenever opportunities arise or can be engineered.

6 The concept of *power* is central to all political theories. The outcomes of the complex decision-making process are likely to be determined according to the relative power of the individuals and interest groups involved in the debate. These participants mobilize resources of power which are deployed in support of their interests and have a significant impact on policy outcomes. 'Power is the medium through which conflicts of interest are ultimately resolved. Power influences who gets what, when and how . . . the sources of power are rich and varied' (Morgan, 1997, pp. 170–1).

The nature and sources of power in education are examined on pages 96–100.

Baldridge's political model

Several of the ideas discussed in the previous section, notably the notion of stages of decision-making, are addressed in the classical political model developed by Baldridge (1971). The author considers the formation of interest

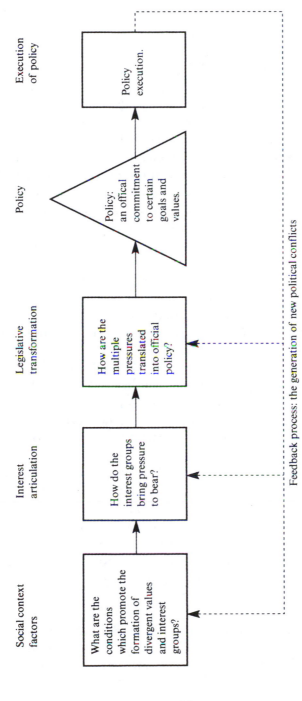

Figure 5.1 A political model (from Baldridge, 1971)

groups and discusses the ways in which policies emerge from the kaleido-scope of conflicting pressures (see Figure 5.1). Baldridge postulates five stages in the policy process:

1 A *social structure* is a configuration of social groups with basically differ-ent lifestyles and political interests. These differences often lead to con-flict, for what is in the interest of one group may damage another. The social structure, with its fragmented groups, divergent goal aspiration, and conflicting claims on the decision-makers, is the setting for political behav-iour. Many conflicts have their roots in the complexity of the social struc-ture and in the complex goals and values held by divergent groups.

2 *Interest articulation* is the process by which interests are advanced. Groups with conflicting values and goals must translate them into effective influ-ence if they are to obtain favourable action by legislative bodies. How does a powerful group exert its pressure, what threats or promises can it make, and how does it translate its desires into political capital? There are many forms of interest articulation and it assumes a multitude of shapes.

3 The *legislative stage* is the process by which articulated interests are trans-lated into policies. Legislative bodies respond to pressures, transforming the conflict into politically feasible policy. In the process many claims are played off against one another, negotiations are undertaken, compromises are forged, and rewards are divided. Committees meet, commissions report negotiators bargain, and powerful people 'haggle' about the policy.

4 The *formulation of policy* is the end result of the legislative stage. The articulated interests have gone through conflict and compromise stages and the final legislative action is taken. The policy is the official climax to the conflict and represents an authoritative, binding decision to commit the organization to one set of possible alternative actions, to one set of goals and values.

5 Finally the execution of policy occurs. The conflict comes to a climax, the battle is at least officially over, and the resulting policy is turned over to the bureaucrats for routine execution. This may not be the end of the matter, however, for two things are likely to happen. First, the major los-ers in the conflict may take up their arms again for a new round of inter-est articulation. Second, the execution of policy inevitably causes a feedback cycle, in which the policy generates new tensions, new vested interests, and a new cycle of political conflict

(Baldridge, 1971, pp. 23–4).

Perhaps the most significant aspect of the Baldridge model is that it is essentially iterative. The policy-making process is rarely straightforward. Rather, it is capable of breakdown at any stage as opposing interests coalesce to defeat proposals and seek to substitute their own plans. This leads to the feedback processes which inevitably follow the breakdown of particular proposals. Ultimately the success or failure of interest groups in promoting their objectives depends on the resources of power which they are able to mobilize.

Sources of power in education

Power may be regarded as the ability to determine the behaviour of others or to decide the outcome of conflict. Where there is disagreement it is likely to be resolved according to the relative resources of power available to the participants.

There are many sources of power but in broad terms a distinction can be made between authority and influence. *Authority* is legitimate power which is vested in leaders within formal organizations. Authority involves a legal right to make decisions which may be supported by sanctions. 'Authorities are defined essentially as the people who are entitled to make binding decisions' (Bolman and Deal, 1991, p. 193). School heads and principals typically have substantial authority by virtue of their formal leadership positions.

Influence represents an ability to affect outcomes and depends on personal characteristics and expertise. Bacharach and Lawler (1980, p. 44) identify seven distinctions between authority and influence:

1 Authority is the static, structural aspect of power in organizations; influence is the dynamic, tactical element.
2 Authority is the formal aspect of power; influence is the informal aspect.
3 Authority refers to the formally sanctioned right to make final decisions; influence is not sanctioned by the organization and is, therefore, not a matter of organizational rights.
4 Authority implies involuntary submission by subordinates; influence implies voluntary submission and does not necessarily entail a superior–subordinate relationship.
5 Authority flows downward, and it is unidirectional; influence is multi-directional and can flow upward, downward, or horizontally.
6 The source of authority is solely structural; the source of influence may be personal characteristics, expertise, or opportunity.
7 Authority is circumscribed, that is, the domain, scope, and legitimacy of the power are specifically and clearly delimited; influence is uncircum-scribed, that is, its domain, scope, and legitimacy are typically ambiguous.

Hoyle (1982, p. 90) points to the ways in which these two aspects of power operate within educational institutions:

> Influence differs from authority in having a number of sources in the organization, in being embedded in the actual relationships between groups rather than located

in an abstract legal source, and is not fixed but is variable and operates through bargaining, manipulation, exchange and so forth. The head teacher in Britain has a high degree of authority; but his [*sic*] exercise of that authority is increasingly modified as teachers' sources of influence . . . increase and thus involves the head in a greater degree of exchange and bargaining behaviour.

There are six significant forms of power relevant to schools and colleges:

1 *Positional power*. A major source of power in any organization is that accruing to individuals who hold an *official position* in the institution. Formal positions confer authority on their holders, who have a recognized right to make decisions or to play a key role in the policy-making process. Handy (1993, p. 128) says that positional power is 'legal' or 'legitimate' power. In schools, the head is regarded as the legitimate leader and possesses legal authority which is inevitably a key determinant of school policy. Other staff who hold senior posts may also exercise positional power. These may include deputy heads, heads of department and pastoral leaders. Chairs of governing bodies or school boards may also exert positional power within self-managing schools and colleges. In a hierarchy the more highly placed individuals exert the greater authority:

> The first and most obvious source of power in an organization is formal authority, a form of legitimized power that is respected and acknowledged by those with whom one interacts . . . legitimacy is a form of social approval that is essential for stabilizing power relations. It arises when people recognize that a person has a right to rule some area of human life and that it is their duty to obey. (Morgan, 1997, p. 172)

2 *Authority of expertise*. In professional organizations there is a significant reservoir of power available to those who possess appropriate *expertise*. Handy (1993, p. 130) says that 'expert power is the power that is vested in someone because of their acknowledged expertise . . . In a meritocratic tradition people do not resent being influenced by those whom they regard as the experts'. Schools and colleges employ many staff who have specialist knowledge of aspects of the curriculum. The music specialist, for example, is regarded as the expert and principals may be cautious in substituting their own judgements for those of their heads of department in curricular matters. In certain circumstances there may be conflict between formal leaders and experts but the outcome is by no means certain: 'Expert power relates to the use of knowledge and expertise as a means of legitimizing what one wishes to do. "The expert" often carries an aura of authority and power that can add considerable weight to a decision that rests in the balance' (Morgan, 1997, p. 181).

3 *Personal power*. Individuals who are charismatic or possess verbal skills or certain other characteristics may be able to exercise *personal power*. Staff who are able to influence behaviour or decisions by virtue of personal abilities or qualities are often thought to possess the attributes of charismatic leadership. These personal skills are independent of the power accruing to individuals by virtue of their position in the organization. In school staff rooms, for example, there are often individuals who command the respect of colleagues because of their perceived wisdom or insight. These teachers may become alternative leaders whose views are sought on the key issues. 'Individuals with charisma, political skills, verbal facility, or the capacity to articulate vision are powerful by virtue of their personal characteristics, in addition to whatever other power they may have' (Bolman and Deal, 1991, p. 197).

4 *Control of rewards*. Power is likely to be possessed to a significant degree by individuals who have *control of rewards*. They are inevitably perceived as powerful by those who value such returns. In education, rewards may include promotion, good references and allocation to favoured classes or groups. Individuals who control or influence the allocation of these benefits may be able to determine the behaviour of teachers who seek one or more of the rewards. Typically, the head or principal is the major arbiter of promotion and references although advice may be sought from heads of department or others who possess relevant knowledge or information. Classes may be allocated by heads of department. This form of power represents a means of control over aspiring teachers but may have little influence on those staff who choose to spurn these rewards. Control of rewards may be regarded as authority rather than influence where it emanates from the leader acting in an official capacity.

5 *Coercive power*. The mirror image of the control of rewards may be *coercive power*. This implies the ability to enforce compliance with a request or requirement. Coercion is backed by the threat of sanctions. 'Coercive power rests on the ability to constrain, to block, to interfere, or to punish' (Bolman and Deal, 1991, p. 196).

Heads and principals may exercise coercive power by threatening not to supply a good reference for external applications or warning about the prospects for internal promotion. In certain circumstances, coercion may be used in conjunction with the control of rewards to manipulate the behaviour of others. This 'carrot and stick' combination may have a powerful double effect on staff and may be a latent factor in all schools and colleges. Wallace and Hall (1994, p. 33) question the legitimacy of such manipulative actions: 'We suggest that action . . . is manipulative either where it is a conscious attempt, covertly, to influence events through means or ends which are not made explicit; or where it is illegitimate, whether or overt or not.'

6 *Control of resources*. Control of the *distribution of resources* may be an important source of power in educational institutions, particularly in self-managing schools and colleges. Decisions about the allocation of resources are likely to be among the most significant aspects of the policy process in such organizations. Resources include revenue and capital finance but also human and material resources such as staff and equipment. Control of these resources may give power over those people who wish to acquire them. There is often competition between interest groups for additional resources and success or failure in acquiring extra finance, staff and other resources is an indicator of the relative power of individuals and groups:

> Resource management is . . . a micropolitical process, providing an arena within which participants compete for the resources which will enable them to develop programmes of activity which embody their values, further their interests and help to provide legitimation for the activities in which they are engaged. (Simkins 1998, p. 110)

While these six forms of power might be regarded as the most significant, Bolman and Deal (1991), Handy (1993) and Morgan (1997) identify several other sources, including:

- physical power;
- developing alliances and networks;
- access to and control of agendas;
- control of meanings and symbols;
- control of boundaries;
- gender and the management of gender relations.

Consideration of all these sources of power leads to the conclusion that heads and principals possess substantial resources of authority and influence. They have the capacity to determine many institutional decisions and to affect the behaviour of their colleagues. However, they do not have absolute power. Other leaders and staff also have power, arising principally from their personal qualities and expertise. Lay governors may also be powerful, particularly if they chair the governing board or one of its important committees. These other sources of power may act as a counterbalance to the head's positional authority and control of rewards.

Political strategies in education

Educational leaders may adopt one or more political strategies in order to maintain or extend their control or to ensure a favoured outcome to a decision process. Using their significant resources of power, they are often able to ensure support for, or compliance with, their preferred position. Hoyle (1986, pp. 140–6) outlines some of the more significant strategies:

1 *Dividing and ruling*. This may involve heads arranging separate deals with individuals or departments, for example in respect of resource allocation.
2 *Co-optation*. This entails the involvement of those who support the leader or whose potential opposition has to be diverted. It may be used simply to involve a certain individual in the decision process or may be an attempt to manipulate the outcome.
3. *Displacement*. This occurs where the apparent issue is used to cloak the real purpose of the participant. A good example is where personal interests, such as status, are presented as 'professional'. This might occur where heads of department argue for more time for their subject.
4 *Controlling information*. Information is an important source of power. Heads and principals are the main recipients of external information and may use this to influence decisions. Curriculum specialists may also receive information related to their specific expertise.
5 *Controlling meetings*. Leaders may be able to control the outcomes of meetings by using one or more of the following devices:

   (a) 'rigging' agendas;
   (b) 'losing' recommendations;
   (c) 'nobbling' members of the group;
   (d) 'invoking' outside bodies;
   (e) 'massaging' minutes.

Political models: goals, structure, environment and leadership

Goals

Political models differ from both the formal and collegial approaches in that they focus primarily on the *goals* of sub-units, or looser groups of individuals, rather than the objectives of the institution itself. Ball (1987, p. 11) claims that the focus on organizational goals in much of the literature is a 'major distortion' and he prefers to emphasize the goal diversity of organizations.

These models assume that groups advance their interests in the form of goals that are pursued vigorously within the institution. Mangham (1979, p. 16) claims that 'organisations may be said to consist of many groups and individuals, multiple coalitions and alliances and each acting so as to achieve its own set of goals and objectives'. The collegial assumption that there is agreement over the goals of the organization is challenged by political theorists who argue that there is no such consensus: 'An assumption of consensus . . . has extremely limited validity in almost all types of organizations' (Ball, 1987, p. 11).

Schools and colleges have multiple goals reflecting the various interest groups. These groups endeavour to promote their own objectives as the official purposes of the institution. Inevitably, the goals of the various groups sometimes conflict with one another because a focus on one objective may be at the expense of another: 'Goals may be inherently in conflict and. . . these conflicts will become manifest when the goals are given a specific form in terms of pedagogy or curriculum' (Hoyle, 1986, p. 58).

Brown, Boyle and Boyle (2000, pp. 253–4) point to the risk of apparently collegial frameworks becoming political. Their research with secondary school departments in England suggests that they develop a sub-culture which leads to the formulation of common aims and enables 'jointly held beliefs and values to flourish', but is separate from that of other departments and from the values of the senior management team, leading to an essentially micropolitical structure.

As a result of this inter-group conflict, goals tend to be ambiguous, unstable and contested. Bolman and Deal (1991, p. 189) stress that 'organisational goals arise not from fiat at the top, but from an ongoing process of negotiation and interaction among the key players in any system'. The capacity to secure institutional backing for group objectives depends crucially on the power of the interest group and the ability of its members to mobilize support from other sub-units and institutional leaders. There is a continuing process of negotiation and alliance building to muster sufficient support for the group's policy objectives. Goals are unstable because alliances break down and new factors are introduced into the bargaining process. The extant objectives may be usurped by purposes advanced by new coalitions of interests.

Ultimately, goals become 'organizational' according to the resources of power that can be mobilized in their support. The purposes of the most powerful groups emerge as organizational goals.

Organizational structure

Political models assume that *organizational structure* emerges from the process of bargaining and negotiation and may be subject to change as the interest groups jockey for position. Formal and collegial approaches present structure as a stable aspect of the organization while political theorists regard it as one of the uncertain and conflictual elements of the institution. The structure is developed not so much for organizational effectiveness, as formal theorists suggest, but rather to determine which interests are to be served by the organization:

Organizational structure[s] . . . are often best understood as products and reflections of a struggle for political control . . . organizational structure is frequently used as a political instrument. (Morgan, 1997, pp. 175–6)

So the groups agree on ways of dividing up power and resources, and those divisions are reflected in the design of the organisation. (Bolman and Deal, 1984, p. 141)

Schools and colleges provide many illustrations of structure being established or adapted following political activity. A management team drawn primarily from heads of department, for example, may be seen as a device to reinforce their baronial power.

Wilkinson (1987) shows how manipulation of the structure by a new head led to a redistribution of power within a secondary school. He abolished the posts of heads of humanities, science and modern languages and promoted teachers to head the relevant subjects within these former departments. He also demoted year heads by introducing heads of lower and middle school. These fundamental changes led to a diminution of formal power amongst staff hostile to the new leader. 'Almost overnight the headteacher had destroyed the most powerful coalition in the school. The newly promoted people would . . . owe their allegiance to him . . . some would say that these are "improper" . . . tactics' (Wilkinson, 1987, p. 54).

Hoyle (1986) argues that schools are particularly prone to political activity because of their 'loosely-coupled' structure (see Chapter 7). The partial autonomy of teachers and their authority of expertise, together with the sectional interests of different sub-units, leads to this structural looseness and the prevalence of 'micropolitics':

The loosely-coupled structure of the school invites micropolitical activity since, although the head has a high degree of authority and responsibility, the relative autonomy of teachers and the norms of the teaching profession serve to limit the pervasiveness and scope of this power . . . Thus heads frequently have recourse to micropolitical strategies in order to have their way. But teachers, too, are not without their micropolitical resources. (Hoyle, 1986, p. 171)

Secondary schools in many countries experience political activity because of a highly differentiated structure. In the Netherlands, for example, there are two parallel structures representing subject departments and student guidance units. Imants, Sleegers amd Witziers (2001, p. 290) argue that these are 'conflicting sub-structures', leading to tension, fragmentation and barriers between teachers of different subjects.

The external environment

Political models emphasize the significance of *external influences* on internal decision-making. The political process includes inputs from outside bodies and individuals which are often mediated by the internal participants. Sergiovanni (1984, p. 6) explains the nature of the interaction between educational institutions and external groups:

> The political perspective is concerned with the dynamic interplay of the organisation with forces in its external environment. Schools and universities, for example, are viewed as open rather than closed systems, as integral parts of a larger environment not as bounded entities isolated from their environment. They receive inputs, process them, and return outputs to the environment. Inputs are presumed to be diverse and output demands often conflicting. As a result there is constant interplay between school and environment.

In this respect political approaches are similar to the open systems theories considered in Chapter 3. The major difference concerns the ways in which external pressures are imported into school or college decision-making. In formal models it is assumed that outside influences are transmitted through heads or principals whose knowledge of the external environment reinforces their official authority. The leaders' interpretation of these pressures may then be a significant element in the decision-making process.

In political models it is thought that external factors may be introduced by interest groups as well as by heads and principals. School or college staff whose courses are vulnerable because of low enrolments may cite evidence from employers who value the threatened courses. These environmental pressures mingle with the internal factors and add to the complexity and ambiguity of decision-making. Baldridge et al. (1978, p. 36) stress the significance of outside interests: 'External interest groups exert a great deal of influence over the policy making process. And external pressures and formal control by outside agencies . . . are powerful shapers of internal governance processes.'

The various groups which have an interest in educational institutions tend to have rather different motivations for their involvement. Official bodies may be concerned about educational standards, or 'value for money', and may exert their authority through the head or principal. Unofficial groups usually pursue sectional interests. Employers may want the school to instil particular skills while parents understandably focus on the progress of their own children. These pressures may be transmitted through the staff most involved with their interests, rather than via the leader. Lindle (1999), referring to the American context, points to the importance of managing the competing demands of diverse community groups:

The school setting is more political due to the increasing and competing demands placed on schooling . . . No one said that public schooling was easy, but its public mission and visibility in the community make it an easy political target. The intimate relationship between schools and communities creates micropolitics. While the context of school is indelibly situated in a larger community, all communities are inherently political. (Lindle, 1999, p. 173)

The management of the external environment is a significant issue for leaders and participants in political organizations. Control of the 'boundary' between schools and their environments is an important source of influence in the debate about policies and resources. Knowledge about the opinions and predilections of clients and interest groups confers power: 'By monitoring and controlling boundary transactions people are able to build up considerable power . . . Most people in leadership positions at all levels of an organization can engage in this kind of boundary management in a way that contributes to their power' (Morgan, 1997, p. 181).

Hoyle (1999, p. 217) adds that 'the nature of micropolitics has changed with the increasing permeability of the school boundary', an explicit recognition that the greater the decentralization of power to self-managing schools, the greater the requirement for effective boundary management within what is essentially a political framework. Governing boards have a political role in representing community interests and harmonizing them with the aims and culture of the school.

Leadership

There are two central facets of *leadership* within political arenas. In the first place the head or principal is a key participant in the process of bargaining and negotiation. Leaders have their own values, interests and policy objectives which they seek to advance as appropriate at meetings of committees and in informal settings. Heads have substantial reserves of power which they may deploy in support of their personal and institutional goals. Leaders also have a significant impact on the nature of the internal decision-making process and can exercise a controlling influence on the proceedings of committees and other decision-making groups. At a new secondary school studied by Wilkinson (1987, pp. 50–1), the head adopted several political strategies to control the apparently participative decision process:

- determining the agenda;
- controlling the contents of discussion documents;
- promoting teachers who shared his values.

West (1999) criticizes the political behaviour of British heads, arguing that they often seem to promote division rather than emphasizing the school as a whole unit. Inappropriate actions include:

- setting group against group, for example in reviewing public examination results;
- generating win–lose competition, for example in bidding for resources;
- isolating groups from the rest of the school, for example in the work of task groups.

> Even at this basic level of micropolitical understanding, all too often school leaders display a niaivety that is likely to lead to frustration and discontent for many of their staff. Deliberately seeking to increase understandings of how the formal and the informal interact and, above all, reducing the 'area of struggle' between groups by creating a commitment to further the school's interests, rather than their own, are priorities for school leaders. (West, 1999, p. 195)

The second facet of leadership concerns heads' responsibility to sustain the viability of the organization and to develop the framework within which policies can be tested and, ultimately, receive the endorsement of the various interest groups. To achieve acceptable outcomes, leaders become mediators who attempt to build coalitions in support of policies. There is a recurring pattern of discussion with representatives of power blocks to secure a measure of agreement. Bennett (1999), drawing on her experience as a principal of two schools in Tasmania, argues that communication is a critical skill for political leaders:

> It is critical to spend the time providing updates to stake-holders through newsletters, promotional material, public relations and marketing so that the various interest groups within the community understand the background behind a decision or an action. Inside the school, developing and maintaining channels of communication . . . assists the principal [in] working with interest groups . . . It is the responsibility of the principal to create opportunities for educational dialogue inviting people to seek clarification and to question how or why an action has occurred or a decision has been made. (Bennett, 1999, p. 199)

Portin (1998, p. 386), referring to research in Belgium, New Zealand, the United Kingdom and the United States, points to the need for principals to develop 'political acumen' as part of their pre-service and in-service preparation:

> Political acumen need not be viewed pejoratively as either manipulative or dominating forms of positional power. Instead, the skills needed here are a deep understanding of the micropolitical dimension of organizational governance, the means by which constituency interests and values are expressed, and an ability to take 'soundings' of the environment in order to inform site decision making. (Ibid., p. 386)

Bolman and Deal (1991) summarize several of the issues in this section, recommending four 'rules' for political leaders:

- Political leaders clarify what they want and what they can get. They are 'realists above all'.
- Political leaders assess the distribution of power and interests. They must 'map the political terrain'.
- Political leaders build linkages to other stakeholders. They 'build relationships and networks'.
- Political leaders persuade first, negotiate second, and use coercion only if necessary. Power needs to be used 'judiciously'.
(Bolman and Deal, 1991, pp. 436–8)

Transactional leadership

The leadership model most closely aligned with micropolitics is that of transactional leadership. This is often contrasted with the transformational leadership model examined in Chapter 4. Miller and Miller (2001, p. 182) explain these twin phenomena:

> Transactional leadership is leadership in which relationships with teachers are based upon an exchange for some valued resource. To the teacher, interaction between administrators and teachers is usually episodic, short-lived and limited to the exchange transaction. Transformational leadership is more potent and complex and occurs when one or more teachers engage with others in such a way that administrators and teachers raise one another to higher levels of commitment and dedication, motivation and morality. Through the transforming process, the motives of the leader and follower merge.

Goldring (1992) points to a shift from transactional to transformational leadership in Israeli schools and attributes this to systemic changes in the requirements imposed on schools and their leaders:

> Until recently, the principal of a typical Israeli neighbourhood school worked in a relatively static organisation. Today, principals in experimental project schools aimed at system-wide diversity are moving towards a dynamic definition of their role. In broad terms, it seems that principals are being required to move from being routine-managers to leader-managers, or from transactional to transformational leaders. (Ibid., p. 52)

Miller and Miller's (2001) definition refers to transactional leadership as an exchange process. Exchange is an established political strategy for members of organizations. Heads and principals possess authority arising from their positions as the formal leaders of their institutions. They also hold power in the form of key rewards such as promotion and references. However, the head requires the co-operation of staff to secure the effective management of the school. An exchange may secure benefits for both parties to the arrangement. The major limitation of such a process is that it does not engage staff beyond the immediate gains arising from the transaction. As Miller and Miller's definition implies, transactional leadership does not produce long-term commitment to the values and vision being promoted by school leaders.

The limitations of political models

Political models are primarily descriptive and analytical whereas most other theories tend to be normative. The focus on interests, conflict between groups and power provides a valid and persuasive interpretation of the decision-making process in schools and colleges. Teachers and managers often recognize the applicability of political models in their own schools and colleges. However, these theories do have five major limitations:

1 Political models are immersed so strongly in the language of power, conflict and manipulation that they neglect other standard aspects of organizations. There is little attempt to discuss the various processes of management or any real acknowledgement that most organizations operate for much of the time according to routine bureaucratic procedures. The focus is heavily on policy formulation while the implementation of policy receives little attention. Political perspectives probably understate the significance of organizational structure as a constraint on the nature of political activity. The outcomes of bargaining and negotiation are endorsed, or may falter, within the formal authority structure of the school or college. Bolman and Deal (1991, p. 238) say that 'the political perspective is so thoroughly focused on politics that it underestimates the significance of both rational and collaborative processes'. Similarly, Baldridge, who is widely recognized as a leading writer on the application of political models to education, acknowledges that modifications are required to accommodate certain aspects of the more formal approaches:

> Our original political model probably underestimated the impact of routine bureaucratic processes. Many decisions are made not in the heat of political controversy but because standard operating procedures dominate in most organizations . . . the model downplayed long-term patterns of decision processes and neglected the way institutional structure shaped and channelled political efforts. (Baldridge et al., 1978, pp. 42–3)

2 Political models stress the influence of interest groups on decision-making and give little attention to the institutional level. The assumption is that organizations are fragmented into groups which pursue their own inde-

pendent goals. These sub-units compete to establish the supremacy of their policy objectives and to secure their endorsement within the institution. This aspect of political models may be inappropriate for most English primary schools which do not have a departmental structure or any other apparatus which could become a focal point for political activity. The institutional level may be the centre of attention for staff in these schools, invalidating the political model's emphasis on interest group fragmentation.

3 In political models there is too much emphasis on conflict and a neglect of the possibility of professional collaboration leading to agreed outcomes. The assumption that staff are continually engaged in a calculated pursuit of their own interests underestimates the capacity of teachers to work in harmony with colleagues for the benefit of their pupils and students. The focus on power as the determinant of outcomes may not be wholly appropriate for a cerebral profession such as teaching. In many situations, staff may well be engaged in genuine debate about the best outcomes for the school rather than evaluating every issue in terms of personal and group advantage: 'The [political] frame is normatively cynical and pessimistic. It overstates the inevitability of conflict and understates the potential for effective collaboration' (Bolman and Deal, 1991, p. 238).

4 Political models are regarded primarily as descriptive or explanatory theories. Their advocates claim that these approaches are realistic portrayals of the decision-making process in schools and colleges. Unlike collegial models, these theories are not intended to be normative or idealistic. There is no suggestion that teachers *should* pursue their own self-interest, simply an assessment, based on observation, that their behaviour is consistent with a political perspective. Nevertheless, the less attractive aspects of political models may make them unacceptable to many educationists:

> The amorality that often characterises political perspectives raises questions of values. To what extent does the political perspective, even as it purports to be simply a description of reality, ratify and sanctify some of the least humane and most unsavoury aspects of human systems? (Bolman and Deal, 1984, p. 146)

Morgan (1997, p. 212) adds that the emphasis on the cynical and the selfish may lead to the notion that there must be winners and losers and that 'the effect is to reduce the scope for genuine openness and collaboration'.

5 Political models offer valid insights into the operation of schools and colleges but it is often difficult to discern what constitutes political behaviour and what may be typical bureaucratic or collegial activity. The interpretation of group processes as either 'collegial' or 'political' is particularly difficult. Campbell and Southworth's (1993, p. 77) research in

primary schools illustrates this point: 'It would be simplistic to say the heads in the collaborative schools controlled what happened there but they certainly exerted a great deal of influence and they sometimes used their power directly . . . the heads . . . revealed a micropolitical dimension to collegiality.'

Conclusion: are political models valid?

Hoyle (1986; 1999) distinguishes between theory-for-understanding, a tool for academics and students, and theory-for-action, a source of guidance for management practice. Political models are important in helping to develop understanding of how educational institutions operate. They provide rich descriptions and persuasive analysis of events and behaviour in schools and colleges. The explicit recognition of interests as prime motivators for action is valid. The acceptance that competing interests may lead to conflict, and that differential power ultimately determines the outcome, is a persuasive element in the analysis of educational institutions: 'The model of interests, conflict, and power . . . provides a practical and systematic means of understanding the relationship between politics and organization and emphasizes the key role of power in determining political outcomes' (Morgan, 1997, p. 209).

Bolman and Deal (1991, p. 237) argue that political models capture several of the essential features of institutions: 'The political frame presents the only realistic portrayal of organizations . . . The political frame says that power and politics are central to organizations and cannot be swept under the rug. This perspective represents an important antidote to the antiseptic rationality sometimes present in structural analysis.'

For many teachers and school leaders, political models fit their experience of day-to-day reality in schools and provide a guide to 'theory-for action'. Bennett (1999), a Tasmanian school principal, shows how politics have influenced practice in her schools:

> Micropolitics exist in schools. It is important to consider how they are manifested and we need to move beyond saying that it is just personality clashes or differences which leads to divisions. We need to understand that staff have different views of the world, that we can see politics in the various groups of school and, if we can recognize actors and ascertain what they are struggling over, this will influence how principals as leaders communicate, collaborate and decide courses of action. (Ibid., p. 200)

Lindle (1999), a school administrator in the United States, makes a similar point about politics-in action, arguing that it is a pervasive feature in schools:

Education is a more overtly contested terrain for communities and governments, teachers, parents and administrators. Schools have become more overtly political arenas in this context. The study of micropolitics is absolutely a question of survival for school leaders and other educators . . . Not only is the study of micropolitics inevitable, advisable and unavoidable, for most school leaders, it is an inherent occupational requirement. (Ibid., p. 176)

In both respects, understanding and action, political models have much to offer in developing an appreciation of the nature of management in schools and colleges. Political theorists rightly draw attention to the significance of groups as a potent influence on policy formulation. The emphasis on conflict may be overdrawn but it is valuable as a counterbalance to the idealistic harmony bias of collegial models. The view that disagreement is likely to be resolved ultimately by the relative power of participants is also a persuasive contribution to understanding and practice in educational institutions. Political models provide valuable insights into the operation of schools and colleges but, as Baldridge et al. (1978, pp. 43–4) demonstrate, they need to be considered alongside the formal and collegial models:

This political model is not a substitute for the bureaucratic or collegial models of academic decision making. In a very real sense each of those addresses a separate set of problems and they often provide complementary interpretations. The political model also has many strengths, however, and we offer it as a strong contender for interpreting academic governance.

References

Bacharach, S.B. and Lawler, E.J. (1980) *Power and Politics in Organisations*, San Francisco, CA: Jossey-Bass.

Baldridge, J.V. (1971) *Power and Conflict in the University*, New York: John Wiley.

Baldridge, J.V., Curtis, D.V., Ecker, G. and Riley, G.L. (1978) *Policy Making and Effective Leadership*, San Francisco, CA: Jossey-Bass.

Ball, S. (1987) *The Micropolitics of the School: Towards a Theory of School Organization*, London: Methuen.

Becher, T. and Kogan, M. (1992) *Process and Structure in Higher Education*, 2nd edn, London: Routledge.

Bennett, J. (1999) 'Micropolitics in the Tasmanian context of school reform', *School Leadership and Management*, 19 (2): 197–200.

Bolman, L.G. and Deal, T.E. (1984) *Modern Approaches to Understanding and Managing Organisations*, San Francisco, CA: Jossey-Bass.

Bolman, L. and Deal, T. (1991) *Reframing Organisations: Artistry, Choice and Leadership*, San Francisco, CA: Jossey-Bass.

Brown, M., Boyle, B. and Boyle, T. (2000) 'The shared management role of the head of department in English secondary schools', *Research in Education*, 63, 33–47.

Campbell, P. and Southworth, G. (1993) 'Rethinking collegiality: teachers' views', in N. Bennett, M. Crawford and C. Riches (eds.), *Managing Change in Education:*

Individual and Organizational Perspectives, London: Paul Chapman Publishing.

Goldring, E.B. (1992) 'System-wide diversity in Israel', *Journal of Educational Administration*, 30 (3): 49–62.

Handy, C. (1993) *Understanding Organizations*, London: Penguin.

Hoyle, E. (1982) 'Micropolitics of educational organisations', *Educational Management and Administration*, 10 (2): 87–98.

Hoyle, E. (1986) *The Politics of School Management*, Sevenoaks: Hodder and Stoughton.

Hoyle, E. (1999) 'The two faces of micropolitics', *School Leadership and Management*, 19 (2): 213–22.

Imants, J., Sleegers, P. and Witziers, B. (2001) 'The tension between organisational sub-structures in secondary schools and educational reform', *School leadership and Management*, 21 (3): 289–308.

Lindle, J. (1999) 'What can the study of micropolitics contribute to the practice of leadership in reforming schools', *School Leadership and Management*, 19 (2): 171–8.

Mangham, I. (1979) *The Politics of Organisational Change*, Associated Business Press, Ludgate House, Fleet Street, London.

Mawhinney, H. (1999) 'Reappraisal: the problems and prospects of studying the micropolitics of leadership in reforming schools', *School Leadership and Management*, 19 (2): 159–70.

Miller, T.W. and Miller, J.M. (2001) 'Educational leadership in the new millennium: a vision for 2020', *International Journal of Leadership in Education*, 4 (2): 181–9.

Milliken, J. (2001) ' "Surfacing" the micropolitics as a potential management change frame in higher education', *Journal of Higher Education Policy and Management*, 23 (1): 75–84.

Morgan, G. (1997) *Images of Organization*, Thousand Oaks, CA: Sage Publications.

Portin, B. (1998) 'From change and challenge to new directions for school leadership', *International Journal for Educational Research*, 29, 381–91.

Sergiovanni, T. J. (1984) 'Cultural and competing perspectives in administrative theory and practice', in T.J. Sergiovanni and J.E. Corbally, *Leadership and Organisational Culture*, Chicago, IL: University of Illinois Press.

Simkins, T. (1998) 'Autonomy, constraint and the strategic management of resources', in D. Middlewood and J. Lumby (eds), *Strategic Management in Schools and Colleges*, London: Paul Chapman Publishing.

Wallace, M. and Hall, V. (1994) *Inside the SMT: Teamwork in Secondary School Management*, London: Paul Chapman Publishing.

West, M. (1999) 'Micropolitics, leadership and all that . . . the need to increase the micropolitical awareness and skills of school leaders', *School Leadership and Management*, 19 (2): 189–96.

Wilkinson, J. (1987) *The Micropolitical Dimensions of Leadership in Secondary Schools*, Sheffield: Sheffield City Polytechnic.

6
Subjective Models

Central features of subjective models

Subjective models incorporate those approaches which focus on individuals within organizations rather than the total institution or its subunits. The individual is placed at the centre of the organization. These perspectives suggest that each person has a subjective and selective perception of the organization. Events and situations have different meanings for the various participants in institutions. Organizations are portrayed as complex units which reflect the numerous meanings and perceptions of all the people within them. Organizations are social constructions in the sense that they emerge from the interaction of their participants. They are manifestations of the values and beliefs of individuals rather than the concrete realities presented in formal models. The definition suggested below captures the main element of these approaches:

> Subjective models assume that organizations are the creations of the people within them. Participants are thought to interpret situations in different ways and these individual perceptions are derived from their background and values. Organizations have different meanings for each of their members and exist only in the experience of those members.

Hermes (1999, p. 198) offers a similar definition in applying subjective models to higher education in Germany, using the term 'construction' to mean interpretation of events: 'Subjective theories presuppose that human beings are autonomous and reflective beings, actively constructing the world around them.'

Subjective models include phenomenological and interactive approaches. While these perspectives are not identical, they are sufficiently close to be treated together and, indeed, are used interchangeably in much of the literature (Innes-Brown, 1993). Hoyle (1986, p. 10) defines phenomenology and explains its link with interactionism:

> [These] perspectives share certain characteristics which constitute a radically different way of conceiving social reality . . . The phenomenological approach gives priority to people and their actions. The social world essentially consists of people

113

interacting with each other, negotiating patterns of relationships and constructing a view of the world.

Subjective models became prominent in educational management as a result of the work of Thomas Greenfield in the 1970s and 1980s. Greenfield was concerned about several aspects of systems theory which he regarded as the dominant model of educational organizations. He argues that systems theory is 'bad theory' and criticizes its focus on the institution as a concrete reality:

> Most theories of organisation grossly simplify the nature of the reality with which they deal. The drive to see the organisation as a single kind of entity with a life of its own apart from the perceptions and beliefs of those involved in it blinds us to its complexity and the variety of organisations people create around themselves. (Greenfield, 1973, p. 571)

Greenfield's criticism of conventional (largely bureaucratic) theory is even more trenchant in his 1986 article on 'the decline and fall of science in educational administration':

> We have a science of administration which can deal only with facts and which does so by eliminating from its consideration all human passion, weakness, conviction, hope, will, pity, frailty, altruism, courage, vice and virtue . . . in its own impotence [it] is inward-looking, self-deluding, self-defeating, and unnecessarily boring. (Greenfield, 1986, p. 61)

Greenfield's work has had a significant impact on theory development in educational management, as Hodgkinson (1993, p. x) suggests: 'It is not possible to properly comprehend the contemporary discipline of educational administration without some familiarity and aquaintanceship with the thoughts of Thomas Barr Greenfield.' Greenfield is closely associated with the application of subjective theories to schools and colleges and much of the theory development has come from him, or from others stimulated or provoked by his work. As Evers and Lakomski (1991, p. 97) put it, 'no adequate understanding of organisations seems possible without some appeal to human subjectivity, to the interpretations people place on their own actions and those of others'.

Subjective models have the following major features:

1 They focus on the beliefs and perceptions of *individual* members of organizations rather than the institutional level or interest groups. While formal and collegial models stress the total institution, and political models emphasize sub-groups, the individual is at the heart of subjective or phenomenological theories. Subjective models 'focus on the individual and emphasize individual perspectives' (Hermes, 1999, p. 198).

Within schools and colleges, subjective theorists point to the different values and aspirations of individual teachers, support staff and pupils. They all experience the institution from different standpoints and interpret events and situations according to their own background and motivations. Ribbins et al. (1981, p. 170) argue that 'The school is not the same reality for all its teachers. Each teacher brings a perspective to the school, and to his place within it, which is to some extent unique. There are ... as many realities as there are teachers.'

The focus on individuals rather than the organization is a fundamental difference between subjective and formal models, and creates what Hodgkinson (1993, p. xii) regards as an unbridgeable divide. 'In the tension between individual and organization ... there is more than a mere dialectical conflict. There can also be a chasm, a Great Divide, an abyss. A fact can *never* entail a value, and an individual can *never* become a collective.' (Original emphases).

Strain (1996) takes a somewhat different view, pointing to the interdependence of individual and collective meanings:

> The social world, of which education is an institutional part, spans the ... individual and the ... collectivity. The relationship between the two is reflexive ... The individual, by virtue of his imagining faculty, power to create meanings, cannot act meaningfully in isolation from the symbolically ordered collectivity ... but neither individual nor collectivity can be conceived of as subordinated to or originated by the other. (Ibid., p. 51)

2 Subjective models are concerned with the *meanings* placed on events by people within organizations. The focus is on the individual interpretation of behaviour rather than the situations and actions themselves. According to Greenfield (1975, p. 83), 'Organisations are to be understood in terms of people's beliefs about their behaviour within them', rather than on the basis of external observations of that behaviour. It is assumed that individuals may have different interpretations of the same event, as Bolman and Deal (1991, p. 244) suggest:

> What is most important about an event is not what happened but what it means. Events and meanings are loosely coupled: the same events can have very different meanings for different people because of differences in the schema that they use to interpret their experience.

In schools there may be differences of interpretation between the head and other staff who often derive divergent meanings from the same event. Hoyle (1981, p. 45) draws attention to one familiar example of such discrepancies:

> When a head talks about his [*sic*] school on public occasions teachers often remark that they do not recognise the place, and, because this view of reality is different from that of the head's they may assume that he is deliberately misleading. But a phenomenological view would hold that we have here *competing* realities, the head and the teachers see the world differently with each perspective having its own legitimacy (original emphasis).

This case illustrates the point that the school or college may be conceptualized differently by the various individuals and groups in the organization. These participants construct a reality out of their interests and any commonality of perspective arises from the fortuitous fact that their interests are held in common (Hoyle, 1986).

In this respect, there are certain similarities between subjective theory and organizational culture. Culture is also an outcome of the meanings and values of the people who inhabit schools and colleges. 'Culture is a useful if intricate and elusive notion. In its broadest sense it is a way of constructing reality and different cultures are simply alternative constructions of reality' (Prosser 1999, p. xii). The main difference between these two concepts is that subjective models focus on individual meanings while culture assumes that these coalesce to produce a distinctive whole-school or sub-unit culture. We shall examine culture in more detail in Chapter 8.

3 The different meanings placed on situations by the various participants are products of their *values, background and experience*. So the interpretation of events depends on the beliefs held by each member of the organization. Holmes (1986, p. 80) argues that it is 'bizarre' to develop a theory of educational administration outside a framework of values:

> The lack of consensus about the purpose of elementary and secondary schools makes it more important rather than less to have a clear framework of goals and values. The modern idea that schools can function in a value-free atmosphere brings the whole educational profession, and particularly administrators, into disrepute.

Strain (1996, p. 59) argues that 'choice . . . is always a subjective affair' and identifies three sets of beliefs in examining the choice behaviour of individuals:

(a) beliefs about the world; how it works and should work;
(b) beliefs about the chooser's own situation; what is feasible and desirable in relation to a set of actions which seem to be available;
(c) beliefs about a range of desirable outcomes (Strain, 1996, p. 54).

116

Greenfield (1979, p. 103) asserts that formal theories make the mistake of treating the meanings of leaders as if they were the objective realities of the organization:

> Life in organisations is filled with contending ideologies... Too frequently in the past, organisation and administrative theory has ... taken sides in the ideological battles of social process and presented as 'theory' the views of a dominating set of values, the views of rulers, elites, and their administrators.

One possible outcome of the different meanings placed on events may be conflict between participants. In this respect, subjective models may take on some of the characteristics of political theories. Where meanings coincide, individuals may come together in groups and engage in political behaviour in pursuit of objectives. Greenfield (1986, p. 72) relates conflict to differences in values: 'Conflict is endemic in organizations. It arises when different individuals or groups hold opposing values or when they must choose between accepted but incompatible values. Administrators represent values, but they also impose them.' In subjective models, then, conflict is regarded as the product of competing values. However, conflict is only one of several possible outcomes and should not be regarded as a norm. Rather the assumption is that meanings are highly personal, often subtle, and subject to the values and experience of participants.

4 Subjective models treat *structure* as a product of human interaction rather than something which is fixed or predetermined. The organization charts which are characteristic of formal models are regarded as fictions in that they cannot predict the behaviour of individuals. Subjective theorists reject the view that people have to conform to the structure of organizations.

> Most managers appear to be of the opinion that structure in organisations is pre-existent, that all organisations have a predetermined structure into which people must fit. This is not so. Structure is simply a description of what people do and how they relate; organisation structure is a grossly simplified description of jobs and relationships... A structure cannot be imposed on an organisation, it can only derive from what people do. (Gray, 1982, p. 34)

Subjective approaches move the emphasis away from structure towards a consideration of behaviour and process. Individual behaviour is thought to reflect the personal qualities and aspirations of the participants rather than the formal roles they occupy. Greenfield (1980, p. 40) claims that the variable nature of human behaviour means that organizations are subject to change: 'There is no ultimate reality about organisations, only a state of constant flux. Organisations are at once both the products of action and its cause. We act out of past circumstances and drive towards those we intend for the future. Social realities are constantly created and re-shaped.'

Subjective theorists are particularly critical of those models which attribute 'human' characteristics to organizations or regard structure as something independent of its members. In this view, schools and colleges do not have an existence which is separate from the actions and behaviours of their staff, students and stakeholders. 'Organisations exist to serve human needs, rather than the reverse' (Bolman and Deal, 1991, p. 121).

This subjective perspective on the relative significance of structure and behaviour has implications for the management of organizations. It suggests that more attention should be given to the theory and practice of staff motivation, and to other aspects of human resource management, and that rather less significance should be attached to issues of organizational structure.

5 Subjective approaches emphasize the significance of individual purposes and deny the existence of organizational *goals*. Greenfield (1973, p. 553) asks, 'What is an organisation that it can have such a thing as a goal?' The view that organizations are simply the product of the interaction of their members leads naturally to the assumption that individuals, and not organizations, have objectives. The formal model's portrayal of organizations as powerful goal-seeking entities is treated with disdain:

> In subjective theory, because organisations have no corporeal existence apart from the experience members have of them, there can be no 'objectives' for an organisation, only objectives for individual members. Furthermore, the nature of organisations as associations of people means that they are at best means to an end; that is they serve purposes. The purposes, however, are individual purposes – whatever members require the organisation to do in order that something or other may be achieved. (Gray, 1982, p. 35)

Applying the subjective model – Rivendell School

The essence of subjective models is the view that the individual participant is at the heart of organizations and should not be regarded as simply a cog within the institution. The meanings placed on events by staff, governors and students are thought to be central to our understanding of schools and colleges. Analysis of educational institutions thus requires a subjective dimension if a complete picture is to emerge. However, there are very few empirical studies of schools or colleges which have adopted a subjective or phenomenological perspective. One significant exception is the classic study of pastoral care at Rivendell School (Best, Ribbins and Jarvis, 1979; Best et al., 1983; Ribbins et al., 1981). Although this is now more than 20 years old, it

118

remains a most valuable illustration of subjective theory in action.

In their two-year study of Rivendell, Best and his colleagues give explicit recognition to the value of subjective approaches while acknowledging the methodological difficulties they pose:

> We accept the force of the argument that to explain any social phenomenon it is necessary to establish the subjective meanings which relevant actors attach to the phenomenon, but it is difficult to see how one can establish *meanings* in any hard and fast way. Meanings are not directly observable in the world like physical objects are, and it would be folly indeed to imagine that imputing meanings to actors or situations was something the researcher could lightly undertake. (Best et al., 1983, p. 58, original emphasis)

The researchers adopted several approaches to ascertain the meanings placed on events by staff at Rivendell. There were interviews with 59 of the 82 staff, supported by observation of teachers in various situations. Any discrepancies between the accounts of different staff, or inconsistencies between teachers' comments and their behaviour, were taken up at subsequent interviews: 'In this way, we were able to reach a position in which we are fairly confident of the validity of the interpretations we finally made' (Best et al., 1983, pp. 61–2). The authors' interpretation of the stated views and behaviour of Rivendell's teachers depended on the context of the statement or action. The implication of the study is that staff may modify their opinions according to the occasion and the nature of the audience. This variation in the manifest positions of teachers makes it difficult to ascertain their real feelings about situations and events:

> What a teacher *says* has to be interpreted in the light of the *context* in which he says it . . . Although at Rivendell many senior staff spoke warmly and supportively of the school's pastoral care arrangements at meetings of feeder school parents, this was not necessarily the case at other times. In the context of interviews and informal discussions with researchers, some of these teachers showed themselves capable of a criticism of the school's pastoral arrangements to which their statements in more public situations gave no clue. (Ribbins et al., 1981, pp. 162–3, original emphasis)

Best and his colleagues were concerned to test the 'conventional wisdom' that teachers have the interests of the children at the heart of their approach to pastoral care. Their hypothesis was that there may be significant differences between the public statements and the reality of pastoral care in schools. The authors' approach to this apparent contradiction was to focus on the subjective interpretations of staff rather than the official version of pastoral care policy.

> In developing an analytical theory of the growth of institutional pastoral care, we have given great weight to the actors and their perceptions of the 'problem' to

which pastoral care is intended to provide the solution. Their perceptions will . . . be influenced by their own interests . . . The naive assumption that pastoral care systems deal only with the problems of the children pre-empts a consideration of the possibility that the creation of pastoral care systems and their posts of responsibility may have been a response to problems confronting teachers, headteachers, LEAs and educational administrators. (Best, Ribbins and Jarvis, 1979, pp. 36–8)

The public statements about pastoral care at Rivendell reflect the conventional wisdom of a child-centred approach. Staff have an obvious interest in maintaining and enhancing the reputation of their school and official pastoral care policy has to be interpreted in that light:

> Headteachers and senior staff have a vested interest in portraying their school as a 'caring' institution because their own public image, and therefore to some extent their self-image, depends in no small measure on the evaluation which the public at large make of the institution for which they are responsible. This is heightened when a school is in the position of Rivendell Comprehensive, battling constantly against what staff believed to be an unjustifiably poor reputation in the local community. (Best et al., 1983, p. 57)

Examples of the discontinuity between the school's official policy and pastoral care practice occurred during the research period at Rivendell. Ribbins et al. (1981, p. 166) record one significant incident which serves to highlight this contrast:

> We once interviewed a fairly senior member of staff who spent some time telling us how much he cared for children and how the 'interests' of his pupils came first with him. At this point a lower school boy knocked, and without waiting for permission, entered the room. He was immediately subjected to a diatribe of impressive proportions and sent from the room to 'wait to be dealt with later'. Once the boy had left, the teacher took up his account exactly where he had left it before the interruption, but to two researchers who were now a good deal more sceptical than they had been a few minutes before.

The numerous perceptions which emerged from the many interviews and observations at Rivendell were classified by the authors into five perspectives on pastoral care:

- child-centred;
- pupil-centred;
- discipline-centred;
- administrator-centred;
- subject-centred.

These perspectives represent clusters of the various interpretations of school policy suggested by the staff. The *child-centred* perspective focuses on the problems of the child as an individual. It centres on issues of personal happiness and adaptation and supports the conventional wisdom of the school as a caring environment for its pupils.

The *pupil-centred* perspective relates primarily to children in their academic roles as pupils. The pastoral provision in the school is evaluated in terms of its function as a facilitator of a pupil's academic performance. Here the concern for pupils' welfare is mainly geared to the promotion of their learning rather than the personal happiness of the children as individuals.

The *discipline-centred* perspective focuses on problems of teachers' control in the classroom and the difficulties created by the failure of other staff to give them support. Here the school's pastoral care provision is perceived as a vehicle for the control of pupils. For certain teachers the pastoral care structure of the school was assessed in terms of discipline and control. Pastoral staff were there to be 'used' by teachers to resolve their problems of control.

The *administrator-centred* perspective relates to the efficiency of the school as an administrative organization. At Rivendell the dual structure of years and houses was criticized by several staff on the grounds of organizational complexity. Teachers who adopt an administrator-centred approach thus evaluate pastoral structures in terms of their administrative efficiency rather than their effectiveness as welfare systems.

The *subject-centred* perspective relates primarily to the academic role of the teacher. Staff are concerned with their work as subject specialists and have little regard to their pastoral responsibilities. The learning situation is perceived as one where distinct subjects are taught by specialists.

The five perspectives identified by the authors are conceptually distinct but few teachers fit neatly into a single category. Nevertheless, the classification provides a useful framework of analysis for pastoral care while serving as a valuable illustration of the subjective model. The study confirms the view of subjective theorists that the school is not a monolithic organization. Each teacher has an individual interpretation of the school and these meanings may cluster into broad perspectives as was the case at Rivendell.

Subjective models and qualitative research

The theoretical dialectic between formal and subjective models is reflected in the often lively debate about positivism and interpretivism in educational research. Positivist research, like the formal models, adheres to a scientific approach. People are the objects of research and 'scientific' knowledge is obtained through the collection of verified facts that are essentially 'value free' and can lead to generalizations (Morrison, 2002). 'Explanation proceeds by way of scientific description' (Cohen, Manion and Morrison, 2000, p. 8).

In contrast, subjective models relate to a mode of research which is predominantly interpretive or qualitative. This approach to enquiry is based on the subjective experience of individuals. The main aim is to seek understanding of the ways in which individuals create, modify and interpret the social world which they inhabit. It is concerned with meanings more than facts and this is one of the major differences between qualitative and quantitative research. The link between qualitative research and subjective models is evident in Cohen, Manion and Morrison's (2000) definition:

> [Qualitative research] stresses the importance of the subjective experience of individuals in the creation of the social world . . . The principal concern is with an understanding of the way in which he or she finds himself or herself. The approach now takes on a qualitative . . . aspect. (Ibid., p. 7)

The main features of interpretive, or qualitative, research echo those of the subjective models:

1 They focus on the perceptions of *individuals* rather than the whole organization. The subject's individual perspective is central to qualitative research (Morrison, 2002, p. 19). Interviews, for example, are respondent centred and have few if any frameworks so that the participant's meanings can predominate.

2 Interpretive research is concerned with the *meanings*, or interpretations, placed on events by participants. The focus is on individual interpretation rather than the situations or actions themselves. 'All human life is experienced and constructed from a subjective perspective. For the interpretivist there cannot be an objective reality which exists irrespective of the meanings human beings bring to it' (Morrison, 2002, p. 19). Cohen, Manion and Morrison (2000, p. 22) add that subjective consciousness has primacy in qualitative research and that 'the central endeavour . . . is to understand the subjective world of human experience'.

3 Research findings are interpreted using 'grounded' *theory* in contrast to positivist researchers who generally 'devise general theories of human behaviour and [seek] to validate them through the use of increasingly complex research methodologies' (Cohen, Manion and Morrison, 2000, p. 23). The use of theory is very different for interpretive researchers: 'Theory is emergent and must arise from particular situations; it should be "grounded" on data generated by the research act. Theory should not precede research but follow it' (ibid., p. 23).

Just as researchers seek the individual perceptions of participants, leaders and managers have to be aware of the individual needs of their colleagues and stakeholders. A recognition of the different values and motivations of the people who work in, or relate to, schools and colleges, is essential if they are to be led and managed effectively.

Subjective models: goals, structure, environment and leadership

Goals

Subjective models differ from other approaches in that they stress the *goals* of individuals rather than the objectives of the institution or its subunits. Members of organizations are thought to have their own personal aims which they seek to achieve within the institution. The notion of organizational objectives, central to formal and collegial models, is rejected, as Coulson (1985, p. 44) suggests:

> It is not schools or organisations but people who pursue goals or aims . . . Teachers, especially perhaps headteachers, hold and pursue their own personal goals within schools, and many of these may be only tenuously linked to the teaching–learning process . . . These individual goals relate to the person's self-esteem, career advancement, and job satisfaction.

As Coulson suggests, individual goals may be related only tangentially to the organization. Often they are not concerned with wider institutional issues but reflect the personal wishes of the staff as individuals. Greenfield (1973, p. 568) argues that, 'Many people do not hold goals . . . in the sense of *ends* that the organisation is to accomplish, but merely hold a set of beliefs about what it is *right* to do in an organisation'. (Original emphases)

The denial of the concept of organizational goals creates difficulties because teachers are usually aware of the purposes and aims of schools and colleges. Many staff acknowledge the existence of school-wide goals such as teaching all children to read or achieving a good record in public examinations. At a common-sense level these are regarded as organizational objectives.

Greenfield (1973, p. 557) suggests that goals which appear to be those of the organization are really the objectives of powerful individuals within the institution: 'The goals of the organisation are the current preoccupations and intentions of the dominant organisational coalition.' In schools it is assumed that headteachers may possess sufficient power to promote their own purposes as the objectives of the institution. Organizational goals are a chimera; they are simply the personal aims of the most powerful individuals. In this respect, subjective models are similar to political theories.

Two of the nine English primary schools researched by Bennett et al. (2000) illustrate the view that school aims are really those of the headteacher:

> The head [of Padingwick] was very much a visionary . . . the head had a clear view of what needed to be done to improve the school and how this created particular priorities at particular times. He spearheaded a series of improvement initiatives. (Ibid., pp. 341 and 343)

123

The head [of Elms] was described as a strong leader, who led from the front but was sympathetic to others . . . there was a clear sense of direction – to improve standards further and provide a lively and supportive learning environment for children. The head was a key figure in this: she was seen as 'knowing what she wants for the school'. (Ibid., p. 342)

These examples support the subjective view that organizational goals are really the personal aims of influential people within schools and colleges. The subjective model's emphasis on individual goals is a valuable counter to the formal assumption about 'organizational' goals.

Organizational structure

Subjective models regard *organizational structure* as an outcome of the interaction of participants rather than a fixed entity which is independent of the people within the institution. Structure is a product of the behaviour of individuals and serves to explain the relationships between members of organizations. 'An organisation structure should be seen as something constructed and sustained through human interaction . . . Structure is a description of behaviour rather than a constraint upon it; structure describes what people do and how they relate' (Cuthbert, 1984, p. 60). Formal and collegial models tend to regard structure as a fixed and stable aspect of organizations while subjective theories emphasize the different meanings placed on structure by the individuals within the institution. The management team might be portrayed as a participative forum by the headteacher but be regarded by other staff as a vehicle for the one-way dissemination of information

Teachers interpret relationships in schools and colleges in different ways and, in doing so, they influence the structures within their institutions. However, there are variations in the amount of power which individuals can wield in seeking to modify structure. In education, heads and principals are often able to impose their interpretations of structure on the institutions they lead. They can introduce a faculty structure to promote inter-departmental co-operation, for example, but the effectiveness of such a change depends crucially on the attitudes of the staff concerned. 'Organisations will change as rapidly (or as slowly) as the ideas of their members' (Crowther, 1990, p. 14).

Lumby's (2001) research with English further education colleges demonstrates the complex relationship between organizational structure and the attitudes of managers and staff. She notes that, in the period following major reform in the early 1990s, most colleges had restructured but the motivation for change owed more to managers' desire for control than to any other factor:

The restructuring process followed the appointment of a new principal or a merger, and did not seem to be in response to particular factors but, rather, the principal's vehicle for making a new start, placing people in new roles where they might have a vested interest in supporting the new order. Restructuring can therefore be seen as both a process for response to the external environment and an internal political process of reshaping power. (Lumby, 2001, p. 89)

Structural change alone may be ineffective if it lacks the support of the people within the organization, as Greenfield, (1973, p. 565) demonstrates:

Shifting the external trappings of organisation, which we may call organisation structure if we wish, turns out to be easier than altering the deeper meanings and purposes which people express through organisation . . . we are forced to see problems of organisational structure as inherent not in 'structure' itself but in the human meanings and purposes which support that structure. Thus it appears that we cannot solve organisational problems by either abolishing or improving structure alone; we must also look at their human foundations.

While accepting the strictures of Greenfield about the limitations of structural change, there are obvious difficulties in understanding and responding to numerous personal interpretations of situations in organizations. The elusive and variable nature of human meanings suggests that organizational change may be a slow and uncertain process because it depends primarily on an understanding of individual wishes and beliefs.

Subjective theorists may be more interested in processes and relationships than in structure. While structure relates to the institutional level, subjective models focus on individuals and their interpretations of events and situations. The emphasis is on small-scale issues of concern to people rather than the macro-level of organizational structure: 'The phenomenologist is less concerned with structures than with processes involved at the microcosmic level as groups construct new realities within the framework of relatively enduring institutions' (Hoyle, 1986, p. 14).

The external environment

In subjective models little attention is paid to relationships between organizations and their *external environments*. This may be because organizations are not portrayed as viable entities. The focus is on the meanings placed on events by people within the organization rather than interaction between the institution and groups or individuals external to it. The notion of outside bodies exerting influence on the school or college makes little sense when subjective models claim that organizations have no existence independent of the individuals within them.

Where subjective models deal with the environment at all, the emphasis is on links between individuals within and outside the organization rather than external pressures on the total institution. The assumption that human behaviour stems from a personal interpretation of events raises the issue of the source of these meanings. Subjective theorists argue that they emanate from the external environment:

> The kinds of organisation we live in derive not from their structure but from attitudes and experiences we bring to organisations from the wider society in which we live. (Greenfield, 1973, p. 558)

In education, the interpretations of individuals may originate from several sources. For teachers a major influence is the socialization that results from their induction into the profession. The process of socialization may be reinforced through interaction with significant individuals who emanate from the same professional background. These may include education officers, inspectors and university lecturers. These professional contacts may be less important for self-managing schools but their historical influence has tended to produce shared meanings and values.

Teachers are also subject to personal influences such as their family, friends and members of clubs and societies external to the school. These sources may lead to a diversity of meanings. Greenfield (1973, p. 559) prefers to emphasize differences in interpretation rather than shared meanings:

> This notion of organisations as dependent upon meanings and purposes which individuals bring to organisations from the wider society does not require that all individuals share the same meanings and purposes. On the contrary, the views I am outlining here should make us seek to discover the varying meanings and objectives that individuals bring to the organisations of which they are a part.

Formal models stress the accountability of organizations, and senior staff within them, to certain groups and individuals in the external environment. Subjective theories give little attention to this issue but the focus is implicitly on the answerability of individual teachers rather than the accountability of the institution itself (Bush, 1994). Accountability may be primarily to the individual's own beliefs and values rather than to organizational leaders. While the focus on individual accountability is legitimate, because it is people who act, the subjective model fails to deal with the expectations of external groups and individuals who often require an explanation of institutional policies and practice.

Leadership

The concept of *leadership* fits rather uneasily within the framework of subjective models. Individuals place different meanings on events and this applies to all members, whatever their formal position in the organization. People who occupy leadership roles have their own values, beliefs and goals. All participants, including leaders, pursue their own interests. A significant difference, however, is that leaders of organizations may be in a position to impose their interpretations of events on other members of the institution. Management may be seen as a form of control, with heads and principals elevating their meanings to the status of school or college policy. These leaders may use their resources of power to require compliance with these interpretations even where other staff do not share those meanings.

Subjective theorists prefer to stress the personal qualities of individuals rather than their official positions in the organization. 'Situations require appropriate behaviours for their resolution and this can only be done by those best fitted to deal with them irrespective of their formal position or status in the organisation' (Gray, 1982, p. 41). This emphasis on the personal attributes of staff suggests that formal roles are an inadequate guide to behaviour. Rather, individuals bring their own values and meanings to their work and interpret their roles in different ways according to their beliefs and experience.

The subjective view is that leadership is a product of personal qualities and skills and not simply an automatic outcome of official authority. However, positional power also remains significant. Perhaps the most effective leaders are those who have positional power *and* the personal qualities to command the respect of colleagues, a combination of the formal and subjective perspectives.

Postmodern leadership

The notion of postmodern leadership aligns closely with the principles of subjective models. This is a relatively recent model of leadership which has no generally agreed definition. For example, Starratt's (2001, p. 34) discussion of 'a postmodern theory of democratic leadership' does not define the concept beyond suggesting that postmodernism might legitimize the practice of democratic leadership in schools.

Keough and Tobin (2001, p. 2) say that 'current postmodern culture celebrates the multiplicity of subjective truths as defined by experience and revels in the loss of absolute authority'. They identify several key features of postmodernism:

- Language does not reflect reality.
- Reality does not exist; there are multiple realities.
- Any situation is open to multiple interpretations.
- Situations must be understood at local level with particular attention to diversity (ibid., pp. 11–13).

Similarly, Sackney and Mitchell (2001) refer to 'widely divergent meanings' (ibid., p. 6) and to 'alternative truth claims' (ibid., p. 9). They add that power is located throughout the organisation and 'enacted by all members' (ibid., p. 11), leading to empowerment.

The postmodern model offers few clues to how leaders are expected to operate. This is also a weakness of the parallel Greenfield (1973) model. The most useful point to emerge from such analyses is that leaders should respect, and give attention to, the diverse and individual perspectives of stakeholders. They should also avoid reliance on the hierarchy because this concept has little meaning in such a fluid organization. Starratt (2001) aligns postmodernity with democracy and advocates a 'more consultative, participatory, inclusionary stance' (ibid., p. 348), an approach which is consistent with collegiality (see Chapter 4).

Sackney and Mitchell (2001, pp. 13–14) stress the centrality of individual interpretation of events while also criticizing transformational leadership as potentially manipulative: 'Leaders must pay attention to the cultural and symbolic structure of meaning construed by individuals and groups . . . postmodern theories of leadership take the focus off vision and place it squarely on voice.' Instead of a compelling vision articulated by leaders, there are multiple visions and diverse cultural meanings.

The limitations of subjective models

Subjective models are prescriptive approaches in that they reflect beliefs about the nature of organizations rather than presenting a clear framework for analysis. Their protagonists make several cogent points about educational institutions but this alternative perspective does not represent a comprehensive approach to the management of schools and colleges. Subjective models can be regarded as 'anti-theories' in that they emerged as a reaction to the perceived limitations of the formal models. Greenfield is zealous in his advocacy of subjective approaches and his rejection of many of the central assumptions of conventional organizational theory.

Although subjective models introduce several important concepts into the theory of educational management, they have four significant weaknesses which serve to limit their validity:

1 Subjective models are *strongly normative* in that they reflect the attitudes and beliefs of their supporters. Greenfield, in particular, has faced a barrage of criticism, much of it fuelled by emotion rather than reason, for his advocacy of these theories. As long ago as 1980, Willower claimed that subjective models are 'ideological':

> [Phenomenological] perspectives feature major ideological components and their partisans tend to be true believers when promulgating their positions rather than offering them for critical examination and test . . . The message is being preached by recent converts who . . . now embrace it wholeheartedly and with the dedication of the convert. (Willower, 1980, p. 7)

This comment serves to illustrate the intensity of feelings engendered by Greenfield's challenge to conventional theory. Nevertheless, there is substance in Willower's criticism. Subjective models comprise a series of principles, which have attracted the committed support of a few adherents, rather than a coherent body of theory: 'Greenfield sets out to destroy the central principles of conventional theory but consistently rejects the idea of proposing a precisely formulated alternative' (Hughes and Bush, 1991, p. 241).

2 Subjective models seem to assume the existence of an *organization* within which individual behaviour and interpretation occur but there is no clear indication of the nature of the organization. It is acknowledged that teachers work within a school or college, but these bodies are not recognized as viable organizations. Educational institutions are thought to have no structure beyond that created by their members. The notion of school and college objectives is dismissed because only people can have goals. So organizations are nothing more than a product of the meanings of their participants. In emphasizing the interpretations of individuals, subjective theorists neglect the institutions within which individuals behave, interact and derive meanings.

3 Subjective theorists imply that *meanings* are so individual that there may be as many interpretations as people. In practice, though, these meanings tend to cluster into patterns which do enable participants and observers to make valid generalizations about organizations. The notion of totally independent perceptions is suspect because individual meanings depend on participants' background and experience. Teachers, for example, emanate from a common professional background which often results in shared meanings and purposes. Ryan (1988, pp. 69–70) criticizes Greenfield's neglect of the 'collective': 'By focusing exclusively on the "individual" as a theoretical . . . entity, he precludes analyses of collective enterprises. Social phenomena cannot be reduced solely to "the individual".'

Subjective models also fail to explain the many similarities between schools. If individual perceptions provide the only valid definitions of organizations, why do educational institutions have so many common features? A teacher from one school would find some unique qualities in other schools but would also come across many familiar characteristics. This suggests that there is an entity called a 'school' which may evoke similar impressions amongst participants and observers.

4 A major criticism of subjective models is that they provide few guidelines for managerial action. Leaders are left with little more substantial than the need to acknowledge the individual meanings placed on events by members of organizations. Formal models stress the authority of heads to make decisions while pointing to the need to acknowledge the place of official groups such as management teams and governing bodies. Collegial models emphasize the desirability of reaching agreement with colleagues and providing opportunities for participation in decision-making. Political models accentuate the significance of building coalitions among interest groups in order to ensure support for policy proposals. Subjective models offer no such formula for the development of leadership strategies but the focus on the individual may provide some guidance. The leader may seek to influence individual behaviour through the application of motivation theory in order to produce a better 'fit' between the participant's personal wishes and the leader's preferences. This stance may help leaders but it is much less secure than the precepts of the formal model. As Greenfield himself acknowledges: 'This conception of organisations does not make them easy to control or to change' (Greenfield, 1980, p. 27).

Conclusion: the importance of the individual

The subjective model has introduced some important considerations into the debate on the nature of schools and colleges. The emphasis on the primacy of individual meanings is a valuable aid to our understanding of educational institutions. A recognition of the different values and motivations of the people who work in organizations is an essential element if they are to be managed successfully. Certainly teachers are not simply automatons carrying out routine activities with mechanical precision. Rather, they deploy their individual skills and talents for the benefit of pupils and students.

The subjective model is also valuable in providing conceptual underpinning for interpretive research methodology. The focus on the individual perceptions of actors is at the heart of qualitative research. Similarly, subjective models have close links with the emerging, but still weakly defined, notion of postmodern leadership. Leaders need to attend to the multiple voices in their organizations and to develop a 'power to' not a 'power over' model of leadership. However, as Sackney and Mitchell (2001, p. 19) note, 'we do not see how postmodern leadership . . . can be undertaken without the active engagement of the school principal'. In other words, the subjective approach works only if leaders wish it to work, a fragile basis for any approach to educational leadership.

Subjective models provide a significant new slant on organizations but the perspective is *partial*. The stress on individual interpretation of events is valid but ultimately it leads to a blind alley. If there are as many meanings as teachers, as Greenfield claims, our capacity to understand educational institutions is likely to be fully stretched. If individual meanings are themselves subject to variation according to the context, as Sackney and Mitchell (2001, p. 8) suggest, then the number of permutations is likely to be overwhelming. In practice, however, interpretations do cluster into patterns, if only because shared meanings emerge from the professional socialization undergone by teachers during training and induction. If there are common meanings, it is possible to derive some generalizations about behaviour.

The subjective perspective does offer some valuable insights which act as a corrective to the more rigid features of formal models. The focus on individual interpretations of events is a useful antidote to the uniformity of systems and structural theories. Similarly, the emphasis on individual aims, rather than organizational objectives, is an important contribution to our understanding of schools and colleges. Greenfield's work has broadened our understanding of educational institutions and exposed the weaknesses of the formal models. His admirers stress the significance of his contribution to organizational theory:

> Greenfield . . . has almost single-handedly led a generation of educational administration theorists to a new perspective on their work. It seems indisputable that a decade from now . . . Greenfield's work will be regarded as truly pioneering. (Crowther, 1990, p. 15)

> To understand Greenfield, whether one agrees with him or not, is to understand the nature of organizational reality better and to be better able to advance the state of the art. (Hodgkinson, 1993, p. xvi)

Despite these eulogies, it is evident that subjective models have supplemented, rather than supplanted, the formal theories Greenfield set out to attack. While his focus on individual meanings is widely applauded, the notion of schools and colleges as organizational entities has not been discarded. There is a wider appreciation of events and behaviour in education but many of the assumptions underpinning the formal model remain dominant in both theory and practice.

The search for a synthesis between formal models and Greenfield's analysis has scarcely begun. One way of understanding the relationship between formal and subjective models may be in terms of scale. Formal models are particularly helpful in understanding the total institution and its relationships with external bodies. In education, the interaction between schools and national or local government may be explained best by using bureaucratic and structural concepts. However, the subjective model may be especially valid in examining individual behaviour and relationships between individuals. Formal and subjective models thus provide complementary approaches to our understanding of organizations. The official structure of schools and colleges should be examined alongside consideration of the individual behaviour and perceptions of staff and students. While institutions cannot be understood fully without an assessment of the meanings of participants, these interpretations are of limited value unless the more formal and stable aspects of organizations are also examined.

References

Bennett, N., Crawford, M., Levačić, R., Glover, D. and Earley, P. (2000) 'The reality of school development planning in the effective primary school: technicist or guiding plan?', *School Leadership and Management*, 20 (3): 333–51.

Best, R., Ribbins, P. and Jarvis, C. (1979) 'Pastoral care: reflections on a research strategy', *British Educational Research Journal*, 5 (1): 35–43.

Best, R., Ribbins, P., Jarvis, C. and Oddy, D. (1983) *Education and Care*, London: Heinemann.

Bolman, L. and Deal, T. (1991) *Reframing Organisations: Artistry, Choice and Leadership*, San Francisco, CA: Jossey-Bass.

Bush, T. (1994) 'Accountability in education', in T. Bush and J. West-Burnham (eds), *The Principles of Educational Management*, Harlow: Longman.

Cohen, L., Manion, L. and Morrison, K. (2000) *Research Methods in Education*, 5th edn, London: RoutledgeFalmer.

Coulson, A. (1985) *The Managerial Behaviour of Primary School Heads*, Collected Original Resources in Education, Abingdon: Carfax.

Crowther, F. (1990) 'The pioneers in administration', *Practicing Administrator*, 12 (3): 14–15.

Cuthbert, R. (1984) *The Management Process, E323 Management in Post Compulsory Education, Block 3, Part 2*, Buckingham: Open University Press.

Evers, C. and Lakomski, G. (1991) 'Educational administration as science: a post-positivist proposal', in P. Ribbins, R. Glatter, T. Simkins and L. Watson (eds), *Developing Educational Leaders*, Harlow: Longman.

Gray H.L. (1982) 'A perspective on organisation theory', in H.L. Gray (ed.), *The Management of Educational Institutions*, Lewes: Falmer Press.

Greenfield, T.B. (1973) 'Organisations as social inventions: rethinking assumptions about change', *Journal of Applied Behavioural Science*, 9 (5): 551–74.

Greenfield, T.B. (1975) 'Theory about organisations: a new perspective and its implications for schools', in M. Hughes (ed.) *Administering Education: International Challenge*, London: Athlone Press.

Greenfield, T.B. (1979) 'Organisation theory is ideology', *Curriculum Enquiry*, 9 (2): 97–112.

Greenfield, T.B. (1980) 'The man who comes back through the door in the wall: discovering truth, discovering self, discovering organisations', *Educational Administration Quarterly*, 16 (3): 26–59.

Greenfield, T.B. (1986) 'The decline and fall of science in educational administration', *Interchange*, 17 (2): 57–80.

Hermes, L. (1999) 'Learner assessment through subjective theories and action research', *Assessment and Evaluation in Higher Education*, 24 (2): 197–204.

Hodgkinson, C. (1993) 'Foreword', in T.B. Greenfield and P. Ribbins (eds), *Greenfield on Educational Administration*, London: Routledge.

Holmes, M. (1986) Comment on 'The decline and fall of science in educational administration', *Interchange*, 17 (2): 80–90.

Hoyle, E. (1981) *The Process of Management, E323 Management of the School, Block 3, Part 1*, Buckingham: Open University Press.

Hoyle, E. (1986) *The Politics of School Management*, Sevenoaks: Hodder and Stoughton.

Hughes, M. and Bush, T. (1991) 'Theory and research as catalysts for change', in W. Walker, R. Farquhar and M. Hughes (eds), *Advancing Education. School Leadership in Action*, London: Falmer Press.

Innes-Brown, M. (1993) 'T. B. Greenfield and the interpretive alternative', *International Journal of Educational Management*, 7 (2): 30–40.

Keough, T. and Tobin, B. (2001) 'Postmodern leadership and the policy lexicon: from theory, proxy to practice', paper for the Pan-Canadian Education Research Agenda Symposium, Quebec, May.

Lumby, J. (2001) *Managing Further Education: Learning Enterprise*, London: Paul Chapman Publishing.

Morrison, M. (2002) 'What do we mean by educational research?', in M. Coleman and A. Briggs (eds), *Research Methods in Educational Leadership and Management*, London: Paul Chapman Publishing.

Prosser, J. (1999) 'Introduction', in J. Prosser (ed.), *School Culture*, London: Paul Chapman Publishing.

Ribbins, P.M., Jarvis, C.B., Best, R.E. and Oddy, D.M. (1981) 'Meanings and contexts: the problem of interpretation in the study of a school', *Research in Educational Management and Administration*, Birmingham: British Educational Management and Administration Society.

Ryan, J. (1988) 'Science in educational administration: a comment on the Holmes-Greenfield dialogue', *Interchange*, 19 (2): 68–70.

Sackney, L. and Mitchell, C. (2001) 'Postmodern expressions of educational leadership', in K. Leithwood and P. Hallinger (eds), *The Second International Handbook of Educational Leadership and Administration*, Dordrecht: Kluwer.

Starratt, R.J. (2001) 'Democratic leadership theory in late modernity: an oxymoron or ironic possibility?', *International Journal of Leadership in Education*, 4 (4): 333–52.

Strain, M. (1996) 'Rationality, autonomy and the social context of education management', *Educational Management and Administration*, 24, (1): 49–63.

Willower, D.J. (1980) 'Contemporary issues in theory in educational administration', *Educational Administration Quarterly*, 16 (3): 1–25.

7
Ambiguity Models

Central features of ambiguity models

Ambiguity models include all those approaches that stress uncertainty and unpredictability in organizations. The emphasis is on the instability and complexity of institutional life. These theories assume that organizational objectives are problematic and that institutions experience difficulty in ordering their priorities. Sub-units are portrayed as relatively autonomous groups which are connected only loosely with one another and with the institution itself. Decision-making occurs within formal and informal settings where participation is fluid. Individuals are part-time members of policy-making groups who move in and out of the picture according to the nature of the topic and the interests of the potential participants. Ambiguity is a prevalent feature of complex organizations such as schools and colleges and is likely to be particularly acute during periods of rapid change. The definition below incorporates the main elements of these approaches:

> Ambiguity models assume that turbulence and unpredictability are dominant features of organizations. There is no clarity over the objectives of institutions and their processes are not properly understood. Participation in policy making is fluid as members opt in or out of decision opportunities.

Ambiguity models are associated with a group of theorists, mostly from the United States, who developed their ideas in the 1970s. They were dissatisfied with the formal models which they regarded as inadequate for many organizations, particularly during phases of instability. March (1982, p. 36) points to the jumbled reality in certain kinds of organization:

> Theories of choice underestimate the confusion and complexity surrounding actual decision making. Many things are happening at once; technologies are changing and poorly understood; alliances, preferences, and perceptions are changing; problems, solutions, opportunities, ideas, people, and outcomes are mixed together in a way that makes their interpretation uncertain and their connections unclear.

Unlike certain other theories, the data supporting ambiguity models have been drawn largely from educational settings. Schools and colleges are characterized as having uncertain goals, unclear technology and fluid participation in decision-making. They are also subject to changing demands from their environments. These factors lead March and Olsen (1976, p. 12) to assert that 'ambiguity is a major feature of decision making in most public and educational organizations'.

Ambiguity models have the following major features:

1 There is a lack of clarity about the *goals* of the organization. Many institutions are thought to have inconsistent and opaque objectives. Formal models assume that organizations have clear purposes which guide the activities of their members. Ambiguity perspectives, by contrast, suggest that goals are so vague that they can be used to justify almost any behaviour. It may be argued that aims become clear only through the behaviour of members of the organization:

> It is difficult to impute a set of goals to the organization that satisfies the standard consistency requirements of theories of choice. The organization appears to operate on a variety of inconsistent and ill-defined preferences. It can be described better as a loose collection of changing ideas than as a coherent structure. It discovers preferences through action more often than it acts on the basis of preferences. (Cohen and March, 1986, p. 3)

Educational institutions are regarded as typical in having no clearly defined objectives. The discretion available to teachers enables them to identify their own educational purposes and to act in accordance with those aims for most of their professional activities. Because teachers work independently for much of their time, they may experience little difficulty in pursuing their own interests. As a result schools and colleges are thought to have no coherent pattern of aims:

> It may not be at all clear what the goals of the school are. Different members of the school may perceive different goals or attribute different priorities to the same goals, or even be unable to define goals which have any operational meaning. Thus while it is commonly expected that those who work in schools should have some overall purpose it is likely that the organizational context of many schools actually renders this either impossible or very difficult. Hence schools face an ambiguity of purpose, the result of which is that the achievement of goals which are educational in any sense cease to be central to the functioning of the school. (Bell, 1989, p. 134)

2 Ambiguity models assume that organizations have a *problematic technology* in that their processes are not properly understood. Institutions are unclear about how outcomes emerge from their activities. This is particularly true of client-serving organizations where the technology is necessarily tailored to the needs of the individual client. In education it is not

clear how pupils and students acquire knowledge and skills so the processes of teaching are clouded with doubt and uncertainty. Bell (1980, p. 188) claims that ambiguity infuses the central functions of schools:

> Teachers are often unsure about what it is they want their pupils to learn, about what it is the pupils have learned about and how, if at all, learning has actually taken place. The learning process is inadequately understood and therefore pupils may not always be learning effectively whilst the basic technology available in schools is often not understood because its purposes are only vaguely recognized . . . Since the related technology is so unclear the processes of teaching and learning are clouded in ambiguity.

3 Ambiguity theorists argue that organizations are characterized by *fragmentation* and *loose coupling*. Institutions are divided into groups which have internal coherence based on common values and goals. Links between the groups are more tenuous and unpredictable. Weick (1976, p. 3) uses the term 'loose coupling' to describe relationships between sub-units:

> By loose coupling, the author intends to convey the image that coupled events are responsive, *but* that each event also preserves its own identity and some evidence of its physical or logical separateness . . . their attachment may be circumscribed, infrequent, weak in its mutual effects, unimportant, and/or slow to respond . . . Loose coupling also carries connotations of impermanence, dissolvability, and tacitness all of which are potentially crucial properties of the 'glue' that holds organizations together. (original emphases)

Weick subsequently elaborated his model by identifying eight particularly significant examples of loose coupling that occur between:

(a) individuals;
(b) sub-units;
(c) organizations;
(d) hierarchical levels;
(e) organizations and environments;
(f) ideas;
(g) activities;
(h) intentions and actions (Orton and Weick, 1990, p. 208).

The concept of loose coupling was developed for, and first applied to, educational institutions. It is particularly appropriate for organizations whose members have a substantial degree of discretion. Client-serving bodies such as schools and colleges fit this metaphor much better than, say, car assembly plants where operations are regimented and predictable. The degree of integration required in education is markedly less than in many other settings, allowing fragmentation to develop and persist.

4 Within ambiguity models *organizational structure* is regarded as problematic. There is uncertainty over the relative power of the different parts of the institution. Committees and other formal bodies have rights and responsibilities which overlap with each other and with the authority assigned to individual managers. The effective power of each element within the structure varies with the issue and according to the level of participation of committee members. The more complex the structure of the organization, the greater the potential for ambiguity. In this view, the formal structures discussed in Chapter 3 may conceal more than they reveal about the pattern of relationships in organizations.

In education, the validity of the formal structure as a representation of the distribution of power depends on the size and complexity of the institution. Many primary schools have a simple authority structure centred on the head and there is little room for misunderstanding. In colleges and large secondary schools, there is often an elaborate pattern of interlocking committees and working parties. Noble and Pym's (1970, p. 436) classic study of decision-making in a college illustrates the ambiguity of structure in large organizations:

> The lower level officials or committees argue that they, of course, can only make recommendations. Departments must seek the approval of inter-departmental committees, these in turn can only submit reports and recommendations to the general management committee. It is there we are told that decisions must be made ... In the general management committee, however, though votes are taken and decisions formally reached, there was a widespread feeling, not infrequently expressed even by some of its senior members, of powerlessness, a feeling that decisions were really taken elsewhere ... as a committee they could only assent to decisions which had been put up to them from one of the lower tier committees or a sub-committee ... The common attribution of effective decision making to a higher or lower committee has led the authors to describe the decision-making structure in this organisation as an involuted hierarchy.

These structural ambiguities lead to uncertainties about the authority and responsibility of individual leaders and managers. Referring to English further education colleges, Gleeson and Shain (1999, p. 469) point to 'the ambiguous territory which middle managers occupy between lecturers and senior managers', a position which also affects middle level leaders in schools (Bush, 2002). One middle manager interviewed by Glesson and Shain (1999, p. 469) illustrates this point: 'The staff don't really know where we fit in and I don't think the senior management really knows either ... I don't know where we fit.' These uncertainties undoubtedly create tension for middle level leaders but also gives them a certain amount of scope to determine their own role. 'Ambiguity ... allows middle managers some room for manoeuvre' (Glesson and Shain, 1999, p. 470).

5 Ambiguity models tend to be particularly appropriate for *professional client-serving* organizations. In education, the pupils and students often demand inputs into the process of decision-making, especially where it has a direct influence on their educational experience. Teachers are expected to be responsive to the perceived needs of their pupils rather than operating under the direct supervision of hierarchical superordinates. The requirement that professionals make individual judgements, rather than acting in accordance with managerial prescriptions, leads to the view that the larger schools and colleges operate in a climate of ambiguity: 'I believe that large and complex, multipurpose, rapidly expanding or otherwise changing organizations are anarchic ... So are organizations with a high degree of professionalisation among their rank and file; service-producing organizations probably fit this picture better than goods-producing enterprises do' (Enderud, 1980, p. 236).

6 Ambiguity theorists emphasize that there is *fluid participation* in the management of organizations. Members move in and out of decision-making situations, as Cohen and March (1986, p. 3) suggest: 'The participants in the organization vary among themselves in the amount of time and effort they devote to the organization; individual participants vary from one time to another. As a result standard theories of power and choice seem to be inadequate.' Bell (1989, pp. 139–40) elaborates this concept and applies it to education:

> The school consists of groups of pupils and teachers all of whom make a wide range of demands on the organization. By their very nature schools gain and lose large numbers of pupils each year and ... staff may move or change their roles ... Membership of the school also becomes fluid in the sense that the extent to which individuals are willing and able to participate in its activities may change over time and according to the nature of the activity itself. In this way schools are peopled by participants who wander in and out. The notion of membership is thus ambiguous, and therefore it becomes extremely difficult to attribute responsibility to a particular member of the school for some areas of the school's activities.

Changes in the powers of governing bodies in schools in England and Wales during the 1980s and 1990s add another dimension to the notion of fluid participation in decision-making. Lay governors now have an enhanced role in the governance of schools. Nominally, they have substantial responsibility for the management of staff, finance, external relations and the curriculum. In practice, however, they usually delegate most of their powers to the headteacher and school staff. The nature of delegation, the extent of the participation of individual governors in committees and working parties, and the relationship between the headteacher and the chair of governors may be unpredictable elements of the relationship.

At Stratford Secondary School in East London, disagreement between the headteacher and chair of governors about the powers of the governing body led to the involvement of the Secretary of State and the courts. In this case, the chair wanted a level of participation in school management much greater than that expected in most other schools (Bush, Coleman and Glover 1993). While this is an extreme case, it serves to illustrate the ambiguity of the relationship between full-time professionals and part-time lay governors in the management of the school.

7 A further source of ambiguity is provided by the signals emanating from the organization's *environment*. There is evidence that educational institutions are becoming more dependent on external groups. Self-managing schools and colleges are vulnerable to changing patterns of parental and student demand. Through the provision for open enrolment, parents and potential parents are able to exercise more power over schools. Funding levels, in turn, are often linked to recruitment, for example in the student-related element of school and college finance in England and Wales. The publication of examination and test results, and of OFSTED inspection reports, also serves to heighten dependence on elements in the external environment.

For all these reasons, institutions are becoming more open to external groups. In an era of rapid change, they may experience difficulties in interpreting the various messages being transmitted from the environment and in dealing with conflicting signals. The uncertainty arising from the external context adds to the ambiguity of the decision-making process within the institution. When there is exceptional environmental turbulence, as with schools and universities in post-apartheid South Africa, the notion of ambiguity is particularly powerful (Bush, 2003).

8 Ambiguity theorists emphasize the prevalence of *unplanned decisions*. Formal models assume that problems arise, possible solutions are formulated and the most appropriate solution is chosen. The preferred option is then implemented and subject to evaluation in due course. Proponents of the ambiguity model claim that this logical sequence rarely occurs in practice. Rather the lack of agreed goals means that decisions have no clear focus. Problems, solutions and participants interact and choices somehow emerge from the confusion.

Hoyle (1986, pp. 69–70) refers to Christensen's (1976) study of a Danish school in which three apparently firm decisions were made but none of these 'decisions' were implemented, apparently for four reasons:

(a) The outcome of a decision may be less important than the process.
(b) Implementation is in the hands of people who may not share the attitudes of the decision-making group.
(c) The high level of attention given to the making of a decision may not be sustained through to its implementation.
(d) Other problems absorb the energies of the organization as new crises arise.

In England and Wales, ambiguity models can be illustrated by the resource allocation process in schools and colleges. Because there is little clarity about the goals of organizations, the notion of linking budgeting to aims is problematic. It is difficult to determine priorities among competing alternatives and the notion of an optimum choice is contentious (Bush, 2000, p. 113). Budgetary decisions are likely to be characterized by ambiguity rather than rationality, as Levačić (1995) research suggests:

> The rational model is undermined by ambiguity, since it is so heavily dependent on the availability of information about relationships between inputs and outputs – between means and ends. If ambiguity prevails, then it is not possible for organizations to have clear aims and objectives. Reliable information about the relationships between different quantities and combinations of inputs and resulting outputs cannot be obtained. This state of affairs would explain why decision-making, particularly in the public sector, does not in fact follow the rational model, but is characterized by incrementalism. (Levačić 1995, p. 82)

Bennett et al.'s (2000) study of development planning in English primary schools also casts doubt on the validity of rational models. They claim that primary schools are working in a highly turbulent environment and that this inevitably affects the planning process: 'It is impossible to predict the environment in which the school must operate, and management is so taken up with day-to-day responses to events as they occur that resources for strategic planning . . . are unlikely to be available (ibid., p. 349).

These examples serve to illustrate the problematic nature of the relationship between the decision-making process and the outcomes of that process. The rational assumption that implementation is a straightforward element in the decision process appears to be flawed. In practice, it is just as uncertain as the process of choice.

9 Ambiguity models stress the advantages of *decentralization*. Given the complexity and unpredictability of organizations, it is thought that many decisions should be devolved to sub-units and individuals. Departments are relatively coherent and may be able to adapt rapidly to changing circumstances. Decentralized decision-making avoids the delays and uncertainties associated with the institutional level. Individual and departmental auton-

omy are seen as appropriate for professional staff who are required to exercise their judgement in dealing with clients. Successful departments are able to expand and thrive, while weaker areas may contract or even close during difficult periods. Weick (1976, p. 7) argues that devolution enables organizations to survive while particular sub-units are threatened:

> If there is a breakdown in one portion of a loosely coupled system then this breakdown is sealed off and does not affect other portions of the organization . . . when any element misfires or decays or deteriorates, the spread of this deterioration is checked in a loosely coupled system . . . A loosely coupled system can isolate its trouble spots and prevent the trouble from spreading.

While decentralization does have certain merits, it may be difficult to sustain when leaders are increasingly answerable for all aspects of the institution. Underperforming departments or units can be identified through the inspection process, and the publication of performance indicators, and this limits the scope for 'sealing off' the weak sub-units. Rather, action must be taken to remedy the weakness if the institution is to thrive in a period of heightened market and public accountability.

The garbage can model

The most celebrated of the ambiguity perspectives is the garbage can model developed by Cohen and March (1986). On the basis of empirical research, they conclude that ambiguity is one of the major characteristics of universities and colleges in the United States. They reject the sequential assumptions of the formal models in which decisions are thought to emanate from a rational process. Rather they regard decision-making as fundamentally ambiguous. They liken the process to that of a 'garbage can':

> A key to understanding the processes within organizations is to view a choice opportunity as a garbage can into which various problems and solutions are dumped by participants. The mix of garbage in a single can depends partly on the labels attached to the alternative cans; but it also depends on what garbage is being produced at the moment, on the mix of cans available, and on the speed with which garbage is collected and removed from the scene. (Cohen and March, 1986, p. 81)

In their analysis of decision-making, the authors focus on four relatively independent streams within organizations. Decisions are outcomes of the interaction of the four streams as follows:

1 *Problems* are the concern of people inside and outside the organization. They arise over issues of lifestyle; family; frustrations of work; careers; group relations within the organization; distribution of status, jobs and

money; ideology; or current crises of mankind as interpreted by the mass media or the next-door neighbour. All require attention. Problems are, however, distinct from choices; and they may not be resolved when choices are made.

2 *Solutions.* A solution is somebody's product. A computer is not just a solution to a problem in payroll management, discovered when needed. It is an answer actively looking for a question. The creation of need is not a curiosity of the market in consumer products; it is a general phenomenon of processes of choice. Despite the dictum that you cannot find the answer until you have formulated the question, you often do not know what the question is in organizational problem-solving until you know the answer.

3 *Participants* come and go. Since every entrance is an exit somewhere else, the distribution of entrances depends on the attributes of the choice being left as much as it does on the attributes of the new choice. Substantial variation in participation stems from other demands on the participants' time (rather than from features of the decision under study).

4 *Choice opportunities.* These are occasions when an organization is expected to produce behaviour that can be called a decision. Opportunities arise regularly, and any organization has ways of declaring an occasion for choice. Contracts must be signed, people hired, promoted or fired, money spent and responsibilities allocated (Cohen and March, 1986, p. 82).

Cohen and March's analysis is persuasive. They argue that problems may well be independent of solutions, which may be 'waiting' for a problem to emerge. Participation in decision-making is fluid in many schools and colleges and the 'decision' emerging from choice opportunities may well depend more on who is present for that meeting than on the intrinsic merits of the potential solutions. French (1989, p. 32) illustrates the vagaries of fluid participation in decision-making:

> Most of us have in our time attended staff meetings, working parties, committee meetings, faculty boards. They may have been important decision-making affairs. How many people attended? All the required staff? Not quite? Ms A sends her apologies, Mr B is ill, Mr C not seen all week . . . Half way through this eminent event we were joined by Mr D and Ms E; then after one hour, two people left . . . we eventually reached a decision.

Cohen and March regard the garbage can model as particularly appropriate for higher education but several of the concepts are also relevant for schools. The major characteristics of ambiguous goals, unclear technology and fluid participation often apply in the secondary sector, although they may be less evident in small primary schools.

The major contribution of the garbage can model is that it uncouples problems and choices. The notion of decision-making as a rational process for finding solutions to problems is supplanted by an uneasy mix of problems, solutions and participants from which decisions may eventually emerge. The garbage can model has a clear application to educational institutions where there are many participants with ready-made solutions to apply to different problems. Levačić (1995, p. 82) contrasts this model with rational approaches: 'In the garbage can model, there is no clear distinction between means and ends, no articulation of organizational goals, no evaluation of alternatives in relation to organizational goals and no selection of the best means.'

Applying the ambiguity model: Oakfields School

The ambiguity model is an important contribution to the theory of educational management. It is a descriptive and analytical model which sets out its proponents' views of how organizations are managed rather than a normative approach extolling the 'right' way to manage institutions. However, there are few empirical studies which employ a conceptual framework drawn from the ambiguity perspective. One important example is Bell's (1989) research at Oakfields, then a newly amalgamated secondary school in the English East Midlands.

Oakfields was formed by the amalgamation of three schools as part of the LEA's strategy for dealing with falling pupil numbers. The new school opened with 1,500 pupils but numbers were expected to fall to about 900 within five years with obvious implications for staffing levels. This uncertainty was aggravated by teachers' union action which meant that planning could not be undertaken at the end of the normal school day. The new school also operated on two sites. These factors created a turbulent environment with a high degree of ambiguity.

Bell refers to a lack of clarity about school aims, technology and school membership. The new head identified the goals but these were not shared by all staff. Attempts to resolve differences of view were inhibited by the teacher action, as the headteacher indicates: 'You may not agree with some of the policies and procedures or even with the long term aims, but until we can discuss these I should like everyone to enforce them for all our sakes, but especially for the sake of the children' (Bell, 1989, p. 135). Bell notes that the lack of clarity about aims emanated from different perceptions held by staff from each of the three constituent schools, particularly in respect of discipline and aspects of the curriculum. It was clear also that teachers' opinions about the nature of the former schools influenced their attitudes: 'Staff . . . interpretation of the goals of the new school, and their stance towards operationalizing those goals, owed as much to their perception of the three constituent schools as it did to any statement of intent from the head of

Oakfields' (Bell, 1989, p. 136). Disagreement about the technology of the school centred around teaching styles and about the relative merits of separate or integrated subjects in science and humanities.

The notion of school membership was highly problematic because many staff retained a loyalty to their former school rather than to the newly amalgamated unit. This was particularly true of teachers at the former secondary school who returned to that school's site for certain lessons. The most potent example concerned the former head of the secondary school who was based at the satellite campus as 'associate head' and also influenced the views of several colleagues:

> He could only be described as being a member of Oakfields school if the notion of membership is used to indicate the most tenuous of connections. Several of his erstwhile colleagues took up a similar position to the extent that they were in the new school but not of it. (Bell, 1989, p. 140)

The ambiguous aims, technology and membership were reflected in the decision-making process which was often unpredictable and irrational. Bell claims that Oakfields illustrates the limitations of formal theories and the salience of the ambiguity model:

> The traditional notion of the school as an hierarchical decision-making structure with a horizontal division into departments and a vertical division into authority levels needs to be abandoned. Such a conceptualization is unsuitable for the analysis of an organization attempting to cope with an unstable and unpredictable environment . . . The fundamental importance of unclear technology, fluid membership and the problematic nature and position of educational goals has to be accorded due recognition in any analysis of the organization and management of a school such as Oakfields. (Bell, 1989, p. 146)

Ambiguity models: goals, structure, environment and leadership

Goals

Ambiguity models differ from all other approaches in stressing the problematic nature of *goals*. The other theories may emphasize the institution, or the sub-unit, or the individual, but they all assume that objectives are clear at the levels identified. The distinctive quality of the ambiguity perspective is that purposes are regarded not only as vague and unclear but also as an inadequate guide to behaviour: 'Events are not dominated by intention. The processes and the outcomes are likely to appear to have no close relation with the explicit intention of actors . . . intention is lost in context dependent flow of problems, solutions, people, and choice opportunities' (Cohen, March and Olsen, 1976, p. 37). Ambiguity theorists argue that decision-making represents an opportunity for discovering goals rather than promoting policies based on existing objectives. The specific choice situation acts as a catalyst in helping individuals to clarify their preferences: 'Human choice behaviour is at least as much a process for discovering goals as for acting on them' (Cohen and March, 1986, p. 220).

Hoyle (1986, pp. 69 and 71) argues that the broad aims of schools are usually very general and uncontroversial but that difficulties arise when these goals are translated into specific commitments. He claims that the concept of organizational goal is 'slippery' and appears to adopt an approach that combines the ambiguity and political models:

> [The ambiguity] approach takes over when it becomes a question of determining by what process particular goals become salient and what factors lead to choices being made . . . Although most schools will certainly move in some broad direction, the notion of a set of goals to which all the components are geared fails to correspond to the reality which is that insofar as a school has specific goals these will emerge from the interplay of interests within the school.

Organizational structure

Ambiguity models regard *organizational structure* as problematic. Institutions are portrayed as aggregations of loosely coupled sub-units with structures that may be both ambiguous and subject to change. In many educational organizations, and certainly in larger schools and colleges, policy is determined primarily by committees rather than by individuals. The various committees and working parties collectively comprise the structure of the organization.

Enderud (1980, p. 248) argues that organizational structure may be subject to a variety of interpretations because of the ambiguity and sub-unit autonomy that exists in many large and complex organizations: 'What really matters to the way in which the formal structure influences the processes is not what the structure formally "looks like", but the way it is actually used.' Enderud (1980) points to four factors which influence the interpretation of structure:

1 Institutions usually classify responsibilities into decision areas which are then allocated to different bodies or individuals. An obvious example is the distinction made between the academic and pastoral structures in many secondary schools. However, these decision areas may not be delineated clearly, or the topics treated within each area may overlap. A pupil's academic progress, for example, may be hampered by personal or domestic

considerations. 'The result is that a given decision may quite reasonably be subject to different classifications of decision area. This again means that the circle of participants who are to deal with the matter is also open to interpretation' (Enderud, 1980, p. 249).

2 Decisions may also be classified in other ways. Issues may be major or minor, urgent or long term, administrative or political, and so on. These distinctions offer the same opportunities for different interpretations as exist with delineation by area.

3 Rules and regulations concerning the decision process within the formal structure may be unclear. The choice of rules for decision-making is often subject to ad hoc interpretation. The adoption of a voting process, or an attempt to reach consensus, or a proposal to defer a decision, may be unpredictable and have a significant influence on the final outcome.

4 Rules and regulations may be disregarded in certain circumstances. Most organizational structures have elements designed to deal with emergencies or procedural conflicts. The formal structure may be circumvented to deal with particular occurrences where participants can agree on such practice (Enderud, 1980).

A further source of ambiguity concerns the extent of *participation* within the organizational structure. Certain individuals within the institution have the right to participate in decision-making through their membership of committees and working parties. Cohen, March and Olsen (1976, p. 27) stress that committee membership is only the starting point for participation in decision-making: 'Such rights are necessary, but not sufficient, for actual involvement in a decision. They can be viewed as invitations to participation. Invitations that may or may not be accepted.'

The elaborate participative structure at Churchfields High School in West Bromwich, England, in the early 1990s illustrates this point well. There were many committees which provided substantial opportunities for staff to influence decisions. In practice, however, teachers were selective about their participation in the decision process. One deputy head explained how staff use the structure: 'Individuals select certain items which interest them particularly and then they will make a statement and make their feelings known on that particular issue; but many day-to-day things go through on the say so of the headteacher' (quoted in Bush, 1993, p. 41).

A basic assumption of ambiguity models is that participation in decision-making is fluid as members underuse their decision rights. One consequence of such structural ambiguities is that decisions may be possible only where there are enough participants. Attempts to make decisions without sufficient participation may founder at subsequent stages of the process.

Lumby's (2001, p. 99) research on English further education colleges sug-

gests that staff roles are likely to be even more problematic than formal structures: 'Whether the official place within the structure of any role had changed
or not, the way the role was seen by the role holder and by others continued to change, and was likely to be subject to ambiguity, conflict and overload.'

The external environment

The *external environment* is a source of ambiguity which contributes to the
unpredictability of organizations. Schools and colleges have a continuing existence only as long as they are able to satisfy the needs of their external constituencies. So educational institutions have to be sensitive and responsive to
the messages transmitted by groups and individuals.

> Perhaps it needs to be recognized more explicitly that organizations, including
> schools, sometimes operate in a complex and unstable environment over which
> they exert only modest control and which is capable of producing effects which
> penetrate the strongest and most selective of boundaries . . . many schools are now
> unable to disregard pressures emanating from their wider environment. They are
> no longer able to respond to the uncertainty which such pressures often bring by
> attempting to buffer themselves against the unforeseen or by gaining control over
> the source of the uncertainty and thus restoring stability. The external pressures
> are, in many cases, too strong for that. (Bell, 1980, pp. 186–7)

The development of a 'market economy' for education in many countries
means that schools and colleges have to be increasingly sensitive to the
demands of clients and potential clients. Institutions which fail to meet the
requirements of their environments may suffer the penalty of contraction or
closure. The demise of certain schools as a result of falling rolls may be
regarded as a failure to satisfy market needs. Closure is often preceded by a
period of decline as parents opt to send their children to other schools which
are thought to be more suitable. One way of assessing these events is to view
the unpopularity of schools as a product of their inability to interpret the
wishes of the environment.

These external uncertainties interact with the other unpredictable aspects
of organizations to produce a confused pattern far removed from the clear,
straightforward assumptions associated with the formal models. A turbulent
environment combines with the internal ambiguities and may mean that management in education is often a hazardous and irrational activity, as Gunter's
(1997) study of 'Jurassic' management suggests:

> Management behaviour is . . . operating in an environment of constant order and
> disorder. The future cannot be visioned as it is unpredictable and depends on
> chance. Feedback can produce behaviour that is complex, in which a direct link

between cause and effect cannot be seen . . . the future is created by the sensitive response to fluctuations in the environment rather than proactive and systematic installations of new structures and tasks. (Ibid., p. 95)

Leadership

In a climate of ambiguity traditional notions of *leadership* require modification. The unpredictable features of anarchic organizations create difficulties for leaders and suggest a different approach to the management of schools and colleges. According to Cohen and March (1986, pp. 195–203), leaders face four fundamental ambiguities:

1 There is an ambiguity of *purpose* because the goals of the organization are unclear. It is difficult to specify a set of clear, consistent goals which would receive the endorsement of members of the institution. Moreover, it may be impossible to infer a set of objectives from the activities of the organization. If there are no clear goals, leaders have an inadequate basis for assessing the actions and achievements of the institution.
2 There is an ambiguity of *power* because it is difficult to make a clear assessment of the power of leaders. Heads and principals do possess authority arising from their position as the formal leaders of their institutions. However, in an unpredictable setting, formal authority is an uncertain guide to the power of leaders. Decisions emerge from a complex process of interaction. Leaders are participants in the process but their 'solutions' may not emerge as the preferred outcomes of the organization.
3 There is an ambiguity of *experience* because, in conditions of uncertainty, leaders may not be able to learn from the consequences of their actions. In a straightforward situation, leaders choose from a range of alternatives and assess the outcome in terms of the goals of the institution. This assessment then provides a basis for action in similar situations. In conditions of ambiguity, however, outcomes depend on factors other than the behaviour of the leaders. External changes occur and distort the situation so that experience becomes an unreliable guide to future action.
4 There is an ambiguity of *success* because it is difficult to measure the achievements of leaders. Heads and principals are usually appointed to these posts after good careers as teachers and middle managers. They have become familiar with success. However, the ambiguities of purpose, power and experience make it difficult for leaders to distinguish between success and failure.

Cohen and March (1986, p. 195) point to the problems for leaders faced with these uncertainties:

These ambiguities are fundamental . . . because they strike at the heart of the usual interpretations of leadership. When purpose is ambiguous, ordinary theories of decision-making and intelligence become problematic. When power is ambiguous, ordinary theories of social order and control become problematic. When experience is ambiguous, ordinary theories of learning and adaptation become problematic. When success is ambiguous, ordinary theories of motivation and personal pleasure become problematic.

These ambiguous features imply that leaders cannot control the institution in the manner suggested by the formal models. Rather they become facilitators of a complex decision-making process, creating opportunities for the discussion of problems, the participation of members and the exposition of solutions.

Two alternative leadership strategies are postulated for conditions of ambiguity. One stratagem involves a participative role for leaders to maximize their influence on policy. Cohen and March (1986) and March (1982) suggest the following approaches for the management of uncertainty:

1 Leaders should be ready to devote *time* to the process of decision-making. By taking the trouble to participate fully, leaders are likely to be present when issues are finally resolved and will have the opportunity to influence the decision.

2 Leaders should be prepared to *persist* with those proposals which do not gain the initial support of groups within the institution. Issues are likely to surface at several forums and a negative reception at one setting may be reversed on another occasion when there may be different participants.

3 Leaders should facilitate the *participation of opponents* of the leader's proposals. Occasional participants tend to have aspirations which are out of touch with reality. Direct involvement in decision-making increases members' awareness of the ramifications of various courses of action. The inclusion of opponents at appropriate forums may lead to the modification or withdrawal of alternative ideas and allow the leader's plans to prosper.

4 Leaders should *overload the system* with ideas to ensure the success of some of the initiatives. When the organization has to cope with a surfeit of issues it is likely that some of the proposals will succeed even if others fall by the wayside.

These tactical manoeuvres may appear rather cynical and they have certain similarities with the political models discussed in Chapter 5. The alternative stratagem is for leaders to forsake direct involvement in the policy-making process and to concentrate on structural and personnel matters. Attention to the formal structure enables leaders to influence the framework of decision-making. In deciding where issues should be discussed there is an effect on the outcome of those discussions.

This second stratagem also requires leaders to pay careful attention to the selection and deployment of staff. If heads or principals recruit teachers who share their educational philosophies, then it is likely that their preferred solutions will become school or college policy. The structural and personnel aspects of management can overlap. Heads may encourage like-minded staff to join committees and working parties to improve the prospects of favourable outcomes.

Both these strategies suggest that leaders in ambiguous situations should proceed by stealth rather than overt proclamation of particular policies. As Baldridge et al. (1978, p. 26) point out, the management of uncertainty requires different qualities from the management of bureaucracies:

> In such fluid circumstances . . . leaders serve primarily as catalysts. They do not so much lead the institutions as they channel its activities in subtle ways. They do not command, they negotiate. They do not plan comprehensively, they try to nudge problems together with pre-existing solutions. They are not heroic leaders, they are facilitators of an ongoing process.

While these strategies may be appropriate for periods of high ambiguity, the tensions inherent in turbulent organizations may be very stressful for heads and principals who have to absorb these pressures both to facilitate institutional development and to foster personal survival and growth. 'Successful heads have a high tolerance of ambiguity. Heads whose personal needs for structuring, continuity and stability are high may find frequent change and constant uncertainty a potent source of frustration and tension' (Coulson, 1986, p. 85).

The most appropriate leadership approach for turbulent conditions is the contingency model.

Contingent leadership

The models of leadership examined in the previous chapters are all partial. They provide valid and helpful insights into one particular aspect of leadership. Some focus on the process by which influence is exerted while others emphasize one or more dimensions of leadership. They are mostly normative and often have vigorous support from their advocates. None of these models provide a complete picture of school leadership. As Lambert (1995, p. 2) notes, there is 'no single best type'.

The contingent model provides an alternative approach, recognizing the diverse nature of school contexts and the advantages of adapting leadership styles to the particular situation, rather than adopting a 'one size fits all' stance:

This approach assumes that what is important is how leaders respond to the unique organizational circumstances or problems . . . there are wide variations in the contexts for leadership and that, to be effective, these contexts require different leadership responses . . . individuals providing leadership, typically those in formal positions of authority, are capable of mastering a large repertoire of leadership practices. Their influence will depend, in large measure, on such mastery. (Leithwood, Jantzi and Steinbach, 1999, p. 15)

Yukl (2002, p. 234) adds that 'the managerial job is too complex and unpredictable to rely on a set of standardised responses to events. Effective leaders are continuously reading the situation and evaluating how to adapt their behaviour to it'.

Bolman and Deal's (1991) 'conceptual pluralism' is similar to contingent leadership. An eclectic stance is required where leaders adapt their styles to the context in which they are operating. Leadership requires effective diagnosis of problems, followed by adopting the most appropriate response to the issue or situation (Morgan 1997). This reflexive approach is particularly important in periods of turbulence when leaders need to be able to assess the situation carefully and react as appropriate rather than relying on a standard leadership model.

The limitations of ambiguity models

Ambiguity models add some important dimensions to the theory of educational management. The concepts of problematic goals, unclear technology and fluid participation are significant contributions to organizational analysis. Most schools and colleges possess these features to a greater or lesser extent, so ambiguity models should be regarded primarily as analytical or descriptive approaches rather than normative theories. They claim to mirror reality rather than suggesting that organizations *should* operate as anarchies.

The turbulence of educational policy in England and Wales, and in many other countries, during the 1990s and into the twenty-first century, lends credence to ambiguity theories. The rapid pace of curriculum change, enhanced government expectations of schools and colleges, and the unpredictable nature of educational funding, lead to multiple uncertainty which can be explained adequately only within the ambiguity framework (Bush, 1994, p. 46). Similarly, Sapre's (2002) analysis of educational reform in India points to the continual failure of top-down reforms, arising largely as a result of ambiguity: 'Repeated failure of reform initiatives is unsettling for practitioners and students. Reformers need a deeper understanding of the dynamics of change, what sustains a reform and what does not' (ibid., p. 106).

The ambiguity model appears to be increasingly plausible but it does have four significant weaknesses:

1 It is difficult to reconcile ambiguity perspectives with the customary structures and processes of schools and colleges. Participants may move in and out of decision-making situations but the policy framework remains intact and has a continuing influence on the outcome of discussions. Specific goals may be unclear but teachers usually understand and accept the broad aims of education.

2 Ambiguity models exaggerate the degree of uncertainty in educational institutions. Schools and colleges have a number of predictable features which serve to clarify the responsibilities of their members. Students, pupils and staff are expected to behave in accordance with standard rules and procedures. The timetable regulates the location and movement of all participants. There are usually clear plans to guide the classroom activities of teachers and pupils. Staff are aware of the accountability patterns, with teachers responsible ultimately to heads and principals who, in turn, are answerable to government and, in self managing institutions, to governing bodies and funding agencies.

 The predictability of schools and colleges is reinforced by the professional socialization which occurs during teacher training, induction and mentoring. Teachers assimilate the expected patterns of behaviour and reproduce them in their professional lives. Socialization thus serves to reduce uncertainty and unpredictability in education. Educational institutions are rather more stable and predictable than the ambiguity perspective suggests: 'The term organised anarchy may seem overly colourful, suggesting more confusion, disarray, and conflict than is really present' (Baldridge et al., 1978, p. 28).

3 Ambiguity models are less appropriate for stable organizations or for any institutions during periods of stability. The degree of predictability in schools depends on the nature of relationships with the external environment. Where institutions are able to maintain relatively impervious boundaries, they can exert strong control over their own processes. Oversubscribed schools, for example, may be able to rely on their popularity to insulate their activities from external pressures.

4 Ambiguity models offer little practical guidance to leaders in educational institutions. While formal models emphasize the head's leading role in policy-making and collegial models stress the importance of team work, ambiguity models can offer nothing more tangible than contingent leadership.

Cohen and March (1986, p. 91) accept that their garbage can model has limitations while proclaiming its relevance to many organizations: 'We acknowledge immediately that no real system can be fully characterized in this way. Nonetheless, the simulated organizations exhibit behaviour that can be observed some of the time in almost all organizations and frequently in some.'

Conclusion: ambiguity or rationality?

Ambiguity models make a valuable contribution to the theory of educational leadership and management. The emphasis on the unpredictability of organizations is a significant counter to the view that problems can be solved through a rational process. The notion of leaders making a considered choice from a range of alternatives depends crucially on their ability to predict the consequences of a particular action. The edifice of the formal models is shaken by the recognition that conditions in schools and colleges may be too uncertain to allow an informed choice among alternatives.

In practice, however, educational institutions operate with a mix of rational and anarchic processes. The more unpredictable the internal and external environment, the more applicable is the ambiguity metaphor: 'Organizations . . . are probably more rational than they are adventitious and the quest for rational procedures is not misplaced. However . . . rationalistic approaches will always be blown off course by the contingent, the unexpected and the irrational' (Hoyle, 1986, p. 72).

The emphasis on development planning provides a rational element in school and college management, although Bennett et al.'s (2000) work demonstrates its limitations in a climate of ambiguity and change. The action plans required of school governing bodies following OFSTED inspections in England and Wales can also be regarded as a rational response to external turbulence. Wallace (1991, pp. 182 and 185) emphasizes that schools have to plan within a framework of uncertainty: 'The nature of many external innovations is liable to change unpredictably. It is in this rather frenetic context, which includes much ambiguity, that planning . . . must take place . . . the context for development planning [is] neither wholly chaotic nor entirely stable.'

The ambiguity model has much to offer but it has to be assessed alongside the formal perspective and other theories of educational management. On its own, it is not sufficiently comprehensive to explain behaviour and events in education. Its relevance is overstated by its adherents but it does offer fascinating and valuable insights into the nature of school and college management:

> In many ways the organized anarchy image is an exceptionally strong and persuasive concept. It breaks through much traditional formality that surrounds discussions of decision making. The imagery of organized anarchy helps capture the spirit of the confused organizational dynamics in academic institutions: unclear goals, unclear technologies, and environmental vulnerability . . . the term helps to expand our conceptions, dislodge the bureaucracy image, and suggest a looser, more fluid kind of organization. (Baldridge et al., 1978, p. 27)

153

References

Baldridge, J.V., Curtis, D.V., Ecker, G. and Riley, G.L. (1978) *Policy Making and Effective Leadership*, San Francisco, CA: Jossey-Bass.

Bell, L. (1980) 'The school as an organisation: a re-appraisal', *British Journal of Sociology of Education*, 1 (2): 183–92.

Bell, L. (1989) 'Ambiguity models and secondary schools: a case study', in T. Bush (ed.), *Managing Education: Theory and Practice*, Buckingham: Open University Press.

Bennett, N., Crawford, M., Levačić, R., Glover, D. and Earley, P. (2000) 'The reality of school development planning in the effective primary school: technicist or guiding plan?', *School Leadership and Management*, 20 (3): 333–51.

Bolman, L. and Deal, T. (1991) *Reframing Organizations: Artistry, Choice and Leadership*, San Francisco, CA: Jossey-Bass.

Bush, T. (1993) *Exploring Collegiality: Theory and Practice, E326 Managing Schools: Challenge and Response*, Buckingham: Open University Press.

Bush, T. (1994) 'Theory and practice in educational management', in T. Bush and J. West-Burnham (eds), *The Principles of Educational Management*, Harlow, Longman.

Bush, T. (2000) 'Management styles: impact on finance and resources', in M. Coleman and L. Anderson (eds), *Managing Finance and Resources in Education*, London: Paul Chapman Publishing.

Bush, T. (2002) *Middle Level Leaders' 'Think Piece'*, Nottingham: NCSL.

Bush, T. (2003) 'Theory and practice in educational management', in T. Bush, M. Coleman and M. Thurlow (eds), *Leadership and Strategic Management in South African Schools*, London: Commonwealth Secretariat.

Bush, T., Coleman, M. and Glover, D. (1993) *Managing Autonomous Schools: The Grant-Maintained Experience*, London: Paul Chapman Publishing.

Christensen, S. (1976) 'Decision-making and socialization', in J.G. March and J.P. Olsen (eds), *Ambiguity and Choice in Organizations*, Bergen: Universitetsforlaget.

Cohen, M.D. and March, J.G. (1986) *Leadership and Ambiguity: The American College President*, Boston, MA: Harvard Business School Press. (First published 1974 by McGraw-Hill, New York.)

Cohen, M.D., March, J.G. and Olsen, J.P. (1976) 'People, problems, solutions and the ambiguity of relevance', in J.G. March and J.P. Olsen (eds), *Ambiguity and Choice in Organisations*, Bergen: Universitetsforlaget.

Coulson, A. (1986) *The Managerial Work of Headteachers*, Sheffield: Sheffield City Polytechnic.

Enderud, H. (1980) 'Administrative leadership in organised anarchies', *International Journal of Institutional Management in Higher Education*, 4 (3): 235–53.

French, B. (1989) *The Hidden Faces of Organisations: Some Alternative Theories of Management*, Sheffield: Sheffield City Polytechnic.

Gleeson, D. and Shain, F. (1999) 'Managing ambiguity: between markets and managerialism – a case study of "middle" managers in further education', *Sociological Review*, 47 (3): 461–91.

Gunter, H. (1997) *Rethinking Education: The Consequences of Jurassic Management*,

London: Cassell.

Hoyle, E. (1986) *The Politics of School Management*, Sevenoaks: Hodder and Stoughton.

Lambert, L. (1995) 'New directions in the preparation of educational leaders', *Thrust for Educational Leadership*, 24 (5): 6–10.

Leithwood, K., Jantzi, D. and Steinbach, R. (1999) *Changing Leadership for Changing Times*, Buckingham: Open University Press.

Lumby, J. (2001) *Managing Further Education Colleges: Learning Enterprises*, London: Paul Chapman Publishing.

Levačić, R. (1995) *Local Management of Schools: Analysis and Practice*, Buckingham: Open University Press.

March, J.G. (1982) 'Theories of choice and making decisions', *Society*, 20 (1). Copyright © by Transaction Inc. Published by permission of Transaction Inc.

March, J.G. and Olsen, J.P. (1976) 'Organisational choice under ambiguity', in J.G. March and J.P. Olsen (eds), *Ambiguity and Choice in Organisations*, Bergen: Universitetsforlaget.

Morgan, G. (1997) *Images of Organisation*, Newbury Park, CA: Sage Publications.

Noble, T. and Pym, B. (1970) 'Collegial authority and the receding locus of power', *British Journal of Sociology*, 21, 431–45.

Orton, J. and Weick, K. (1990) 'Loosely coupled systems: a reconceptualization', *Academy of Management Review*, 15 (2): 203–23.

Sapre, P. (2002) 'Realizing the potential of educational management in India', *Educational Management and Administration*, 30 (1): 101–8.

Wallace, M. (1991) 'Flexible planning: a key to the management of multiple innovations', *Educational Management and Administration*, 19 (3): 180–92.

Weick, K.E. (1976) 'Educational organisations as loosely coupled systems', *Administrative Science Quarterly*, 21 (1): 1–19.

Yukl, G.A. (2002) *Leadership in Organizations*, 5th edn, Upper Saddle River, NJ: Prentice-Hall.

8

Cultural Models

What do we mean by culture?

Cultural models emphasize the informal aspects of organizations rather then their official elements. They focus on the values, beliefs and norms of individuals in the organization and how these individual perceptions coalesce into shared organizational meanings. Cultural models are manifested by sym-

---

Cultural models assume that beliefs, values and ideology are at the heart of organizations. Individuals hold certain ideas and value-preferences which influence how they behave and how they view the behaviour of other members. These norms become shared traditions which are communicated within the group and are reinforced by symbols and ritual

---

bols and rituals rather than through the formal structure of the organization. The definition below captures the main elements of these approaches:

Cultural models have become increasingly significant in education since the first edition of this book was published in 1986. Harris (1992, p. 4) claims that educational writers attach considerable value to culture: 'Theorists argue that educational administration has a technical management aspect but is mainly about the culture within an organization. This culture includes the rituals which occur (or should occur) within an organization . . . Educational managers . . . are taken to be those capable of shaping ritual in educational institutions.' This extract demonstrates that culture may be both operational and normative ('occur (or should occur)') and that leaders have a central role in influencing culture.

The increasing interest in culture as one element in school and college management may be understood as another example of dissatisfaction with the limitations of the formal models. Their emphasis on the technical aspects of institutions appears to be inadequate for schools and colleges aspiring to excellence. The stress on the intangible world of values and attitudes is a useful counter to these bureaucratic assumptions and helps to produce a more balanced portrait of educational institutions.

The developing importance of cultural models arises partly from a wish to understand, and operate more effectively within, this informal domain of the values and beliefs of teachers and other members of the organization. Morgan (1997) and O'Neill (1994) both stress the increasing significance of cultural factors in management. The latter charts the appearance of cultural 'labels' and explains why they became more prevalent in the 1990s:

> The increased use of such cultural descriptors in the literature of educational management is significant because it reflects a need for educational organizations to be able to articulate deeply held and shared values in more tangible ways and therefore respond more effectively to new, uncertain and potentially threatening demands on their capabilities. Organizations, therefore, articulate values in order to provide form and meaning for the activities of organizational members in the absence of visible and certain organizational structures and relationships. In this sense the analysis and influence of organizational culture become essential management tools in the pursuit of increased organizational growth and effectiveness. (O'Neill, 1994, p. 116)

Beare, Caldwell and Millikan (1989, p. 173) claim that culture serves to define the unique qualities of individual organizations: 'An increasing number of . . . writers . . . have adopted the term "culture" to define that social and phenomenological uniqueness of a particular organisational community . . . We have finally acknowledged publicly that uniqueness is a virtue, that values are important and that they should be fostered.'

The international trend towards self-managing institutions reinforces the notion of schools and colleges as unique entities. It is likely that self-management will be accompanied by greater diversity and, in England, this is one of the explicit aims of the government's educational policy. Caldwell and Spinks (1992, p. 74) argue that there is 'a culture of self-management'. The essential components of this culture are the *empowerment* of leaders and their acceptance of *responsibility*.

Societal culture

Most of the literature on culture in education relates to organizational culture and that is also the main focus of this chapter. However, there is also an emerging literature on the broader theme of national or societal culture. Dimmock and Walker (2002a, p. 3) claim that 'the field of educational administration . . . has largely ignored the influence of societal culture' but their work has contributed to an increasing awareness of this concept.

Given the globalization of education, issues of societal culture are increasingly significant. Walker and Dimmock (2002, p. 1) refer to issues of context and stress the need to avoid 'decontextualized paradigms' in researching and analysing educational systems and institutions:

The field of educational leadership and management has developed along ethno-centric lines, being heavily dominated by Anglo-American paradigms and theories ... Frequently, either a narrow ethnicity pervades research and policy, or an implicit assumption is made that findings in one part of the world will necessarily apply in others. It is clear that a key factor missing from many debates on educational administration and leadership is context ... context is represented by societal culture and its mediating influence on theory, policy and practice. (Walker and Dimmock, 2002, p. 2)

Walker and Dimmock are by no means alone in advocating attention to issues of context. Crossley and Broadfoot (1992, p. 100) say that 'policies and practice cannot be translated intact from one culture to another since the mediation of different cultural contexts can quite transform the latter's salience' while Bush, Qiang and Fang (1998, p. 137) stress that 'all theories and interpretations of practice must be "grounded" in the specific context ... before they can be regarded as useful'.

Dimmock and Walker (2002b) have given sustained attention to these issues and provide a helpful distinction between societal and organizational culture:

Societal cultures differ mostly at the level of basic values, while organizational cultures differ mostly at the level of more superficial practices, as reflected in the recognition of particular symbols, heroes and rituals. This allows organizational cultures to be deliberately managed and changed, whereas societal or national cultures are more enduring and change only gradually over longer time periods. School leaders influence, and in turn are influenced by, the organizational culture. Societal culture, on the other hand, is a given, being outside the sphere of influence of an individual school leader. (Ibid, p. 71)

Dimmock and Walker (2002b) identify seven 'dimensions' of societal culture, each of which is expressed as a continuum:

1 *Power-distributed/power concentrated*: power is either distributed more equally among the various levels of a culture or is more concentrated.
2 *Group-oriented/self-oriented*: people in self-oriented cultures perceive themselves to be more independent and self-reliant. In group-oriented cultures, ties between people are tight, relationships are firmly structured and individual needs are subservient to the collective needs.
3 *Consideration/aggression*: in aggression cultures, achievement is stressed, competition dominates and conflicts are resolved through the exercise of power and assertiveness. In contrast, consideration societies emphasize relationship, solidarity and resolution of conflicts by compromise and negotiation.
4 *Proactivism/fatalism*: this dimension reflects the proactive or 'we can change things around here' attitude in some cultures, and the willingness to accept things as they are in others – a fatalistic perspective.

158

5 *Generative/replicative*: some cultures appear more predisposed towards innovation, or the generation of new ideas and methods, whereas other cultures appear more inclined to replicate or to adopt ideas and approaches from elsewhere.

6 *Limited relationship/holistic relationship*: in limited relationship cultures, interactions and relationships tend to be determined by explicit rules which are applied to everyone. In holistic cultures, greater attention is given to relationship obligations, for example kinship, patronage and friendship, than to impartially applied rules.

7 *Male influence/female influence*: in some societies, the male domination of decision-making in political, economic and professional life is perpetuated. In others, women have come to play a significant role.
(adapted from Dimmock and Walker, 2002b, pp. 74–6)

This model can be applied to educational systems in different countries. Bush and Qiang's (2000) study shows that most of these dimensions are relevant to Chinese education:

- *Power is concentrated* in the hands of a limited number of leaders. 'The principal has positional authority within an essentially bureaucratic system . . . China might be regarded as the archetypal high power-distance (power-concentrated) society' (ibid., p. 60).
- Chinese culture is *group-oriented*. 'Collective benefits [are] seen as more important than individual needs' (ibid., p. 61).
- Chinese culture stresses *consideration* rather than aggression. 'The Confucian scholars advocate modesty and encourage friendly co-operation, giving priority to people's relationships. The purpose of education is to mould every individual into a harmonious member of society' (ibid., p. 62).
- *Patriarchal leadership* dominates in education, business, government and the Communist Party itself. There are no women principals in the 89 secondary schools in three counties of the Shaanxi province. Coleman, Qiang and Li (1998, p. 144) attribute such inequalities to the continuing dominance of patriarchy.

Similar outcomes are evident in Hallinger and Kantamara's (2000) research in Thailand. They show that Thailand is a power-concentrated culture with collectivist values, replicative rather than generative approaches, and a focus on relationship-building in local communities.

Societal culture is one important aspect of the context within which school leaders must operate. They must also contend with organizational culture which provides a more immediate framework for leadership action. Principals and others can help to shape culture but they are also influenced by it. We turn now to examine the main features of organizational culture.

Central features of organizational culture

Organizational culture has the following major features:

1 It focuses on the *values and beliefs* of members of organizations. These values underpin the behaviour and attitudes of individuals within schools and colleges but they may not always be explicit. In Nias, Southworth and Yeomans's (1989, p. 11) research in primary schools, beliefs were often difficult to discern: 'Because group members share and understand them, they have little need to articulate them. Many beliefs are indeed so deeply buried that individuals do not even know what they are.' The assumption of 'shared' values is reflected in much of the literature on culture: 'Shared values, shared beliefs, shared meaning, shared understanding, and shared sensemaking are all different ways of describing culture . . . These patterns of understanding also provide a basis for making one's own behaviour sensible and meaningful' (Morgan, 1997, p. 138).

The sharing of values and beliefs is one way in which cultural models may be distinguished from the subjective perspective. While Greenfield (1973) and other subjective theorists stress the values of individuals, the cultural model focuses on the notion of a single or dominant culture in organizations. This does not necessarily mean that individual values are always in harmony with one another. Morgan suggests that 'There may be different and competing value systems that create a mosaic of organizational realities rather than a uniform corporate culture' (Morgan, 1997, p. 137).

Large, multipurpose organizations, in particular, are likely to have more than one culture. 'Our experience with large organizations tells us that at a certain size, the variations among the sub-groups are substantial . . . any social unit will produce subunits that will produce subcultures as a normal process of evolution' (Schein, 1997, p. 14).

Within education, sub-cultures are more likely in large organizations such as universities and colleges, but they may also exist in primary education. Nias, Southworth and Yeomans (1989) note that, in relation to two of their case-study schools, there were sub-groups which had their own cultures separate from that held by their heads. Fullan and Hargreaves (1992, pp. 71–2) argue that some schools develop a 'balkanized' culture made up of separate and sometimes competing groups:

> Teachers in balkanized cultures attach their loyalties and identities to particular groups of their colleagues. They are usually colleagues with whom they work most closely, spend most time, socialize most often in the staffroom. The existence of such groups in a school often reflects and reinforces very different group outlooks on learning, teaching styles, discipline and curriculum.

2 Organizational culture emphasizes the development of *shared norms and meanings*. The assumption is that interaction between members of the organization, or its subgroups, eventually leads to behavioural norms that gradually become cultural features of the school or college: 'The nature of a culture is found in its social norms and customs, and that if one adheres to these rules of behaviour one will be successful in constructing an appropriate social reality' (Morgan, 1997, p. 139). Nias, Southworth and Yeomans's (1989, pp. 39–40) research shows how group norms were established in their case-study schools:

> As staff talked, worked and relaxed together, they began to negotiate shared meanings which enabled them to predict each others' behaviour. Consequently each staff developed its own taken-for-granted norms. Because shared meanings and ways of behaving became so taken for granted, existing staff were largely unaware of them. But they were visible to newcomers . . . Researchers moving between schools were constantly reminded of the uniqueness of each school's norms.

These group norms sometimes allow the development of a monoculture in a school with meanings shared throughout the staff – 'the way we do things around here'. We have already noted, however, that there may be several sub-cultures based on the professional and personal interests of different groups. These typically have internal coherence but experience difficulty in relationships with other groups whose behavioural norms are different. Wallace and Hall (1994, pp. 28 and 127) identify senior management teams (SMTs) as one example of group culture with clear internal norms but often weak connections to other groups and individuals:

> SMTs in our research developed a 'culture of teamwork' . . . A norm common to the SMTs was that decisions must be reached by achieving a working consensus, entailing the acknowledgement of any dissenting views . . . there was a clear distinction between interaction inside the team and contact with those outside . . . [who] were excluded from the inner world of the team.

In this respect cultural models are similar to collegiality where loyalty may be to a department or other sub-unit rather than to the school or college as an entity.

3 Culture is typically expressed through *rituals and ceremonies* which are used to support and celebrate beliefs and norms. Schools, in particular, are rich in such symbols as assemblies, prize-givings and, in many voluntary schools, corporate worship. Hoyle (1986, pp. 150 and 152) argues that ritual is at the heart of cultural models: 'Symbols are a key component of the culture of all schools . . . [they] have expressive tasks and symbols which are the only means whereby abstract values can be conveyed . . .

Symbols are central to the process of constructing meaning.' Beare, Caldwell and Millikan (1989, p. 176) claim that culture is symbolized in three modes:

(a) *Conceptually or verbally*, for example through use of language and the expression of organizational aims.
(b) *Behaviourally*, through rituals, ceremonies, rules, support mechanisms, and patterns of social interaction.
(c) *Visually or materially*, through facilities, equipment, memorabilia, mottoes, crests and uniforms.

Schein (1997, p. 248) argues that 'rites and rituals [are] central to the deciphering as well as to the communicating of cultural assumptions'. Wallace and Hall (1994, p. 29) refer to rituals developed by SMTs, including seating arrangements for meetings and social occasions for team members.

4 Organizational culture assumes the existence of *heroes and heroines* who embody the values and beliefs of the organization. These honoured members typify the behaviours associated with the culture of the institution. Campbell-Evans (1993, p. 106) stresses that heroes or heroines are those whose achievements match the culture: 'Choice and recognition of heroes . . . occurs within the cultural boundaries identified through the value filter . . . The accomplishments of those individuals who come to be regarded as heroes are compatible with the cultural emphases.' Beare, Caldwell and Millikan (1989, p. 191) stress the importance of heroes for educational organizations:

> The heroes (and anti-heroes) around whom a saga is built personify the values, philosophy and ideology which the community wishes to sustain . . . The hero figure invites emulation and helps to sustain group unity. Every school has its heroes and potential heroes; they can be found among principals and staff, both present and past; among students and scholars who have gone on to higher successes; and among parents and others associated with the school. Every school honour board contains hero material.

In practice, only those heroes whose achievements are consistent with the culture are likely to be celebrated. 'Whether religion or spirituality, pupils' learning, sporting achievements, or discipline are emphasized in assemblies provides a lens on one facet of school culture . . . [schools] are making statements about what is considered important' (Stoll, 1999, p. 35). In South Africa, for example, the huge interest in school sport means that sporting heroes are frequently identified and celebrated. This was evident in a Durban school visited by the author, where former student Shaun Pollock, the South African cricket captain, had numerous photographs on display and a room named after him.

Handy's four culture model

Each school and college has its own distinctive culture, dependent on the mix of values, beliefs and norms prevalent in the organization. We have also noted that larger schools and colleges may have several sub-cultures, operating simultaneously. Each culture has its own features which differentiate one school from another and give it a unique ethos. However, it is possible to identify certain 'ideal types' of culture. Organizations may typify one of these models through most if not all of their characteristics. The best known typology is that by Handy (1985), applied to schools by Handy and Aitken (1986). He identifies four cultures as follows:

- club culture;
- role culture;
- task culture;
- person culture.

Club culture is illustrated by the spider's web. The person at the head of the organization is located at the centre of the web, surrounded by concentric circles of associates. The organization is there as an extension of the head. Club cultures are rich in personality and abound in mythical stories and folk-lore from the past. Their danger lies in the dominance of the central figure. It works well when the organization is relatively small and when the leader is good. Handy and Aitken (1986) suggest that some primary schools may be benevolent club cultures.

Role culture is represented by the organization charts familiar to larger schools and colleges and discussed in Chapter 3. The formal structure is evident from the chart which identifies roles, and assigns responsibilities largely on the basis of official position. Communications are formalized and go from role to role rather than person to person. Role organizations are suitable for periods of stability and for routine tasks but less appropriate when there is rapid change. The focus is on organizational design and people are trained to fulfil their specific role. Handy and Aitken (1986) claim that secondary schools are often role cultures and this also applies to some colleges.

In *task cultures* a group or team is applied to a problem or task. The task culture is usually warm and friendly because it is co-operative rather than hierarchical. It has certain similarities with the collegial model. This culture thrives in problem-solving situations but may be very time-consuming. Working parties are examples of task cultures whereas standing committees are typical of role cultures. Handy's research (Handy and Aitken, 1986) suggests that many primary teachers regard their schools as task cultures. Clark (1992, p. 65) illustrates the task culture in education: 'We seem to have abandoned committees and sub-committees in the last three years and gone in

163

for many more working parties. These are set up, make reports and close down again quickly, then before you know it another one springs up on another problem.'

The *person culture* puts the individual first and makes the organization the resource for individual talents. This is consistent with the subjective model. The managers of the organization are of lower status than the individual professionals whose talents are at the heart of the organization. Expert or personal power is decisive because the star individuals are critical to the success of the organization. Few schools or colleges can be typified as person cultures although it may apply to heads of very successful departments which perform exceptionally well. It is relevant within universities where the talents of individual professors may be vital in securing the organization's reputation and research income.

Handy and Aitken (1986) stress that cultures are not inherently good or bad because they are situational. The important point is that culture should be appropriate for the organization and the people within it.

Bennett (1993, p. 36) accepts that the Handy model is a useful representation of organizational forms but argues persuasively that it does not explain culture: 'I do not think it is actually about cultures . . . It seems to marry well with theories of management, and to provide a useful way of characterizing the structure of organizations. But it does not address what makes a particular school . . . what it is.' Despite Bennett's reservations, the Handy model is useful in connecting culture and structure. It shows how structure may represent certain aspects of culture but it does not explain how values and beliefs coalesce to create the distinctive cultures of individual schools and colleges.

Developing a culture of learning in South Africa

The predominant culture in South African schools reflects the wider social structure of the post-apartheid era. Decades of institutionalized racism and injustice have been replaced by an overt commitment to democracy in all aspects of life, including education. The move from four separate and unequal education systems to integrated educational provision was underpinned by the rhetoric of democracy.

Badat (1995) traces the nature of educational transition since 1990 and links it to democratic values. He points out the difficulties involved in switching from racist and ethnic education to a system restructured 'along progressive and democratic lines' (ibid., p. 141). Education was an important battleground in the struggle for national liberation, encapsulated in slogans such as 'Equal Education' and 'Education towards Democracy', and linked to the wider objective of political rights:

> The form and content of struggles around education have been shaped by a social structure characterized by severe economic and social inequalities of a race, class, gender and geographic nature, political authoritarianism and repression, and the ideology, politics, and organizational strengths and weaknesses of the social movements and organizations that have waged the struggle around apartheid education. (Badat, 1995, p. 145)

The years of struggle against apartheid inevitably affected schools, particularly those in the townships. One of the 'weapons' of the black majority was for youngsters to 'strike' and demonstrate against the policies of the white government. Similarly, teacher unions were an important aspect of the liberation movement and teachers would frequently be absent from school to engage in protest activity. It is perhaps inevitable that a culture of learning was difficult to establish in such a hostile climate.

As long ago as 1955, the education clause of the South African 'Freedom Charter' emphasized that 'the doors of learning and culture shall be open to all' (Johnson, 1995, p. 131). In practice, however, it has been difficult to shift from struggle and protest to a culture of learning. Badat (1995, p. 143) claims that 'the crisis in black education, including what has come to be referred to as the "breakdown" in the "culture of learning" . . . continued unabated' while the National Education Policy Investigation links this problem to poor conditions in schools:

> South African teachers, especially those in black education, have had to contend with severe difficulties in rendering professional service to their clients, frequently because of the wretched physical conditions prevailing in their schools. Most teachers in black education have experienced a weakening of the social fabric in their communities, and the consequent disintegration of the culture of learning within their institutions. Most have experienced the trauma of having their bona fides questioned and their service rejected by their clients, as well as the humiliation of not being able to offer an adequate defence against these charges. (National Education Policy Investigation, 1992, p. 32)

This issue surfaced in the author's survey of school principals in the KwaZuluNatal province. In response to a question about the aims of the school, principals stated that the school is striving:

- to instil in the minds of learners that 'education is their future';
- to show the importance of education within and outside the school;
- to provide a conducive educational environment;
- to develop a culture of learning.

The absence of a culture of learning in many South African schools illustrates the long-term and uncertain nature of cultural change The long years of resistance to apartheid education have to be replaced by a commitment to teaching and learning if South Africa is to thrive in an increasingly competitive world economy. However, educational values have to compete with the still prevalent discourse of struggle and it seems likely that the development of a genuine culture of learning will be slow and dependent on the quality of leadership in individual schools (Bush and Anderson, 2003).

Organizational culture: goals, structure, environment and leadership

Goals

The culture of a school or college may be expressed through its *goals*. The statement of purposes, and their espousal in action, serve to reinforce the values and beliefs of the organization. Where goals and values are consistent the institution is likely to cohere: 'A clear description of the aims of a school, college or any section within it helps to provide a common vision and set of values. Well-stated aims will seize everybody's interest. Such aims will help in creating a strong culture' (Clark, 1992, p. 74). Clark suggests that the process of goal-setting should be linked to organizational values. The core values help to determine the vision for the school or college. The vision is expressed in a mission statement which in turn leads to specific goals. This essentially rational process is similar to that set out in the formal models but within a more overt framework of values. In practice, however, the link between mission and goals is often tenuous:

> Consensus on the core mission does not automatically guarantee that the members of the group will have common goals. The mission is often understood but not well articulated. To achieve consensus on goals, the group needs a common language and shared assumptions about the basic logical operations by which one moves from something as abstract and general as a sense of mission to the concrete goals. (Schein, 1997, p. 56)

As Schein implies, official goals are often vague and tend to be inadequate as a basis for guiding decisions and action. Much then depends on the interpretation of aims by participants. This is likely to be driven by the values of the interpreter. Where there is a monoculture within the organization, a consistent policy is likely to emerge. If there are competing cultures, or 'balkanization' (Fullan and Hargreaves, 1992), the official aims may be subverted by members of sub-units who will interpret them in line with their own sectional values and goals.

Organizational structure

Structure may be regarded as the physical manifestation of the culture of the

166

organization. 'There is a close link between culture and structure: indeed, they are interdependent' (Stoll, 1999, p. 40). The values and beliefs of the institution are expressed in the pattern of roles and role relationships established by the school or college. Handy's four culture model (Handy and Aitken, 1986), discussed earlier, is the best-known typology linking structure with the culture of the organization.

Schein (1997, pp. 180–1) cautions against a simplistic analysis of the relationship between structure and culture: 'The problem with inferring culture from an existing structure is that one cannot decipher what underlying assumptions initially led to that structure. The same structure could result from different sets of underlying assumptions . . . The structure is a clear, visible artifact, but its meaning and significance cannot be deciphered without additional data.'

Morgan (1997, pp. 141–2) argues that a focus on organizations as cultural phenomena should lead to a different conceptualization of structure based on shared meanings. He adopts a perspective similar to the subjective model in discussing the link between culture and structure:

> Culture . . . must be understood as an active, living phenomenon through which people create and recreate the worlds in which they live . . . we must root our understanding of organization in the processes that produce systems of shared meaning . . . organizations are in essence socially constructed realities that are as much in the minds of their members as they are in concrete structures, rules and relations. (Ibid.)

Structure is usually expressed in two distinct features of the organization. Individual roles are established and there is a prescribed or recommended pattern of relationships between role holders. There is also a structure of committees, working parties and other bodies which have regular or ad hoc meetings. These official encounters present opportunities for the enunciation and reinforcement of organizational culture. Hoyle (1986, pp. 163–4) stresses the importance of 'interpretation' at meetings:

> Ostensibly formal meetings are called to transact school business either in a full staff meeting or in various sub-committees and working parties. But meetings are rich in symbolic significance both *as* meetings and in the forms they take . . . The teachers have the task of interpreting the purposes of the meeting and they may endow a meeting with functions which are significant to them (original emphasis).

The larger and more complex the organization the greater the prospect of divergent meanings leading to the development of sub-cultures and the possibility of conflict between them:

> The relationship between organizational structure and culture is of crucial importance. A large and complex organizational structure increases the possibility of

several cultures developing simultaneously within the one organization. A minimal organizational structure, such as that found in most primary schools, enhances the possibility of a solid culture guiding all areas of organizational activity. (O'Neill, 1994, p. 108)

The development of divergent cultures in complex organizations is not inevitable but the establishment of a unitary culture with wide and active endorsement within the institution requires skilled leadership to ensure transmission and reinforcement of the desired values and beliefs (see 'Leadership' section below).

The external environment

The external environment may be regarded as the source of many of the values and beliefs that coalesce to form the culture of the school or college. The professional background and experience of teachers yield the educational values that provide the potential for the development of a common culture. However, there is also the possibility of differences of interpretation, or multiple cultures, arising from the external interests, professional or personal, of teachers and other staff.

O'Neill (1994, p. 104) charts the links between the external environment and the development of organizational culture (see Figure 8.1). The environment is the source of the values, norms and behaviours that collectively represent culture:

> The well-being of schools and colleges depends increasingly on their ability to relate successfully to their external environments. As such they are open rather than closed systems. It is therefore fundamentally important that the organization is able to offer visible and tangible manifestations of cultural 'match' to that environment. (Ibid.)

O'Neill (1994) argues that the existence of complementary values should be publicized to external groups in order to sustain their sponsorship and support. This stance is particularly significant for autonomous colleges and schools whose success, or very survival, is dependent on their reputation with potential clients and the community. Caldwell and Spinks (1992) stress the need for self-managing schools to develop a concept of marketing that allows for the two-way transmission of values between the school and its community.

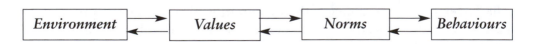

Figure 8.1 The development of organizational culture

Leadership

Leaders have the main responsibility for generating and sustaining culture and communicating core values and beliefs both within the organization and to external stakeholders (Bush, 1998, p. 43). Heads and principals have their own values and beliefs arising from many years of successful professional practice. They are also expected to embody the culture of the school or college. Hoyle (1986, pp. 155–6) stresses the symbolic dimension of leadership and the central role of heads in defining school culture:

> Few heads will avoid constructing an image of the school. They will differ in the degree to which this is a deliberate and charismatic task. Some heads . . . will self-consciously seek to construct a great mission for the school. Others will convey their idea of the school less dramatically and construct a meaning from the basic materials of symbol-making: words, actions, artefacts and settings.

Schein (1997, p. 211) argues that cultures spring primarily from the beliefs, values and assumptions of founders of organizations. Nias, Southworth and Yeomans (1989, p. 103) suggest that heads are 'founders' of their school's culture. They refer to two of their case-study schools where new heads dismantled the existing culture in order to create a new one based on their own values. The culture was rebuilt through example: 'All the heads of the project schools were aware of the power of example. Each head expected to influence staff through his/her example. Yet their actions may also have been symbolic of the values they tried to represent.' Nias, Southworth and Yeomans (1989) also mention the significance of co-leaders, such as deputy heads and curriculum co-ordinators, in disseminating school culture.

Deal (1985, pp. 615–18) suggests several strategies for leaders who wish to generate culture:

- Document the school's history to be codified and passed on.
- Anoint and celebrate heroes and heroines.
- Review the school's rituals to convey cultural values and beliefs.
- Exploit and develop ceremony.
- Identify priests, priestesses and gossips and incorporate them into mainstream activity. This provides access to the informal communications network.

However, it should be noted that cultural change is difficult and problematic. Turner (1990, p. 11) acknowledges the pressures on leaders to 'mould' culture but rejects the belief that 'something as powerful as culture can be much affected by the puny efforts of top managers'. Hargreaves (1999, p. 59) makes a similar point, claiming that 'most people's beliefs, attitudes and values are far more resistant to change than leaders typically allow'. He identifies three circumstances when culture may be subject to rapid change:

- The school faces an obvious crisis, for example a highly critical inspection report or falling pupil numbers, leading to the prospect of staff redundancies or school closure.
- The leader is very charismatic, commanding instant trust, loyalty and followership. This may enable cultural change to be more radical and be achieved more quickly.
- The leader succeeds a very poor principal. Staff will be looking for change to instil a new sense of direction.
(adapted from Hargreaves, 1999, pp. 59–60)

Hargreaves (1999, p. 60) concludes that, 'if none of these special conditions applies, assume that cultural change will be rather slow'.

Leaders also have responsibility for sustaining culture, and cultural maintenance is often regarded as a central feature of effective leadership. Sergiovanni (1984a, p. 9) claims that the cultural aspect is the most important dimension of leadership. Within his 'leadership forces hierarchy', the cultural element is more significant than the technical, human and educational aspects of leadership:

> The net effect of the cultural force of leadership is to bond together students, teachers, and others as believers in the work of the school . . . As persons become members of this strong and binding culture, they are provided with opportunities for enjoying a special sense of personal importance and significance. (Ibid.)

Moral leadership

The leadership model most closely linked to organizational culture is that of moral leadership. This model assumes that the critical focus of leadership ought to be on the values, beliefs and ethics of leaders themselves. Authority and influence are to be derived from defensible conceptions of what is right or good (Leithwood, Jantzi and Steinbach, 1999, p. 10). These authors add that this model includes normative, political/democratic and symbolic concepts of leadership.

Sergiovanni (1984b, p. 10) says that 'excellent schools have central zones composed of values and beliefs that take on sacred or cultural characteristics'. Subsequently, he adds that 'administering' is a 'moral craft' (Sergiovanni, 1991, p. 322). The moral dimension of leadership is based on 'normative rationality; rationality based on what we believe and what we consider to be good' (ibid., p. 326):

> The school must move beyond concern for goals and roles to the task of building purposes into its structure and embodying these purposes in

everything that it does with the effect of transforming school members from neutral participants to committed followers. The embodiment of purpose and the development of followership are inescapably moral. (Ibid., p. 323)

West-Burnham (1997) discusses two approaches to leadership which may be categorized as 'moral'. The first he describes as 'spiritual' and relates to 'the recognition that many leaders possess what might be called "higher order" perspectives. These may well be . . . represented by a particular religious affiliation' (ibid., p. 239). Such leaders have a set of principles which provide the basis of self-awareness.

West-Burnham's (1997) second category is 'moral confidence', the capacity to act in a way that is consistent with an ethical system and is consistent over time. The morally confident leader is someone who can:

- demonstrate causal consistency between principle and practice;
- apply principles to new situations;
- create shared understanding and a common vocabulary;
- explain and justify decisions in moral terms;
- sustain principles over time;
- reinterpret and restate principles as necessary.
  (West-Burnham, 1997, p. 241)

Gold et al.'s (2003) research in English primary, secondary and special schools provides some evidence about the nature of the values held and articulated by heads regarded as 'outstanding' by OFSTED inspectors. These authors point to the inconsistency between 'the technicist and managerial view of school leadership operationalised by the Government's inspection regime' and the heads' focus on 'values, learning communities and shared leadership' (ibid., p. 127).

The heads in Gold et al.'s (2003) research demonstrated the following values and beliefs through their words and deeds:

- inclusivity;
- equal opportunities;
- equity or justice;
- high expectations;
- engagement with stakeholders;
- co-operation;
- teamwork;
- commitment;
- understanding.

171

Gold et al. (2003, p. 136) conclude that their case study heads 'mediate the many externally generated directives to ensure, as far as possible, that their take-up was consistent with what the school was trying to achieve'.

Grace (2000) adopts a temporal perspective in linking moral and managerial leadership in England and Wales. He asserts that, for more than 100 years, 'the position of the headteacher was associated with the articulation of spiritual and moral conceptions' (ibid., p. 241). Subsequently, the requirements of the Education Reform Act led to the 'rising dominance' (ibid., p. 234) of management, exemplified by the National Professional Qualification for Headship. Grace (2000, p. 244) argues, prescriptively, that 'the discourse and understanding of management must be matched by a discourse and understanding of ethics, morality and spirituality'.

Sergiovanni (1991) takes a different approach to the leadership/management debate in arguing for both moral and managerial leadership. His conception points to the vital role of management but also shows that moral leadership is required to develop a learning community:

> In the principalship the challenge of leadership is to make peace with two competing imperatives, the managerial and the moral. The two imperatives are unavoidable and the neglect of either creates problems. Schools must be run effectively if they are to survive . . . But for the school to transform itself into an institution, a learning community must emerge . . . [This] is the moral imperative that principals face. (Ibid., p. 329)

Greenfield (1991) also stresses that managerial leadership must have a moral base:

> Values lie beyond rationality. Rationality to *be* rationality must stand upon a value base. Values are asserted, chosen, imposed or believed. They lie beyond quantification, beyond measurement. (Ibid., p. 208, original emphasis)

Moral leadership is consistent with organizational culture in that it is based on the values, beliefs and attitudes of principals and other educational leaders. It focuses on the moral purpose of education and on the behaviours to be expected of leaders operating within the moral domain. It also assumes that these values and beliefs coalesce into shared norms and meanings that either shape or reinforce culture. The rituals and symbols associated with moral leadership support these values and underpin school culture.

Limitations of organizational culture

Cultural models add several useful elements to the analysis of school and college leadership and management. The focus on the informal dimension is a valuable counter to the rigid and official components of the formal models.

By stressing the values and beliefs of participants, cultural models reinforce the human aspects of management rather than their structural elements. The emphasis on the symbols of the organization is also a valuable contribution to management theory while the moral leadership model provides a useful way of understanding what constitutes a values-based approach to leadership. However, cultural models do have three significant weaknesses:

1 There may be ethical dilemmas in espousing the cultural model because it may be regarded as the imposition of a culture by leaders on other members of the organization. The search for a monoculture may mean subordinating the values and beliefs of some participants to those of leaders or the dominant group. 'Shared' cultures may be simply the values of leaders imposed on less powerful participants. Morgan (1997, pp. 150–1) refers to 'a process of ideological control' and warns of the risk of 'manipulation': 'Ideological manipulation and control is being advocated as an essential managerial strategy ... such manipulation may well be accompanied by resistance, resentment and mistrust ... where the culture controls rather than expresses human character, the metaphor may thus prove quite manipulative and totalitarian in its influence.'

   Prosser (1999, p. 4) refers to the 'dark underworld' of school culture and links it to the micropolitical ideas addressed in Chapter 5. 'The micropolitical perspective recognized that formal powers, rules, regulations, traditions and rituals were capable of being subverted by individuals, groups or affiliations in schools.' Hargreaves (1999, p. 60) uses the term 'resistance group' to refer to sub-units seeking to subvert leaders and their intended cultural change.

2 The cultural model may be unduly mechanistic, assuming that leaders can determine the culture of the organization (Morgan, 1997). While they have influence over the evolution of culture by espousing desired values, they cannot ensure the emergence of a monoculture. As we have seen, secondary schools and colleges may have several sub-cultures operating in departments and other sections. This is not necessarily dysfunctional because successful sub-units are vital components of thriving institutions.

   In an era of self-managing schools and colleges in many countries, lay influences on policy are increasingly significant. Governing bodies often have the formal responsibility for major decisions and they share in the creation of institutional culture. This does not mean simple acquiescence to the values of the head or principal. Rather, there may be negotiation leading to the possibility of conflict and the adoption of policies inconsistent with the leader's own values. Nias, Southworth and Yeomans (1989) refer to the dissatisfaction of two heads who experienced difficulty in gaining acceptance for their preferred ways of working.

3 The cultural model's focus on symbols such as rituals and ceremonies may mean that other elements of organizations are underestimated. The symbols may misrepresent the reality of the school or college. Hoyle (1986, p. 166) illustrates this point by reference to 'innovation without change'. He suggests that schools may go through the appearance of change but the reality continues as before:

> A symbol can represent something which is 'real' in the sense that it . . . acts as a surrogate for reality . . . there will be a mutual recognition by the parties concerned that the substance has not been evoked but they are nevertheless content to sustain the fiction that it has if there has been some symbolization of the substance . . . in reality the system carries on as formerly.

Schein (1997, p. 249) also warns against placing too much reliance on ritual: 'When the only salient data we have are the rites and rituals that have survived over a period of time, we must, of course, use them as best we can . . . however . . . it is difficult to decipher just what assumptions leaders have held that have led to the creation of particular rites and rituals.'

Conclusion: values and action

The cultural model is a valuable addition to our understanding of organizations. The emerging focus on societal culture provides the framework within which school and college leaders must operate. It also serves to re-emphasize the significance of context at a time when globalization threatens to undermine it. Values and beliefs are not universal, as Dimmock and Walker's (2002a) work demonstrates. A 'one size fits all' model does not work for nations any more than it does for schools.

The recognition that school and college development needs to be preceded by attitudinal change is also salutary, and consistent with the oft-stated maxim that teachers must feel 'ownership' of change if it is to be implemented effectively. Externally imposed innovation often fails because it is out of tune with the values of the teachers who have to implement it. 'Since organization ultimately resides in the heads of the people involved, effective organizational change always implies cultural change' (Morgan, 1997, p. 150).

The emphasis on values and symbols may also help to balance the focus on structure and process in many of the other models. The informal world of norms and ritual behaviour may be just as significant as the formal elements of schools and colleges. Morgan (1997, p. 146) stresses the symbolic aspects of apparently rational phenomena such as meetings: 'Even the most concrete and rational aspects of organization – whether structures, hierarchies, rules, or organizational routines – embody social constructions and meanings that are crucial for understanding how organization functions day to day. For example meetings are more than just meetings. They carry important aspects of organizational culture.'

Cultural models also provide a focus for organizational action, a dimension that is largely absent from the subjective perspective. Leaders often adopt a moral approach and may focus on influencing values so that they become closer to, if not identical with, their own beliefs. In this way, they hope to achieve widespread support for, or 'ownership' of, new policies. By working through this informal domain, rather than imposing change through positional authority or political processes, heads and principals are more likely to gain support for innovation. An appreciation of the relevance of both societal and organizational culture, and of the values, beliefs and rituals that underpin them, is an important element in the leadership and management of schools and colleges.

References

Badat, S. (1995) 'Educational politics in the transition period', *Comparative Education*, 31 (2): 141–59.

Beare, H., Caldwell, B. and Millikan, R. (1989) *Creating an Excellent School: Some New Management Techniques*, London: Routledge.

Bennett, N. (1993) *Effectiveness and the Culture of the School, E326 Managing Schools: Challenge and Response*, Buckingham: Open University Press.

Bush, T. (1998) 'Organisational culture and strategic management', in D. Middlewood and J. Lumby (eds), *Strategic Management in Schools and Colleges*, London: Paul Chapman Publishing.

Bush, T. and Anderson, L. (2003) 'Organizational culture', in T. Bush, M. Coleman and M. Thurlow (eds), *Leadership and Strategic Management in South African Schools*, London: Commonwealth Secretariat.

Bush, T. and Qiang, H. (2000) 'Leadership and culture in Chinese education', *Asia Pacific Journal of Education*, 20 (2): 58–67.

Bush, T., Qiang, H. and Fang, J. (1998) 'Educational management in China: an overview', *Compare*, 28 (2): 133–40.

Caldwell, B. and Spinks, J. (1992) *Leading the Self-Managing School*, London: Falmer Press.

Campbell-Evans, G. (1993) 'A values perspective on school-based management', in C. Dimmock (ed.), *School-Based Management and School Effectiveness*, London: Routledge.

Clark, J. (1992) *Management in Education*, Lancaster: Framework Press.

Coleman, M., Qiang, H. and Li, Y. (1998) 'Women in educational management in China: experience in Shaanxi province, *Compare*, 28 (2): 141–54.

Crossley, M. and Broadfoot, P. (1992) 'Comparative and international research in education: scope, problems and potential', *British Educational Research Journal*, 18: 99–112.

Deal, T. (1985) 'The symbolism of effective schools', *Elementary School Journal*, 85 (5): 605–20.

Dimmock, C. and Walker, A. (2002a) 'An international view of the principalship and its development: allowing for cultural context – no one "best practice" model', paper presented at the National College for School Leadership International Conference, Nottingham, October.

Dimmock, C. and Walker, A. (2002b) 'School leadership in context – societal and organizational cultures', in T. Bush and L. Bell (eds), *The Principles and Practice of Educational Management*, London: Paul Chapman Publishing.

Fullan, M. and Hargreaves, A. (1992) *What's Worth Fighting for in Your School?* Buckingham: Open University Press.

Gold, A., Evans, J., Earley, P., Halpin, D. and Collarbone, P. (2003) 'Principled principals? Values-driven leadership: evidence from ten case studies of "outstanding" leaders', *Educational Management and Administration*, 31 (2): 127–38.

Grace, G. (2000) 'Research and the challenges of contemporary school leadership: the contribution of critical scholarship', *British Journal of Educational Studies*, 48 (3): 231–47.

Greenfield, T. (1973) 'Organisations as social inventions: rethinking assumptions about change', *Journal of Applied Behavioural Science*, 9 (5): 551–74.

Greenfield, T. (1991) 'Re-forming and re-valuing educational administration: whence and when cometh the Phoenix?', *Educational Management and Administration*, 19 (4): 200–17.

Greenfield, T.B. (1973) 'Organisations as social inventions: rethinking assumptions about change', *Journal of Applied Behavioural Science*, 9 (5): 551–74.

Hallinger, P. and Kantamara, P. (2000) 'Leading at the confluence of tradition and globalization: the challenge of change in Thai schools', *Asia Pacific Journal of Education*, 20 (2): 46–57.

Handy, C. (1985) *Understanding Organization*, London: Penguin.

Handy, C. and Aitken, R. (1986) *Understanding Schools as Organizations*, London: Penguin.

Hargreaves, D. (1999) 'Helping practitioners explore their school's culture', in J. Prosser (ed.), *School Culture*, London: Paul Chapman Publishing.

Harris, C. (1992) 'Ritual and educational management: a methodology', *International Journal of Educational Management*, 6 (1): 4–9.

Hoyle, E. (1986) *The Politics of School Management*, Sevenoaks: Hodder and Stoughton.

Johnson, D. (1995) 'Introduction: the challenges of educational reconstruction and transformation in South Africa', *Comparative Education*, 31 (2): 131–40.

Leithwood, K., Jantzi, D. and Steinbach, R. (1999) *Changing Leadership for Changing Times*, Buckingham: Open University Press.

Morgan, G. (1997) *Images of Organization*, Newbury Park, CA: Sage.

National Education Policy Investigation (1992) *Teacher Education*, Cape Town: Oxford University Press.

Nias, J., Southworth, G. and Yeomans, R. (1989) *Staff Relationships in the Primary School*, London: Cassell.

O'Neill, J. (1994) 'Organizational structure and culture', in T. Bush and J. West-Burnham (eds), *The Principles of Educational Management*, Harlow: Longman.

Prosser, J. (ed.) (1999) *School Culture*, London: Paul Chapman Publishing.

Schein, E. (1997) *Organizational Culture and Leadership*, San Francisco, CA: Jossey-Bass.

Sergiovanni, T. (1984a) 'Cultural and competing perspectives in administrative theory and practice', in T. Sergiovanni and J. Corbally (eds), *Leadership and Organizational Culture*, Chicago, IL: University of Illinois Press.

Sergiovanni, T. (1984b) 'Leadership and excellence in schooling', *Educational Leadership*, 41 (5): 4–13.

Sergiovanni, T.J. (1991) *The Principalship: a reflective practice perspective*, Needham Heights, MA: Allyn and Bacon.

Stoll, L. (1999) 'School culture: black hole or fertile garden for school improvement?', in J. Prosser (ed.), *School Culture*, London: Paul Chapman Publishing.

Walker, A. and Dimmock, C. (2002) 'Introduction', in A. Walker and C. Dimmock (eds), *School Leadership and Administration: Adopting a Cultural Perspective*, London: RoutledgeFalmer.

Wallace, M. and Hall, V. (1994) *Inside the SMT: Teamwork in Secondary School Management*, London: Paul Chapman Publishing.

West-Burnham, J. (1997) 'Leadership for learning: reengineering "mind sets"', *School Leadership and Management*, 17 (2): 231–43.

9

Conclusion

Comparing the management models

The six management models discussed in this book represent different ways of looking at educational institutions. They are analogous to windows, offering a view of life in schools or colleges. Each screen offers valuable insights into the nature of management in education but none provides a complete picture. The six approaches are all valid analyses but their relevance varies according to the context. Each event, situation or problem may be understood by using one or more of these models but no organization can be explained by using only a single approach. In certain circumstances a particular model may appear to be applicable while another theory may seem more appropriate in a different setting. There is no single perspective capable of presenting a total framework for our understanding of educational institutions:

> [T]he search for an all-encompassing model is simplistic, for no one model can delineate the intricacies of decision processes in complex organizations such as universities and colleges . . . there is a pleasant parsimony about having a single model that summarises a complicated world for us. This is not bad except when we allow our models to blind us to important features of the organization. (Baldridge et al. 1978, p. 28)

The formal models dominated the early stages of theory development in educational management. Formal structure, rational decision-making and 'top-down' leadership were regarded as the central concepts of effective management and attention was given to refining these processes to increase efficiency. Since the 1970s, however, there has been a gradual realization that formal models are 'at best partial and at worst grossly deficient' (Chapman, 1993, p. 215).

The other five models featured in this volume all developed in response to the perceived weaknesses of what was then regarded as 'conventional theory'. They have demonstrated the limitations of the formal models and put in place alternative conceptualizations that provide different portrayals of school and college management. While these more recent models are all valid, they are just as partial as the dominant perspective their advocates seek to replace.

178

There is more theory and, by exploring different dimensions of management, its total explanatory power is greater than that provided by any single model: 'Traditional views . . . still dominate understandings of theory, research and administrative practice but there are now systematic alternatives to this approach. As a result, educational administration is now theoretically much richer, more diverse and complex than at any other time in its short history' (Evers and Lakomski, 1991, p. 99).

The six models presented in this book are broad categories, encompassing a variety of different perspectives on management in education. Each has elements that provide a 'shock of recognition' and seem to be essential components of theory.

Collegial models are attractive because they advocate teacher participation in decision-making. The author's experience in postgraduate teaching, and as a consultant, suggests that most heads aspire to collegiality, a claim which rarely survives rigorous scrutiny. The collegial framework all too often provides the setting for political activity or 'top-down' decision-making.

The cultural model's stress on values and beliefs, and the subjective theorists' emphasis on the significance of individual meanings, also appear to be both plausible and ethical. In practice, however, these may lead to manipulation as leaders seek to impose their own values on schools and colleges.

The increasing complexity of the educational context may appear to lend support to the ambiguity model with its emphasis on turbulence and anarchy. However, this approach provides few guidelines for managerial action and leads to the view that 'there has to be a better way'.

The six models differ along crucial dimensions but taken together they do provide a comprehensive picture of the nature of management in educational institutions. Throughout the book, four main aspects of management have been addressed:

- goals;
- organizational structure;
- the external environment;
- leadership.

A review of these themes provides the focus for a comparative analysis of the six models.

Goals

There are significant differences in the assumptions made about the *goals* of educational organizations. In formal models, objectives are set at the institutional level. Goals are determined by senior staff and the support of other teachers is taken for granted. The activities of schools and colleges are evaluated in the light of these official purposes.

The advocates of collegial models claim that members of an organization agree on its goals. These approaches have a harmony bias in that they assume that it is always possible for staff to reach agreement based on common values. Unlike formal perspectives, the aims are not imposed from above but emerge from a participative process.

Political models differ from both the formal and collegial perspectives in stressing the goals of sub-units or departments rather than those of the institution. There is assumed to be conflict as groups seek to promote their own purposes. Goals are unstable as sub-units engage in negotiation and alliances form and break down.

Subjective models emphasize the goals of individuals rather than institutional or group purposes. The concept of organizational objectives is supplanted by the view that individuals have personal aims. Schools and colleges are regarded as the subjective creations of the people within them and the only reality is their individual perceptions of the organization. Goals attributed to organizations are thought to be the purposes of the most powerful individuals within them.

Ambiguity theorists claim that goals are problematic. While other perspectives assume that objectives are clear at institutional, group or individual levels, the ambiguity approach assumes that goals are opaque. Aims are also regarded as an unreliable guide to behaviour. In this view it is a mistake to regard policies or events as a corollary of the goals of the institution.

In cultural models, goals are an expression of the culture of the organization. The statement of purposes, and their espousal in action, serve to reinforce the beliefs of the institution. The core values help to determine a vision for the school or college. This vision is expressed in a mission statement which in turn leads to specific goals.

Organizational structure

The notion of *organizational structure* takes on different meanings within the various perspectives. Formal and collegial models regard structures as objective realities. Individuals hold defined positions in the organization and working relationships are assumed to be strongly influenced by these official positions. Formal models treat structures as hierarchical with decision-making as a 'top-down' process. Collegial models present structures as lateral with all members having the right to participate in the decision process.

Political models portray structure as one of the unstable and conflictual elements of the institution. The design of the structure is thought to reflect the interests of the dominant groups and individuals within the school or college. Committees and working parties may provide the framework for conflict between interest groups anxious to promote their policy objectives.

Subjective models regard organizational structure as a fluid concept that arises from relationships between individuals, rather than an established framework constraining the behaviour of its members. The emphasis is on the participants rather than the roles they occupy. The interaction of people within the organization is reflected in the structure which is valid only as long as it represents those relationships accurately.

Ambiguity models assume that organizational structure is problematic because of the uncertain nature of the relationships between loosely coupled sub-units. It may not be clear which group has the power to determine outcomes. Committees and working parties are characterized by the fluid participation of their members. Attendance is variable and decisions may be compromised by the absence of certain individuals who may challenge outcomes on other occasions.

In cultural models, structure may be regarded as the physical manifestation of the culture of the organization. The values and beliefs of the institution are thought to be expressed in the pattern of roles and role relationships established by the school or college. Committees and whole staff meetings provide opportunities for the enunciation and reinforcement of organizational culture.

The external environment

Relations with external groups are an increasingly important consideration for educational institutions if they are to survive and prosper. These links with the *environment* are portrayed in very different ways by the various models. Some of the formal approaches tend to regard schools and colleges as 'closed systems', relatively impervious to outside influences. Other formal theories typify educational organizations as 'open systems', responding to the needs of their communities and building a positive image to attract new clients.

Collegial models tend to be inadequate in explaining relationships with the environment. Policy is thought to be determined within a participatory framework which can make it difficult to locate responsibility for decisions. Heads may be held accountable for outcomes which do not enjoy their personal support, a position which is difficult to sustain for both the leader and the external group. Collegial approaches gloss over this difficulty by the unrealistic assumption that heads are always in agreement with decisions.

Political models tend to portray relationships with the environment as unstable. External bodies are regarded as interest groups which may participate in the complex bargaining process that characterizes decision-making.

Internal and external groups may form alliances to press for the adoption of certain policies. Interaction with the environment is seen as a central aspect of an essentially political decision process.

In subjective models, the environment is treated as a prime source of the meanings placed on events by people within the organization. Individuals are thought to interpret situations in different ways and these variations in meaning are attributed in part to the different external influences upon participants.

Ambiguity models regard the environment as a source of the uncertainty which contributes to the unpredictability of organizations. The signals from outside groups are often unclear and contradictory, leading to confusion inside schools and colleges. Interpretation of messages from a turbulent environment may be difficult, adding to the ambiguity of the decision process.

In cultural models, the external environment may be regarded as the source of many of the values and beliefs that coalesce to form the culture of the school or college. The professional background and experience of teachers yield the educational values that provide the potential for the development of a common culture. However, there is also the possibility of multiple cultures arising from the divergent external interests, professional or personal, of teachers and other staff.

Leadership

The perceived styles of *leadership* inevitably reflect the particular features of the diverse models of management. Within formal perspectives, the official leader is thought to have the major role in goal-setting, decision-making and policy formulation. Heads and principals are located at the apex of a hierarchy and they are acknowledged as the leaders both inside and outside the institution. The positional leader is assumed to be the most powerful person in the organization.

In collegial models, policies are thought to emerge from a complex process of discussion at committees and in other formal and informal settings. Influence is distributed widely within the institution and the leader is one participant in a collegial style of decision-making. Principals are assumed to have the prime responsibility for the promotion of consensus among their fellow professionals. A hierarchical approach is thought to be inappropriate for participative organizations and the leader is portrayed as *primus inter pares*.

Political models assume that leaders are active participants in the process of bargaining and negotiation which characterizes decision-making in organizations. Heads and principals have significant resources of power which they are able to deploy in support of their interests and objectives. Leaders may also mediate between groups in order to develop acceptable policy outcomes.

Subjective models de-emphasize the concept of leadership, preferring to stress the personal attributes of individuals rather than their official positions in the organization. All participants, including leaders, are assumed to have their own values and objectives which necessarily influence their interpretation of events. Heads and principals may be able to exert control over colleagues by enunciating institutional policies in line with their own personal interests and requiring the compliance of staff with these interpretations.

Ambiguity models stress the uncertainty facing leaders and the difficulties associated with the management of unpredictability. There are two schools of thought about the most appropriate leadership strategies for conditions of ambiguity. One mode involves active participation, with the leader engaging in various tactical machinations, an approach similar to that assumed in the political models. The alternative stance is to adopt an unobtrusive style with an emphasis on personnel and structural issues. Here the leader sets the framework for decision-making but avoids direct involvement in the policy-making process.

In cultural models, the leader of the organization has the main responsibility for developing and sustaining its culture. Heads and principals have their own values and beliefs arising from many years of successful professional practice and these may become the fulcrum of institutional culture. Leaders are expected to communicate the organization's core values and beliefs, both internally and to external stakeholders. Promotion and maintenance of the culture are regarded as central features of effective leadership.

The six perspectives differ significantly in the ways in which they treat the various components of institutional management, including goals, structure, environment and leadership. The major features of the six models are compared, and linked to the leadership models, in Figure 9.1.

Comparing the leadership models

Leadership can be understood as a process of influence based on clear values and beliefs and leading to a 'vision' for the school. The vision is articulated by leaders who seek to gain the commitment of staff and stakeholders to the ideal of a better future for the school, its students and stakeholders.

Each of the leadership models discussed in this book is partial. In this respect, they are similar to the management models. They provide distinctive but unidimensional perspectives on school leadership. Sergiovanni (1984, p. 6) adds that much 'leadership theory and practice provides a limited view, dwelling excessively on some aspects of leadership to the virtual exclusion of others'.

Elements of management	Type of model					
	Formal	Collegial	Political	Subjective	Ambiguity	Cultural
Level at which goals are determined	Institutional	Institutional	Subunit	Individual	Unclear	Institutional or subunit
Process by which goals are determined	Set by leaders	Agreement	Conflict	Problematic May be imposed by leaders	Unpredictable	Based on collective values
Relationship between goals and decisions	Decisions based on goals	Decisions based on agreed goals	Decisions boased on goals of dominant coalitions	Individual behaviour based on personal objectives	Decisions unrelated to goals	Decisions based on goals of the organisation or its subunits
Nature of decision process	Rational	Collegial	Political	Personal	Garbage can	Rational within a framework of values
Nature of structure	Objective reality hierarchial	Objective reality Lateral	Setting for subunit	Constructed through human interaction	Problematic	Physical manifestation of culture
Links with environment	May be 'closed' or 'open' Head accountable	Accountability blurred by shared decision making	Unstable external bodies portrayed as interest groups	Source of individual meanings	Source of uncertainty	Source of values and beliefs
Style of leadership	Head establishes goals and initiates policy	Head seeks to promote consensus	Head is both participant and mediator	Problematic May be perceived as a form of control	May be tactical or unobtrusive	Symbolic
Related leadership model	Managerial	Transformational Participative Interpersonal	Transactional	Postmodern	Contingent	Moral

Note: 1 Figure 9.1 has certain similarities with Cuthbert's (1984) tabular representation of five models using the criteria noted on page 30 above.

Figure 9.1

Conclusion

The nine models, adapted from Leithwood, Jantzi and Steinbach (1999) and presented by Bush and Glover (2002), collectively suggest that concepts of school leadership are complex and diverse. They provide clear normative frameworks by which leadership can be understood but relatively weak empirical support for these constructs. They are also artificial distinctions, or 'ideal types', in that most successful leaders are likely to embody most or all of these approaches in their work.

Hallinger (1992) provides a helpful, although dated, temporal perspective on what are probably the three most important models; managerial, instructional and transformational. He argues that there has been a shift in expectations of American principals which can be explained as changing conceptions of school leadership. These three phases were:

1 *Managerial*. During the 1960s and 1970s, principals came to be viewed as change agents for government initiatives:

> These categorical programmes and curriculum reforms represented innovations conceived and introduced by policymakers outside the local school . . . the principal's role, though apparently crucial, was limited to *managing* the implementation of an externally devised solution to a social or educational problem. (Ibid., p. 36, original emphasis)

2 *Instructional*. By the mid-1980s, the emphasis had shifted to the 'new orthodoxy' of instructional leadership. 'The instructional leader was viewed as the primary source of knowledge for development of the school's educational programme' (ibid., p. 37).

As noted earlier, this model is primarily about the direction rather than the process of influence. This view is reflected in two contemporary criticisms of instructional leadership:

(a) an inability 'to document the processes by which leaders helped their schools to become instructionally effective' (ibid., pp. 37–8).
(b) principals did not have 'the instructional leadership capacities needed for meaningful school improvement' (ibid., p. 38).

3 *Transformational*. During the 1990s, a new conception of leadership emerged based on the assumption that schools were becoming the 'unit responsible for the initiation of change, not just the implementation of change conceived by others' (ibid., p. 40). This led to the notion of transformational leadership, as principals sought to enlist support from teachers and other stakeholders to participate in a process of identifying and addressing school priorities.

Hallinger (1992) claims that instructional leadership should not be the predominant role of principals:

> The legitimate instructional leaders . . . ought to be teachers. And principals ought

to be leaders of leaders: people who develop the instructional leadership in their teachers. (Ibid., p. 41)

In this view, transformational leadership is the vehicle for promoting and developing the instructional leadership capabilities of classroom teachers and those leaders with direct responsibility for promoting learning.

The Hallinger (1992) distinction provides a starting point for an assessment of school leadership in the twenty-first century, beginning with an overview of the nine leadership models.

Managerial leadership

Managerial leadership is analogous to the formal models of management. It has been discredited and dismissed as limited and technicist but it is an essential component of successful leadership, ensuring the implementation of the school's vision and strategy. When vision and mission have been defined, and goals agreed, they have to be converted into strategic and operational management. The implementation phase of the decision process is just as crucial as the development of the school's vision. Management without vision is rightly criticized as 'managerialist' but vision without effective implementation is bound to lead to frustration. Managerial leadership is a vital part of the armoury of any successful principal.

Instructional leadership

Instructional leadership is different to the other models in focusing on the direction rather than the process of leadership. In Chapter 1, there is a firm emphasis on the purpose of education and the instructional leadership model stresses the need to focus on teaching and learning as the prime purpose of educational institutions. This model has been endorsed by the English National College for School Leadership, which has included it as one of its ten leadership propositions (NCSL, 2001), but it has two major weaknesses:

- It underestimates the other important purposes of education, including pupil welfare, socialization and the process of developing young people into responsible adults. It also de-emphasizes the less academic aspects of education, including sport, drama and music.
- It says little about the process by which instructional leadership is to be developed. It focuses on the 'what' rather than the 'how' of educational leadership. In this respect, it is a limited and partial model.

Transformational leadership

Transformational leadership is currently in vogue as it accords closely with the present emphasis on vision as the central dimension of leadership. Successful leaders are expected to engage with staff and other stakeholders to produce higher levels of commitment to achieving the goals of the organization which, in turn, are linked to the vision. As Miller and Miller (2001, p. 182) suggest, 'through the transforming process, the motives of the leader and follower merge'.

There is evidence to suggest that transformational leadership is effective in improving student outcomes (Leithwood, 1994) but this model also has two major limitations:

- It may be used as a vehicle for the manipulation or control of teachers who are required to support the 'vision' and aims of the leader.
- In England, the government uses the language of transformation but this is about the implementation of centrally determined policies not the identification of, and commitment to, school-level vision and goals.

Participative leadership

Participative leadership is an attractive model because it appears to provide for teachers and other stakeholders to become involved in the decision-making process. It is a normatively preferred approach in the early twenty-first century and may be described as shared, distributed, dispersed, collaborative or collegial, as well as participative. The model may be manifested in collective decision-making and/or in the allocation of responsibility for decision-making to specific individuals and groups.

This model is likely to be effective in increasing the commitment of participants, and in the development of team work, but the price may be an increase in the time taken to reach agreement, and there may be difficulties for the formal leader, who remains accountable for decisions reached through the collective process.

Interpersonal leadership

Interpersonal leadership involves a process of self-awareness leading to successful engagement with school stakeholders. As with collegiality, it stresses the importance of collaboration and interpersonal relationships. Leaders require high level personal and interpersonal skills to work effectively and collaboratively with staff, students and other stakeholders. Bennett et al.'s (2000) research with English primary schools suggests that this model can be effective in developing a conducive environment for learning and teamwork.

Transactional leadership

In transactional leadership, relationships with teachers and other stakeholders are based on a process of exchange. Leaders offer rewards or induce-ments to followers rather than seeking to improve their commitment or moti-vation, as in the transformational model. At its most basic, this model is demonstrated in contracts of employment where the employee's terms and conditions of work are articulated and the rewards structure and process clar-ified. In day-to-day management, principals may offer inducements, such as promotion or discretionary salary increments, to persuade others to support their plans or to undertake certain tasks.

The main limitation of the transactional model is that the exchange is often short-term and limited to the specific issue under discussion. It does not have a wider impact on the behaviour of the teacher or on school outcomes. Transactional leadership does not produce long-term commitment to the val-ues and vision being promoted by school leaders.

Postmodern leadership

Postmodern leadership is very similar to the subjective model of management in focusing on multiple individual perceptions rather than objective reality. There can be as many meanings as there are people in the organization, with power being distributed throughout the school rather than being the pre-serve of the formal leader. Each participant has a unique view of the insti-tution. There is no absolute truth, only a set of individual insights. There are multiple visions and diverse cultural meanings instead of a single vision enunciated by leaders.

The main limitation of this model, as with the parallel subjective per-spective, is that it offers few guidelines for leadership action. Its main con-tribution to leadership theory is its focus on individual perceptions and its emphasis on the need to deal with people as individuals rather than as an undifferentiated group.

Contingent leadership

Contingent leadership acknowledges the diverse nature of school contexts and the advantages of adapting leadership styles to the particular situation, rather than adopting a 'one size fits all' stance. As Leithwood, Jantzi and Steinbach (1999, p. 15) suggest, 'what is important is how leaders respond to the unique organizational circumstances or problems'. The educational context is too complex and unpredictable for a single leadership approach to be adopted for all events and issues. Given the turbulent environment, leaders need to be able to read the situation and adopt the most appropri-ate response.

Contingent leadership, then, is not a single model but represents a mode of responsiveness which requires effective diagnosis followed by careful selection of the most appropriate leadership style. It is analogous to selecting the right club for each golf shot or the appropriate clothes for each occasion. It is pragmatic rather than principled and can be criticized for having no overt sense of the 'big picture'.

Moral leadership

Moral leadership is based on the values, beliefs and ethics of leaders themselves. Leaders are expected to operate on the basis of what is 'right' or 'good'. It has similar characteristics to transformational leadership, in its emphasis on developing the commitment of followers, but its distinctive element is the focus on values and moral purpose. Leaders are expected to behave with integrity and to develop and support goals underpinned by explicit values. Such leadership may be found in religious schools, where the values are those of the particular group concerned, or may be a product of the leader's own background and experience. The main difficulty arises when staff or stakeholders do not support the values of leaders. This is likely to be uncomfortable for the people concerned and may lead to dissonance within the school.

Applying the models to schools and colleges

The six management models represent conceptually distinct approaches to the management of educational institutions. Similarly, the nine leadership models illustrate different approaches to educational leadership. However, as we have seen, it is rare for a single theory to capture the reality of leadership or management in any particular school or college. Rather, aspects of several perspectives are present in different proportions within each institution. The applicability of each approach may vary with the event, the situation and the participants. The validity of the various models also depends on five overlapping considerations:

1 Size of the institution.
2 Organizational structure.
3 Time available for management.
4 The availability of resources.
5 The external environment.

We first examine the impact of institutional size.

1 The *size of the institution* is an important influence on the nature of management structure and process. A small two-teacher primary school necessarily operates very differently from a large multipurpose college. The two primary teachers are likely to determine policy by informal agreement

while the head is acknowledged as the official leader by external groups and individuals. It may be appropriate to regard the management of such schools as comprising elements of both the collegial and formal models.

In large and complex institutions, such as colleges and most secondary schools, there are numerous decision points leading to the development of alternative power centres. Staff may owe their first loyalty to their discipline and their department. These sub-units compete for the resources they require to advance their objectives in a process encapsulated by the political model. In certain circumstances the situation may be so fluid that the ambiguity perspective appears to be appropriate.

Size may also be a factor influencing leadership styles. It is easier to adopt a participative approach in small organizations while managerial leadership is likely to be an essential dimension in larger schools and colleges. It is straightforward to be sensitive to individual meanings in smaller schools, making the postmodern model salient in such settings. The interpersonal model may also be more applicable in small units where personal knowledge of all staff and some stakeholders is possible. Transactional approaches are likely to be most useful in large institutions where leaders may have to bargain with staff as individuals or in groups. Transformational and moral leadership models may be applicable in both large and small organizations although it may be easier to secure the adherence of followers in smaller units.

2 The nature of the *organizational structure* is likely to have a significant impact on school and college management. Heads who establish participative machinery may be motivated by a desire to involve professional colleagues in decision-making. The intention, then, is to create a collegial framework for policy formulation and to lead in a participative style. However, the introduction of committees and working parties also provides several focal points for political behaviour and transactional leadership. Interest groups seek representation on these bodies, engage in bargaining and attempt to build coalitions in order to secure favourable outcomes.

Leadership styles may also be influenced by organizational structure although leaders do have the power to modify structure to achieve their own policy objectives. For example, committees and working parties could be restructured to ensure a stronger focus on teaching and learning, a strategy consistent with the instructional leadership model.

3 The nature of the leadership and management process depends on the *time available for management*. Participants differ in the amount of time they are able and willing to devote to the wider organizational and managerial aspects of their work. In the primary sector in England and Wales, teach-

ers have full-time classroom responsibilities and only the head may be available to deal with management issues during the school day. This factor contributes to the limited influence of subject leaders in many primary schools (Campbell and Neill, 1997). Limited time is also a major problem for heads of department in English secondary schools (Wise and Bush, 1999). The limited time available for management may serve to reinforce the 'top-down' leadership style associated with the formal model and managerial leadership. It also exacerbates the fluid participation in decision-making which is one of the central characteristics of the ambiguity model.

4 *The availability of resources* is likely to play a part in determining the relevance of the various models. In periods of expansion it may be possible to adopt a rational approach to the distribution of resources or to rely on a collegial stance. When funding is limited, departments may face the possibility of reductions in real resources such as staff, books or equipment. In these circumstances, units are likely to seek to defend their interests. Committees and working parties may begin to resemble political arenas as sub-units seek to retain existing resource levels. Simkins (1998, p. 71) shows how political models and transactional leadership are likely to thrive when resource allocation is being decided:

> Resource management is . . . a micropolitical process, providing an arena within which participants compete for the resources which will enable them to develop programmes of activity which embody their values, further their interests and help to provide legitimation for the activities in which they are engaged.

5 *The external environment* inevitably influences the process of management inside schools and colleges. The shift to self management and a 'market economy' in many countries means that schools and colleges have to be responsive to signals from their environment if they are to thrive. Hoy and Miskel (1987, p. 103) stress the links between the environment and school management: 'The emergence of open-systems theory during the past two decades has highlighted the importance [of the] external environment on internal school structures and processes.'

In periods of relative stability, organizations may be able to adopt formal or collegial approaches. This may be true of institutions with good reputations; they may have an assured clientele and be insulated from environmental turbulence. Fluctuating levels of recruitment in many schools and colleges, however, lead to unpredictable funding with clear implications for staffing and other real resources. The ambiguity model is particularly salient in such an unstable climate and leaders may need to adopt a contingent approach.

While these issues are important influences on management structure and process, it is rarely appropriate to label any school or college as typifying a single model. Rather, elements of many or all of the models may be found in almost all organizations. In any one institution, certain models may be more prevalent than the others but it is a question of relative not absolute significance.

This caution is important but it may be possible to conclude that small schools are likely to possess most of the characteristics of formal or collegial organizations, particularly in periods of stability, and be able to operate with a mix of transformational, participative, interpersonal and managerial leadership. Large, multipurpose colleges undergoing rapid change may display many of the features of the political and ambiguity theories and leaders may adopt transactional and contingent models. Many secondary schools have elements of all these models, whose significance varies from time to time according to the nature of the activity and the nature and level of participation. Adherents of the subjective and cultural models, and the postmodern and moral leadership approaches, would add that much depends on the values, perceptions and interpretations of individuals and groups in the organization.

Attempts at synthesis

Each of the models discussed in this volume offers valid insights into the nature of leadership and management in schools and colleges. Yet all the perspectives are limited in that they do not give a complete picture of educational institutions. Rather, they turn the spotlight on particular aspects of the organization and consequently leave other features in the shade. As we have seen, most educational institutions display features from most or all of the models: 'Organizations are many things at once! They are complex and multifaceted. They are paradoxical. That's why the challenges facing management are so difficult. In any given situation there may be many different tendencies and dimensions, all of which have an impact on effective management' (Morgan, 1997, p. 347).

The inadequacies of each theory, taken singly, have led to a search for a comprehensive model that integrates concepts to provide a coherent analytical framework. Ellstrom (1983, p. 236) makes the case for such a synthesis: 'Each model emphasises certain variables, while others are de-emphasised or ignored. Consequently, each model can be expected to give only partial understanding of the organisational reality . . . it might be possible to obtain a more comprehensive understanding of organisations by integrating the . . . models into an overarching framework.'

The attempt to develop coherence is not just a matter of esoteric interest for educational theorists. Chapman (1993, p. 212) stresses the need for leaders to develop this broader perspective in order to enhance organizational effectiveness: 'Visionary and creative leadership and effective management in education require a deliberate and conscious attempt at integration, enmeshment and coherence.'

Enderud (1980), and Davies and Morgan (1983), have developed integrative models incorporating ambiguity, political, collegial and formal perspectives. These syntheses are based on the assumption that policy formation proceeds through four distinct phases which all require adequate time if the decision is to be successful. Attempts by leaders to omit certain stages or to proceed too fast with initiatives may lead to a breakdown of the decision process or create the necessity for a 'loopback' to earlier phases.

These authors assume an initial period of high ambiguity as problems, solutions and participants interact at appropriate choice opportunities. This anarchic phase serves to identify the issues and acts as a preliminary sifting mechanism. If conducted properly it should lead to an initial coupling of problems with potential solutions.

The output of the ambiguous period is regarded as the input to the political phase. This stage is characterized by bargaining and negotiations, and usually involves relatively few participants in small, closed committees. The outcome is likely to be a broad measure of agreement on possible solutions.

In the third collegial phase, the participants committed to the proposed solution attempt to persuade less active members to accept the compromise reached during the political stage. The solutions are tested against criteria of acceptability and feasibility, and may result in minor changes. Eventually this process should lead to agreed policy outcomes and a degree of commitment to the decision.

The final phase is the formal or bureaucratic stage during which agreed policy may be subject to modification in the light of administrative considerations. The outcome of this period is a policy which is both legitimate and operationally satisfactory.

Enderud (1980, p. 241) emphasizes that the significance of each phase varies according to the different perceptions of participants as well as the nature of the issue:

> With its four phases, the model . . . reflects a mix of different realities in . . . decision making – an anarchistic, a political, a collegial and a bureaucratic reality – which may all be part of any one joint decision process. This composite picture will be one of the reasons why different participants often can interpret the same decision as largely anarchic, political, collegial or bureaucratic, according to the phase which is most visible to them, because of their own participation or for other reasons.

Although Enderud acknowledges that the individual interpretations of participants may influence the visibility of the models, the subjective perspective is not featured explicitly in the syntheses discussed by him, or by Davies and Morgan (1983). Theodossin (1983, p. 88), however, does link the subjective or phenomenological approach to the formal or systems model using an analytical continuum. He argues that a systems perspective is the most appropriate way of explaining national developments while individual and sub-unit activities may be understood best by utilizing the individual meanings of participants:

> Asked to account for and to explain national movements . . . we are more likely to find that a systems perspective is an appropriate form of conceptual organization: to think in terms of thousands of private biographies of the participating individuals is clearly to concern oneself with more detail than one can handle conceptually, let alone collect, and to segment the experience into an incoherent fragmentation. However, asked to explain the emergence of mixed-ability grouping in a particular school . . . we are likely to find the phenomenological approach more helpful: we are here dealing with change agents whose activities spring from personal, individual experience. (Ibid.)

Theodossin's analysis is interesting and plausible. It helps to delineate the contribution of the formal and subjective models to educational management theory. In focusing on these two perspectives, however, it necessarily ignores the contribution of other approaches, including the cultural model which has not been incorporated into any of the syntheses applied to education

The Enderud (1980), and Davies and Morgan (1983), models are valuable in suggesting a plausible sequential link between four of the major theories. However, it is certainly possible to postulate different sets of relationships between the models. For example, a collegial approach may become political as participants engage in conflict instead of seeking to achieve consensus. It is perhaps significant that there have been few attempts to integrate the management models since the 1980s. There are probably too many potential combinations for an integration of the nine leadership models to be a profitable activity.

Using theory to improve practice

The six models present different approaches to the management of education and the syntheses indicate a few of the possible relationships between them. However, the ultimate test of theory is whether it improves practice. Theory which is arid and remote from practice will not improve leadership and management or help to enhance teaching and learning, which should be at the heart of the educational process.

There should be little doubt about the *potential* for theory to inform practice. School and college managers generally engage in a process of implicit theorizing in deciding how to formulate policy or respond to events. Theory provides the analytical basis for determining the response to events and helps in the interpretation of management information. Facts cannot simply be left to speak for themselves. They require the explanatory framework of theory in order to ascertain their real meaning.

The multiplicity of competing models means that no single theory is sufficient to guide practice. Rather, managers need to develop 'conceptual pluralism' (Bolman and Deal, 1984, p. 4) in order to be able to select the most appropriate approach to particular issues and avoid a unidimensional stance: 'Understanding organizations is nearly impossible when the manager is unconsciously wed to a single, narrow perspective . . . Managers in all organizations . . . can increase their effectiveness and their freedom through the use of multiple vantage points. To be locked into a single path is likely to produce error and self-imprisonment.'

Conceptual pluralism is similar to the notion of contingent leadership. Both recognize the diverse nature of educational contexts and the advantages of adapting leadership styles to the particular situation rather than adopting a 'one size fits all' stance. Leaders should choose the theory most appropriate for the organization and for the particular situation under consideration. Appreciation of the various models is the starting point for effective action. It provides a 'conceptual tool-kit' for the manager to deploy as appropriate in addressing problems and developing strategy. The explicit acquisition of a range of theoretical perspectives should lead to 'the wise manager making the most informed and appropriate selection of the multiple "truths" available' (French, 1989, p. 49).

This eclectic approach may be illustrated by reference to the task of chairing a meeting. The chair may begin by adopting the normatively preferable collegial model and a participative leadership style. If consensus cannot be achieved, s/he may need to adopt the political strategy of mediation to achieve a compromise. If the emerging outcome appears to contradict governing body policy, it may be necessary to stress accountability, a central concept in both the formal model and managerial leadership. During the meeting, there may be different interpretations of the same phenomena and sensitivity may be required to this essentially subjective or postmodern position. There may also be elements of the ambiguity model, particularly if there is fluid participation in the discussion. Throughout the process, the chair may seek to ensure that the tone of the debate, and any policy proposals, are consistent with the values and cultural norms of the organization.

Morgan (1997, p. 359) argues that organizational analysis based on these multiple perspectives comprises two elements:

- a diagnostic reading of the situation being investigated, using different metaphors to identify or highlight key aspects of the situation;

- a critical evaluation of the significance of the different interpretations resulting from the diagnosis.

These skills are consistent with the concept of the 'reflective practitioner' whose managerial approach incorporates both good experience and a distillation of theoretical models based on wide reading and discussion with both academics and fellow practitioners. This combination of theory and practice enables the leader to acquire the overview required for strategic management. Middlewood (1998, p. 8) claims that this 'helicopter' quality is a central element of strategic thinking.

While it is widely recognized that appreciation of theory is likely to enhance practice, there remain relatively few published accounts of how the various models have been tested in school or college-based research. More empirical work is needed to enable judgements on the validity of the models to be made with confidence. As Bell (1984, p. 199) indicates, detailed observations are required to establish how decisions are made: 'These observations are the key to understanding those forces of power and influence, both inside and outside schools, which control and regulate them. Only in this way can the internal organization of schools be fully understood.'

While observation is important, it may not be sufficient to judge the validity of the models: 'Empirical adequacy is not a sufficient criterion for deciding the merits of competing theories: the same empirical foundation may adequately confirm any number of different theories' (Evers and Lakomski, 1991, p. 101). Adherents of the subjective model, and postmodern leadership, would argue that observation is inadequate because it overlooks the perceptions of participants, whose interpretations of events are central to any real understanding of educational institutions. Research is required which combines observation and participants' perceptions to provide a comprehensive analysis of school and college management. The objectives of such a research programme would be to test the validity of the models presented in this volume and to develop an overarching conceptual framework. It is a tough task but if awareness of theory helps to improve practice, as we have sought to demonstrate, then more rigorous theory should produce more effective practitioners and better schools and colleges.

References

Baldridge, J.V., Curtis, D.V., Ecker, G. and Riley, G.L. (1978) *Policy Making and Effective Leadership*, San Francisco, CA: Jossey-Bass.

Bell, L. (1984) 'The sociology of school organisation: impossible or irrelevant?', *British Journal of Sociology of Education*, 5 (2): 187–204.

Bennett, N., Crawford, M., Levačić, R., Glover, D. and Earley, P. (2000) 'The reality of school development planning in the effective primary school: technicist or guiding plan', *School Leadership and Management*, 20 (3): 333–51.

Bolman, L. and Deal, T. (1984) *Modern Approaches to Understanding and Managing Organizations*, San Francisco, CA: Jossey-Bass.

Bush, T. and Glover, D. (2002) *School Leadership: Concepts and Evidence*, Nottingham: National College for School Leadership.

Campbell, R. and Neill, S. (1997) 'Managing teachers' time under systemic reform', in T. Bush and D. Middlewood (eds), *Managing People in Education*, London: Paul Chapman Publishing.

Chapman, J. (1993) 'Leadership, school-based decision-making and school effectiveness', in C. Dimmock (ed.), *School-based Management and School Effectiveness*, London: Routledge.

Cuthbert, R. (1984) *The Management Process, E324 Management in Post Compulsory Education, Block 3, Part 2*, Buckingham: Open University Press.

Davies, J.L. and Morgan, A.W. (1983) 'Management of higher education in a period of contraction and uncertainty', in O. Boyd-Barrett, T. Bush, J. Goodey, I. McNay and M. Preedy (eds), *Approaches to Post School Management*, London: Harper and Row.

Ellstrom, P.E. (1983) 'Four faces of educational organisations, *Higher Education*, 12: 231–41.

Enderud, H. (1980) 'Administrative leadership in organised anarchies', *International Journal of Institutional Management in Higher Education*, 4 (3): 235–53.

Evers, C. and Lakomski, G. (1991) 'Educational administration as science: a post-positivist proposal', in P. Ribbins, R. Glatter, T. Simkins and L. Watson (eds), *Developing Educational Leaders*, Harlow: Longman.

French, B. (1989) *The Hidden Face of Organisations: Some Alternative Theories of Management*, Sheffield: Sheffield City Polytechnic.

Hallinger, P. (1992) 'The evolving role of American principals: from managerial to instructional to transformational leaders, *Journal of Educational Administration*, 30 (3): 35–48.

Hoy, W. and Miskel, C. (1987) *Educational Administration: Theory, Research and Practice*, New York: Random House.

Leithwood, K. (1994) 'Leadership for school restructuring', *Educational Administration Quarterly*, 30 (4): 498–518.

Leithwood, K., Jantzi, D. and Steinbach, R. (1999) *Changing Leadership for Changing Times*, Buckingham: Open University Press.

Middlewood, D. (1998) 'Strategic management in education: an overview', in D. Middlewood and J. Lumby (eds), *Strategic Management in Schools and Colleges*, London: Paul Chapman Publishing.

Miller, T.W. and Miller, J.M. (2001) 'Educational leadership in the new millennium: a vision for 2020', *International Journal of Leadership in Education*, 4 (2): 181–9.

Morgan, G. (1997) *Images of Organization*, Newbury Park, CA: Sage Publications.

National College for School Leadership (NCSL) (2001) *Leadership Development Framework*, Nottingham: NCSL.

Sergiovanni, T. (1984) 'Leadership and excellence in schooling', *Educational Leadership*, 41 (5): 4–13.

Simkins, T. (1998) 'Autonomy, constraint and the strategic management of resources', in D. Middlewood and J. Lumby (eds), *Strategic Management in Schools and Colleges*, London: Paul Chapman Publishing.

Theodossin, E. (1983) 'Theoretical perspectives on the management of planned organizational change', *British Educational Research Journal*, 9 (1): 81–90.

Turner, C. (1990) *Organisational Culture*, Blagdon: Mendip Papers, p. 127.

Wise, C. and Bush, T. (1999) 'From teacher to Manager: the role of the academic middle manager in secondary schools', *Educational Research*, 41 (2): 183–96.

Subject index

Added to the page number 'f' denotes a figure

199

Author index

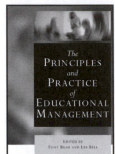

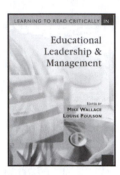